Ardoyne '69

'A crucial text for future generations trying to make sense of what were often senseless acts of violence perpetrated by one group of people on another group of people (sometimes neighbours) – simply because they were "the Other"...

The author isn't concerned with political point-scoring or making moral judgements – nor does he seek to identify 'victims' and 'perpetrators'. What he does, and does effectively, is give voice to ordinary people telling their stories – sharing their struggles and how their experiences during those tumultuous days of August 1969 changed their lives forever. The drama involving many "actors" and "extras" unfolds and we are told in a series of gripping narratives how, in a matter of days, the world seemed to shift on its axis, after which things would never be quite the same again – relationships shattered, lives ended prematurely, intentionally or not by the actions of others....'

Rev Bill Shaw

(Presbyterian Minister and CEO of 174 Trust, Belfast,
a social justice organisation with a distinct Christian
ethos active in the work of peace and reconciliation)

'For those who do not come from Ardoyne, or whose recollection of the events of August 1969 may be different from those who have shared their stories in this book, *Ardoyne '69: Stories of Struggle and Hope* may well be an uncomfortable read. But for those who have contributed to this account of the chilling events of 1969 it is their story, their memory, and this is what must be respected. I expect though that even within the Ardoyne community, this book will also be uncomfortable reading as it presents a wide range of experiences that can be overlooked as we search for an agreed narrative.

This is the story of a community dominated by fear, murder and mayhem, within which vulnerable young people were faced with life-and-death decisions from which most of us were protected. Decisions which took each of the story-tellers on very different journeys, some of which might well have been discouraged and others which offered alternative and challenging opportunities for those who dared to look beyond what was happening within and beyond the confines of their beloved but beleaguered Ardoyne of the day – from President of the State to the heading of a national network, and lesser known but no less fulfilling opportunities in between. Some of these people joined the IRA while others rejected this path and ideology, and chose starkly different roads in life. Above all though, this book speaks of a community which never lost hope, or the affection of its children.

As the author suggests, as well as the story of Ardoyne in the most troubled of times, this is an invitation for others to share their stories, from whatever perspective or tradition they may come. Not in the negative spirit of "what-aboutry", but in the listening to each other's stories we may understand more clearly what was happening up the road and across the road from where we may have lived. Above all, in the sharing of our stories may we share a commitment to ensure that for the sake of our children and theirs, our painful histories will never be repeated.'

'*Ardoyne '69: Stories of Struggle and Hope* is an important collection of rich testimonies. Fourteen individuals who lived through the heady days of 14–16 August 1969 share their stories of this time and a very different life after it. Each reflection demonstrates the very different path many residents of Ardoyne took both during and after the violence of August 1969. Ardoyne, an area which has proportionally the highest number of sectarian deaths of any place in Northern Ireland, stood at the crossroads between and betwixt communities.

The Catholic, Nationalist island of Ardoyne witnessed some of the most intense violence of the conflict, the legacy of which remains with each of the contributors to this day. How each individual dealt with that trauma remains evident in all fourteen of the stories shared in this touching collection. These stories share the themes of loss, desperation, fear, but, above all, resilience. One hopes this thoughtful collection will inspire other areas to create their own collection of memories from this chaotic time.'

'The danger for historians and other commentators on what we euphemistically refer to as "the Troubles" is that they find themselves a degree or two removed from the realities as experienced by people on the ground. By default they write as "outsiders" and can easily fall into the trap of using labels, an example of which is Ardoyne being often referred to as "the Ardoyne". This is perceived as a derogatory term for a very proud people.

Historical accounts become weakened with the creation of labels and of putting people and areas into boxes that belie the real truth that lies beneath. Brian McKee bypasses such labels and boxes, and the stories within this book tell a very different and richer truth. They portray a community of proud, talented, industrious people.

It is refreshing to hear from the people who were present on the ground at the time and the diversity of backgrounds only serves to enrich the story.

Brian McKee opens up an opportunity to dispense with labels and judgements and to hear a truth seldom heard. For this I congratulate him. His own background in Ardoyne facilitated those interviewed to tell their story honestly, when often they were forgotten people. The diversity of these fourteen witnesses gives us one of the most rounded insights into what it was like to be present in Ardoyne in August 1969.

Despite the different paths in life taken by these fourteen people, the one obvious unifying sentiment is their love and pride of Ardoyne – not "the Ardoyne".

Rev Gary Donegan CP
(Former rector and parish priest of Holy Cross,
Ardoyne and currently Director of the
Passionist Peace and Reconciliation Office)

Ardoyne '69

Stories of Struggle and Hope

Brian McKee

Published by
Red Stripe Press

an imprint of
Orpen Press
Upper Floor, Unit B3
Hume Centre
Hume Avenue
Park West Industrial Estate
Dublin 12
Ireland

email: info@orpenpress.com
www.orpenpress.com

Paperback ISBN 978-1-78605-100-4
ePub ISBN 978-1-78605-101-1

Printed in Dublin by SPRINTprint Ltd

This book is dedicated to:

My mum and dad, Rose and Barney McKee. People of immense courage and integrity who did more for Ardoyne than most people will ever know. The green glens of Antrim are calling to me!

Ciceam Ard Eoin CLG. Ardoyne Kickhams were at the heart of this community in 1969, and continue that proud tradition to this day. No club suffered loss and struggle in 'the Troubles' to the extent of the Kickhams, and they gave so many of us a love and sense of pride for our Gaelic games and culture. Ard Eoin Abu!

In Memory

In memory of Conor McMahon. Died peacefully 14 October 2020 aged 38. One of life's true gentlemen. Alive forever in the hearts and memories of those who loved him. Ar dheis Dé go raibh a anam.

Acknowledgements

This book has been three years in the making, but is the fulfilment of a long-time dream to write about the community from which I come. It would not have been possible without the support of my wife, Elizabeth. Without her this book would never have happened and I am indebted to her for her patience and tolerance over the past few years.

So many people offered me encouragement along the way. However, to those who gave me their precious time to share their memories of August 1969 and the impact of those few days on the rest of their lives I owe a great debt of gratitude. I hope this book does them justice and that I have captured their stories faithfully. If mistakes have been made I apologise but dealing with peoples' memories of traumatic events can be difficult to negotiate. Some of the stories I heard, for varying reasons, did not find their way into the finished book, and people from Ardoyne will understand that statement more than most. However, they all filled out the tapestry of those three days and the events that surrounded them, and listening to them pushed me on to complete this work.

I am indebted to Dr Eamon Phoenix for putting so much time and thought into the foreword that situates these three days of August 1969 into the wider historical and political context. I also thank Harold Good, Bill Shaw, Gary Donegan and Maggie Scally for their kind words of review.

Photographs tell so much about the story of Ardoyne that words could simply never capture. I therefore want to give a special thanks to the family of Jim Moreland (FBIPP.FMPA.FRPS.) for permission to use the treasured photos taken by Jim and to Frankie Quinn (Belfast Archives Project) for use of the wonderful photographs of Hugh McKeown. Other photographs were provided with the kind permission of

Acknowledgements

Thomas McMullan (*North Belfast News*), Peadar Whelan (*An Phoblacht*) and Pacemaker Press. The *Irish News* allowed me access to their 1969 archives, which filled in so much of the story captured by their reporters and editorial team at the time, and I am indebted to them for doing so.

From the legal profession I want to thank Paidí O'Muirigh (Padraig O'Muirigh Solicitors) and Niall O'Murchú (Kinnear and Co.) for their advice but also for access to material that filled in so many gaps in the story.

To Joe Lavery, whose love and enthusiasm for all things Ardoyne was inspirational in completing this work.

To Michael Brennan, Eileen O'Brien and Gerry Kelly at Red Stripe Press, thank you for all your advice and guidance in bringing this book to completion.

I finally want to give a special word of thanks to Fr Gary Donegan CP, who has given me the opportunity over the past ten years to work in the community that people call Ardoyne, that Ardoyne people call heaven, and that I call home!

Foreword

The ancient townland of Ardoyne (from the Irish, *Ard Eoin*, signifying 'Eoin's Height') is recorded on maps and title deeds going back as far as the 1500s, but its growth as a community has its origins in 1815, when Michael Andrews moved his linen and damask mill from Little York Street to the scarp of the Belfast hills to avail of the water power and bleach greens. By the 1850s there were several mills in the village and these attracted a flood of landless Catholic labourers from all over the north of Ireland in the wake of the Great Famine. At the turn of the twentieth century there was an influx of migrants from County Cork where a linen mill had closed and its workforce were offered employment in this northern suburb of Belfast.

In 1868 the Passionist congregation arrived in response to an invitation from Bishop Dorrian to care for the parish, with the current Holy Cross Church being built in 1902, establishing Ardoyne as one of the city's main Nationalist enclaves. The community largely supported the Home Rule Party and established a GAA club, a Gaelic League branch, a division of the Ancient Order of Hibernians and a detachment of the Irish Volunteers, while their cultural activities included Irish drama, Gaelic games and soccer, and concerts in the local church hall. Seán Mac Diarmada, the Irish revolutionary, executed for his part in the 1916 Rising and a native of County Leitrim, lived in the area in the early 1900s.

Belfast, however, had a long history of sectarian strife and Ardoyne suffered severely in the anti-Catholic violence which marked the partition of Ireland during 1920–1922. Hundreds of local people, men and women, were expelled from their jobs in the shipyards, linen mills and engineering factories in 1920 and found themselves on the verge of starvation. Sectarian violence erupted once again in 1935, and Catholic families evicted from their homes in the York Street area sought refuge in the newly built Glenard estate at Ardoyne and were eventually accepted as tenants. This part of the district became known as 'New Ardoyne'.

But it is with the transformative events of 14–16 August 1969 that Brian McKee is concerned in this probing and timely book. In those frightful, almost dystopian days in high summer, Ardoyne and its close-knit, supportive community would be changed forever. The searing, indeed life-changing, effects of those events are recalled here by fourteen individuals who experienced them personally, responded to them differently and went on to pursue a range of diverse and contrasting paths in life.

Some found high-profile careers in public administration, others in influential media positions, several in business, one as a senior officer in the former Royal Ulster Constabulary (RUC), one as principal of the local girls' primary school. Mary McAleese (née Lenaghan) became President of Ireland at a critical moment in the peace process, while yet another contributor, Brendan ('Bik') McFarlane, would become a leading figure in the IRA and Officer Commanding during the 1981 Republican Hunger Strike, which marked a serious escalation in the conflict. Some, including Brian McKee, were children about to transfer to secondary school; one was training to be a Catholic missionary in North Wales; one was about to read Law at university while two others were embarking on teaching careers.

Their highly personal, incisive and reflective memories, written at a distance of fifty years, cover the prelude to the Troubles both in this society and in Ardoyne, the suddenness and sheer savagery of the mob violence, murders and eviction of those August days, and the responses of themselves, their families and the local community to these unprecedented events.

Several recall the peaceful, carefree pre-Troubles days of the mid 1960s when they enjoyed cordial relations with Protestant neighbours and played football and hurling, without fear, at Ballysillan and in the nearby Shankill area. This was the 'era of good feelings' when the Stormont Prime Minster, Terence O'Neill, met the Taoiseach and 1916 veteran, Seán Lemass, and the Ardoyne area had a non-sectarian Labour MP at Stormont.

Yet despite the surface calm, most of writers recall a sharp awareness of discrimination in employment: 'As a young Catholic you had to keep your horizons low', recalls Brian McCargo, then a 27-year-old sports-mad mill worker. Others recall the anti-Catholic fulminations of 'a man called Paisley'.

With the emergence of the Civil Rights Movement by 1968, there was a perceptible rise in tension. John McKeague had emerged as the leader of the Loyalist Woodvale Defence Association in the nearby Shankill Road. For one contributor,

Eugene McEldowney, a young teacher at the time, the Loyalist attack on the student marchers at Burntollet in January 1969 was the turning point. Within weeks a series of mysterious explosions (instigated by the illegal UVF) had figuratively blown O'Neill from office. As the British Labour government insisted on the introduction of basic reforms such as 'one man, one vote' and the fair allocation of houses, Unionism remained bitterly divided while Paisley warned of betrayal.

By the onset of the tense marching season that summer all eyes were on the Apprentice Boys' parade in Derry on 12 August which the Unionist government had refused to ban. Within hours predictable clashes between the RUC and Nationalist youths had escalated into the 'Battle of the Bogside'.

As tensions rose across the North on 13 August, the Taoiseach, Jack Lynch, warned in a television broadcast that the Irish government 'could not stand by and see innocent people injured and perhaps worse', and the violence spread to Belfast. The city, in Churchill's immortal phrase from 1922, was always 'a powder-keg with violent passions of its own'. Several of the eye-witnesses in this book recall hearing talk of 'taking the pressure off Derry' as hasty civil rights protests were mounted at RUC stations across Belfast. On the Shankill and Crumlin Roads the 'B' Specials (members of the State's auxiliary and exclusively Protestant police force) were mobilized and mobs began to gather at the interfaces.

Then came the horrendous events of 14–16 August when, in the chilling headline of the *Irish News*, Belfast became 'a city convulsed'. Some contributors recall how their elders had feared a re-run of the sectarian mob attacks which Ardoyne had experienced in the early 1920s: 'Granny spoke of the 1920s pogroms and how it was happening all over again', recalls Sharon O'Connor, then aged eleven.

For all of the contributors to this book, 14 August 1969 was a day of frightfulness and sectarian barbarism. That evening, as an eighteen-year-old Mary McAleese returned to her Crumlin Road home after a meal to celebrate her A-level success, she and her parents watched in horror as uniformed and armed 'B' Specials set fire to Catholic homes. From her vantage point in Chief Street that same night, as gunfire and mob fury filled the air, Anne Tanney, a young married teacher, observed groups of men with white armbands trying to set fire to the Catholic church. It was, she believed, 'a determined attempt by Loyalist gangs to wipe out the Catholic population'.

From his family home nearby, fifteen-year-old Cathal Goan watched with his father and brother as 'the RUC, along with thugs' tossed petrol bombs into the homes of their neighbours. There followed heavy machine-gun fire by the RUC – 'very scary from little whippet cars'. The defence of the area was left to young men who manned makeshift barricades and the local clergy who worked tirelessly to give support to those who had been driven from their homes. What shocked people most was the suddenness of the onslaught and the rapid transition from a demand for civil rights to 'a situation of complete destruction and death being visited on the community'.

Later there would be much anger in Ardoyne as the Northern Ireland Prime Minister, James Chichester-Clark, told a bemused world press that the violence of those three days was an 'IRA uprising to subvert the State'. Yet several contributors recall that 'a real tit-for-tat went on afterwards' as inoffensive Protestant families in Hooker Street were forced out of their homes in retaliation for the expulsion of Catholics in Protestant streets. 'I found it heart-breaking' notes Brian McCargo, who had many friends in both communities.

All the Ardoyne eye-witnesses are agreed on one point. 'There were no guns, no protection', as former President McAleese remembers. There was no IRA. That night two local men were shot dead: Sammy McLarnon was killed by shots fired into in his own home and Michael Lynch was shot by the RUC as he walked home.

In the aftermath of the sectarian onslaught many initially welcomed the arrival of British troops, whose deployment was not only called for by the Stormont regime but by Nationalist politicians and the Catholic hierarchy. Many joined the hastily-formed Citizens' Defence Committee, set up with the blessing of the Church and including 'GAA types', youths and old IRA men from the 1940s. There was a determination that the local community would 'stand their ground' and that Ardoyne would rise again.

Yes, as the British Labour Government of Harold Wilson issued the 'Downing Street Declaration', reaffirming the commitment of the two governments to the Reform Programme on 19 August 1969, and the first Peace Lines were established, few could have realised that these events marked the beginning of 'the Troubles'. Within months, the Provisional IRA and Loyalist paramilitaries had emerged and the relationship between the Catholic community and the British Army rapidly deteriorated. Over the next 25 years, 3,500 people – civilians, paramilitaries, police and troops – would die violently in Northern Ireland. In Ardoyne 99 members of the community died and in a small area of 6,000 people, few families escaped unscathed. It would take almost thirty years before peace was finally achieved with the signing of the Good Friday Agreement in 1998.

For all fourteen eye-witnesses featured in these pages, things would never be the same again. Three would see their family homes destroyed by mobs over the next two years as the Troubles escalated. A number channeled their energies into their studies and gained the skills which would propel them to senior positions in Irish society, North and South. A few joined the IRA, convinced that its 'armed struggle' was justified, with Bik McFarlane abandoning his priestly training to become a Volunteer. Brian McCargo, determined to serve the whole community, joined the RUC (then disarmed under the Hunt reforms) only to find that he had effectively 'burned his bridges' with the local community as the Troubles developed. One young woman, Anne Tanney, continued to serve her community as an educationist and community leader.

Several contributors, notably Mary McAleese, speak movingly of the 'wastefulness' and futility of the violence which engulfed Ardoyne and the North from 1969 onwards. Cathal Goan, a later controller of RTE, regrets that glaring wrongs such as discrimination in housing and an unfair voting system could not have been righted before the situation escalated out of control.

Anne Tanney, who experienced at first hand both the horrors of 1969 and the sectarian obscenity of the Holy Cross School Dispute some thirty years later, speaks for many when she highlights two lessons she has drawn from those events: 'The first is that peace is precious and that we must work for peace based on justice and mutual respect. The second is that all our children have the right to grow up free from fear in a secure, loving environment.' Anne's remarks are as eloquent as they are inspiring and point the way to a brighter future for this place and all its citizens.

Dr Éamon Phoenix
Historian, broadcaster and a member of the Taoiseach's Expert Advisory Group on Commemorations

Contents

Contributors

Brian McKee – Brian is a qualified teacher and youth worker. After teaching for a number of years in primary and secondary schools, he became director of Youth Ministry in the diocese of Down and Connor. Since 2010 Brian has worked in peace and reconciliation in the parish of Holy Cross, Ardoyne, as well as in the Passionist Retreat Centre at Tobar Mhuire near Downpatrick. Brian has been a proud member of Ardoyne Kickhams GAC since the age of ten and still plays an active role in promoting hurling within the club

Brendan (Bik) McFarlane – Brendan began studies with the Divine Word Missionaries in 1968. He left the seminary in 1970 and returned home to Ardoyne. He was involved in the defence of the district before eventually joining the IRA. He was appointed OC of the IRA in Long Kesh during the 1981 Hunger Strikes and played a leading role in the escape of 38 prisoners from Long Kesh in 1983. He is a keen musician and singer and is heavily involved in the Féile and other cultural events in Belfast.

Brian McCargo – Brian was born in Ardoyne where he was a key part of the local Gaelic football and hurling team. He was also a keen boxer. He took part in the defence of the Ardoyne area in 1969 before joining the RUC in 1970. He introduced Gaelic football and hurling into the RUC and latterly the PSNI. In his retirement Brian played a major role with the Special Olympics in the North of Ireland.

Mary McAleese – The oldest of nine children, Mary graduated in Law from Queen's University Belfast in 1973 and was called to the Bar in 1974. In 1994 she became the first female Pro-Vice Chancellor of Queen's University. On 11 November 1997 Mary was inaugurated as the eighth President of Ireland. She was re-elected on Friday 1 October 2004. The theme for her presidency was 'Building Bridges'. She holds a licentiate and doctorate in canon law, and her memoirs were published in 2020 with the title *Here's the Story: A Memoir*.

Ciarán Goan – Ciarán's paternal grandfather came from Cloghbolie, Co. Donegal, a house in which his own family now live. He worked with his father in the bar trade before eventually joining the civil service. He joined the Citizens' Defence Committee when it was formed in 1969 to defend the area against attack from loyalists. He later moved to a mixed area close to Ardoyne, but following an increase in sectarian murders his family moved to Dublin, where Ciarán followed a career in the food distribution business.

Sharon O'Connor – Sharon is a chartered director and chartered fellow of the Institute of Personnel Development. She is also professionally qualified in marketing. Sharon led the acclaimed Derry/Londonderry UK City of Culture 2013 as the town clerk and Chief Executive of Derry City Council. With a background in business, she joined local government in 2000 and was named Public Sector Director of the Year in 2009/2010 by the Institute of Directors NI. Sharon's family were evicted from their home on the outskirts of Ardoyne in 1970 and her family home was burned to the ground.

Davy Wasson – Davy's family were at heart of community and parish life in Ardoyne. He was an altarboy in Holy Cross Church and captain of the Ardoyne Kickhams under-16 Gaelic football team which won the championship just one week after the events of 14–16 August 1969. Davy helped Catholic families to move out of their homes following intimidation from Loyalist mobs. Like many of his contemporaries, Davy left Ardoyne for what seemed like a better life in Sydney, Australia in 1971 but came back two-and-a-half years later to build a life in Belfast.

Jackie Donnelly – Jackie's grandfather was a soldier in the British Army, but his father joined the IRA and was interned during the Second World War. So while his grandfather was serving in the British Army, Jackie's father was interned in Belfast. Jackie was also interned in 1973 while his younger brother was killed in an explosion in Ardoyne in 1979. Jackie is now dedicated to caring for ex-prisoners and enjoys fishing in his spare time.

Eugene McEldowney – Eugene was born in Ardoyne in 1943 at a time when Belfast was being bombarded by Luftwaffe bombing raids. He moved to London in 1963 for a job in the civil service. Here his interest in politics developed with membership of the Young Socialists, but he returned home to Ardoyne in 1964 to pursue studies at Queen's University. Eugene took part in the People's Democracy march to Derry in January 1971 and found himself wading in the River Faughan to escape as the protestors were attacked by Loyalists at Burntollet Bridge. He pursued a career in journalism and was news editor and later night editor with the *Irish Times*. Eugene enjoys folk music and has written and released several songs.

Anne Tanney – Anne was born in Ardoyne in 1945 and married her husband Pat in 1968. She qualified as a teacher and spent her entire teaching career in Holy Cross Girl's School, including nine years as vice-principal and seventeen years as principal. Anne and Pat were involved with the SDLP and the People's Assembly in Ardoyne, set up by Passionist priest Fr Myles Kavanagh during the early years of the Troubles. Anne was thrust into the headlines during the Holy Cross School Blockade in 2001. She was described by the BBC as 'the best-known teacher in Northern Ireland and the headmistress of the most-photographed school in the UK'.

Rab McCallum – Rab was born in the shadow of Holy Cross Church, Ardoyne. As a child his big interests were snooker, football and heading over the mountains that surround Belfast. At the age of fourteen he was caught up in the violence that erupted in the streets around him as his home area was attacked by Loyalists. Early thoughts of a life on the boats disappeared following the riots of 27 June 1970 when he joined the Fianna, the youth wing of the IRA, and eventually the main IRA. Rab was first imprisoned at the age of seventeen, and spent a total of twelve years in prison. Today he is committed to his work aimed at removing the so-called 'Peace Walls' that still blight the face of his community and in building peace and reconciliation across the community divide.

Pat Murphy – Pat was born into a family that had strong Republican connections on his mother's side, along with a deep commitment to socialism. His paternal grandfather, though, had served in the British Army during the Boer War and the First World War. Alongside his interest in politics from an early age, Pat was a committed member of the Ardoyne Kickhams Gaelic club. Pat played in the Ardoyne under-16 football team that won the championship in 1969. His younger brother, Ciarán, was also a member of that squad but was murdered by the Protestant Action Force on 13 October 1973.

Malachy Toner – Malachy was born just outside Newry in 1948. His father was a farmer but due to ill health moved into the off-licence trade. This career move saw the family move to Ardoyne in 1954. Malachy got deeply involved with the local Ardoyne Kickhams Gaelic team along with his brother Charlie. The family home in Cambrai Street and their licensed premises was regularly attacked during the 'marching season', but they were eventually burned out in August 1969. The family were left homeless and they moved in with relatives. While friends were killed and others ended up in prison as a result of the violence that surrounded them, Malachy rejected violence and pursued a career in the bar trade that continues to this day.

Cathal Goan – Cathal is a younger brother of Ciarán Goan and the fifth of eight children. As a teenager he was a member of Ardoyne Kickhams Gaelic club and shared a great love of Irish music with his friends Pat Murphy and Brendan McFarlane. Following the outbreak of the Troubles Cathal, like many of his age in Ardoyne, joined the Fianna. However his father, a former internee in the 1940s, heard about this and brought that part of his career to a quick end. Cathal's great love of and commitment to the Irish language saw him study Celtic Studies at University College Dublin. He rose to the position of Director General of RTE, the national Irish broadcasting corporation, from 2003 to 2011, and played a prominent role in the launch of the Irish language station TG4.

Glossary

Chapter 1

'Kick The Pope' bands: Usually flute bands within the Loyalist community known for blatantly sectarian/anti-Catholic songs.

The Ulster Special Constabulary (commonly called the 'B' Specials or 'B' Men): A quasi-military reserve police force in Northern Ireland that was set up in 1920, shortly before the partition of Ireland. The force was almost exclusively Ulster Protestant and was viewed with great mistrust by Catholics. The Special Constabulary was disbanded in May 1970, after the Hunt Report, which advised re-shaping Northern Ireland's security forces to attract more Catholic recruits and disarming the police.

Burntollet: Approximately 40 People's Democracy supporters left Belfast on New Year's Day 1969 on a protest march to Derry. Following a series of incidents along the route, the march, now with approximately 500 participants, was stopped just before its final leg to Derry at Burntollet Bridge and came under a bombardment of missiles from Loyalists and 'B' Specials. As many marchers fled into the fields they were pursued by attackers and the RUC made no attempt to intervene. Other marchers were thrown into the nearby River Faughan.

Woodvale Defence Association: A Loyalist paramilitary group based in the Woodvale area, close to Ardoyne. Its members received military training, mostly with legally held weapons. It combined with a number of other locally based paramilitary units to form the Ulster Defence Association in 1972, and became known as 'B' Company in the restructured organisation.

Scarman Tribunal: A Tribunal under the Chairmanship of Mr Justice Scarman constituted by the Northern Ireland Assembly under the Tribunals of Inquiry (Evidence) Act 1921 to investigate seven different incidents that occurred during rioting in 1969. It sat for 172 days hearing evidence and published its report in April 1972.

The International Commission of Jurists: An international human rights non-governmental organisation. It is a standing group of 60 eminent jurists – including senior judges, attorneys and academics – who work to develop national and international human rights standards through the law.

Chapter 2

Toby's Hall: A hall located in Butler Street that was used for community activities.

Felden House: Originally used to provide training for men returning from the Second World War, particularly for the shipyards and aircraft factory, but later used for training young men in trades such as bricklaying, plumbing and joinery.

Bombay Street: Located within the Clonard area of West Belfast, Bombay Street was burnt to the ground by a Loyalist mob on 15 August 1969. It was one of the key events of the early days of the Troubles.

Mills bomb: The popular name for a type of British Army hand grenade that was originally used in the First World War.

.303: The .303 rifle was the commonly used name for the Lee Enfield rifle.

Ard Fhéis: The name used by many Irish political parties for their annual party conference.

CCDC: The Central Citizens' Defence Committee was founded on 16 August 1969 to coordinate various Belfast community and defence groups in Nationalist areas.

Battle of the Short Strand: The Battle of the Short Strand (or St Matthew's) took place on the night of 27–28 June 1970 between the fledgling Provisional IRA and Loyalists from the Ballymacarrett/Newtownards Road area following Loyalist marches. The battle lasted about five hours and ended at dawn on 28 June. The British Army and police were deployed nearby but did not intervene. Three people were killed and at least 26 wounded in the fighting.

Cage 11: Following the introduction of internment in August 1971, Long Kesh – a disused Second World War airfield near Lisburn – was used as an internment camp. It was divided into compounds (also known as 'cages'). Each cage was surrounded by razor-wire fencing and generally consisted of four Nissen huts. Each hut was designed to accommodate 80 men, with half of each hut designated as a dining/recreational area. The cages were segregated along political lines, but as well as Republicans and Loyalists being held in separate cages, so also were the various organisations, including the Provisional IRA, Official IRA, UDA, UVF. Free association was allowed within each cage/compound from 8 a.m. until 'lock-up' at 9 p.m.

Brownie: IRA prisoners were engaged in critical debate during the conflict and would smuggle statements and articles out of the prisons that contributed to a wider debate within the Republican movement outside the prisons. These articles became known as the 'Brownie papers' and it is now widely accepted that 'Brownie' was a pseudonym for Gerry Adams, the author of the articles.

H-Blocks: Getting their name from their distinctive shape, the H-Blocks were used to hold prisoners convicted of scheduled offences after 1 March 1976. Merlyn Rees, then Secretary of State for Northern Ireland, announced that people convicted of causing terrorist offences would no longer be entitled to special category status but were to be treated as ordinary criminals. On 14 September 1976 Kieran Nugent was the first prisoner to be sentenced under the new regime and he refused to wear prison clothes, choosing instead to wrap a blanket around himself, marking the start of the 'Blanket Protest'.

By 1978, more than 300 men had joined the protest and in March 1978 some prisoners refused to leave their cells to shower or use the lavatory, and were provided with wash-hand basins in their cells. Following the refusal by prison authorities to install showers in their cells, prisoners refused to use the wash-hand basins, leading to the 'no wash' protest. A fight took place between a prisoner and prison guards when he was removed to solitary confinement and prisoners responded by smashing the furniture in their cells, forcing the prison authorities to remove the remaining furniture from the cells, leaving only blankets and mattresses. The prisoners responded by refusing to leave their cells and, as a result, the prison officers were unable to clear them. This resulted in the blanket protest escalating into the 'dirty protest' where prisoners would not leave their cells to 'slop out', leading to excrement being smeared on the cell walls.

OC: Officer Commanding. The most senior IRA Volunteer in a specified location.

Irish Commission for Justice and Peace: The Irish Commission for Justice and Peace (ICJP) was an organisation established by the Catholic Bishops Conference based in Maynooth who tried unsuccessfully to mediate between prisoners and prison authorities.

Chapter 3

Glenard: Built in the 1930s, Glenard was seen as the 'newer' part of Ardoyne and a great local rivalry developed between residents of Glenard and those of 'Old' Ardoyne.

Ard Scoil: The Ard Scoil was a building located in Divis Street, Falls Road that was run by the Gaelic League and fostered the growth of the Irish language and culture.

Gerrymandering: Gerrymandering is the deliberate manipulation of electoral boundaries designed to ensure a particular group, especially one that is in a minority, retains political power. Although Catholics were a clear majority of the Derry population, Unionists were able to maintain control of the Council by severe gerrymandering. Although working-class people from both communities suffered from poor housing and unemployment, Catholics were significantly more likely to live in crowded and generally inadequate housing and have lower employment. The housing situation was caused in part by Unionist politicians wishing to keep Catholics concentrated in a small number of electoral wards, thus confining the Nationalist vote to these wards.

Lenadoon: A housing estate developed on a green-field site in West Belfast to provide larger and improved homes than Belfast's inner city, which had more cramped terraced housing. Lenadoon estate became an area of significant sectarian conflict. The IRA ceasefire of 1972 ended in Lenadoon when the British Army blocked Republicans from moving Catholics into the lower end of the estate. The Army established billets in houses and flats in the estate. Many houses were damaged by gunfire.

Eddie McAteer: Irish Nationalist politician elected to Derry City Council in 1952. He became leader of the Nationalist Party in Stormont in 1964 but lost his seat in the 1969 general election to John Hume. With the growth of the SDLP and the decline of the Nationalist Party, he joined the Irish Independence Party in 1978.

RUC Reserve: The RUC Reserve was set up in 1970 as an auxiliary group of Northern Ireland police officers to support the regular force in mainly security-related policing work.

Rule 21: Rule 21 was brought into the GAA in 1897 and it banned members of the British security forces from membership of the GAA. It was intended to allay fears that members of the Royal Irish Constabulary (RIC) were joining GAA clubs to spy on members' political activities. The affected organisations included the British Armed Forces and the RUC, and prior to partition the RIC and Dublin Metropolitan Police. It also applied to police forces in Britain. The rule was abolished after the establishment of the Police Service of Northern Ireland (PSNI) as part of the Northern Ireland peace process.

Newforge: A country club in Belfast founded in 1956 for members of the Royal Ulster Constabulary Athletic Association (RUC AA). Originally a private club for serving and retired police officers, membership eventually opened to non-police members and it has developed into an open club with multiple sports facilities.

Shankill Butchers: A Loyalist gang based in the Shankill area that was active between 1975 and 1982. Mostly members of the Ulster Volunteer Force (UVF), they were responsible for the deaths of at least 23 people, most of whom were killed in sectarian attacks.

Special Patrol Group: The Special Patrol Group (SPG) of the Royal Ulster Constabulary was a tactical reserve of approximately 150 officers. They were the first policemen trained by the British Army in the use of riot equipment and tactics which it had developed since arriving in the North in 1969. They were given upgraded weaponry and dispersed in units across the region and had the particular role of policing riot situations and engaging in 'anti-terrorist' activity.

Castlereagh Barracks: RUC holding station used during the Troubles. Known as the headquarters for Special Branch, it was also associated with torture and mistreatment within the Nationalist community.

CID: In the UK Criminal Investigation Department (CID) is the generic name for the branch of a police force to which most plainclothes detectives belong and is concerned with finding out who has committed crimes.

Chapter 4

Millies: A name given to mill workers. 'Doffers' was the name given to the mostly women who 'doffed' or tied up the full spindles of linen thread and quickly replaced this with a fresh empty spindle.

The Fenian Brotherhood: An Irish Republican organisation founded in the United States in 1858 by John O'Mahony and Michael Doheny. It was a precursor to Clan na Gael, a sister organisation to the Irish Republican Brotherhood. Members were commonly known as 'Fenians'. The term 'Fenian' today is seen as a derogatory sectarian term in Ireland to refer to Irish Nationalists and/or Catholics, particularly in Northern Ireland.

The Hammer: A strong Loyalist area on the Shankill Road, situated between Malvern Street and Agnes Street.

Daniel O'Connell: Often referred to as 'The Liberator' or 'The Emancipator', Daniel O'Connell was an Irish political leader in the first half of the nineteenth century. He campaigned for Catholic Emancipation, including the right of Catholics to sit in Parliament (at that time banned for over 100 years), and a repeal of the Acts of Union which combined the parliaments of Great Britain and Ireland.

Billy McMillen: Billy McMillen stood for the Republican Clubs in the 1964 Westminster election in the Belfast West constituency. His office was in Divis Street, where he flew the Irish tricolour alongside the Starry Plough (the flag of James Connolly's Citizen Army) in the window. The Flags and Emblems Act gave the police power to remove any flag or emblem from public or private property that was considered to be likely to cause a breach of the peace. Ian Paisley threatened to organise a protest march and remove it himself if the police did not remove it. Street unrest followed the removal of the flags.

Lost Lives: A book edited by Chris Thornton, Seamus Kelters, Brian Feeney, David McKittrick and published by Mainstream, Edinburgh (1999) that tells the stories of the men, women and children who died as a result of the Northern Ireland Troubles.

Historical Enquiries Team (HET): The HET was set up in September 2005 as a unit of the Police Service of Northern Ireland to investigate the 3,269 unsolved murders committed during the Troubles, specifically those that happened between 1968 and 1998. It was wound up in September 2014 due to budget cuts in the PSNI.

McGurk's Bar: On 4 December 1971, the UVF detonated a bomb at McGurk's Bar in the New Lodge area of Belfast. The explosion caused the building to collapse, killing fifteen Catholic civilians, including two children, and wounding seventeen more. Despite evidence to the contrary, the security forces initially asserted that the explosion had been caused by a bomb being carried by IRA members who were in the pub. In 1977, UVF member Robert Campbell was sentenced to life imprisonment for his part in the bombing and served fifteen years.

The Kingsmill Massacre: A shooting that took place on 5 January 1976 near the village of Whitecross, County Armagh. Gunmen stopped a minibus carrying eleven Protestant workmen, lined them up against the bus and shot them. Only one victim survived, despite having been shot eighteen times. The only Catholic man on the minibus was allowed to go free. The Kingsmill Massacre was the climax of a string of tit-for-tat killings in the area during the mid-1970s. A 2011 report by the Historical Enquiries Team (HET) found that the attack was carried out by the IRA, despite the organisation being on ceasefire. The weapons used were linked to 110 other attacks.

Chapter 5

Voice of the North: Following the walk out from the Sinn Féin Ard Fhéis in 1969 by Republicans who were dissatisfied with the then current leadership (later to form the Provisional IRA), the *Voice of the North* newspaper was set up mainly to discuss the defence of Catholic districts in Belfast. It was eventually replaced by the *Republican News* in the North, and *An Phoblacht* in the South.

Knights of Malta: The Order of Malta is an ancient Catholic lay religious order, formed in Jerusalem in 1048 with two main missions: the first to nurture, witness and protect the Catholic faith; the second to serve the poor and the sick. The Order's Ambulance Corps (known as the Knights of Malta) played a significant role in helping the injured during the Troubles and the distinctive Maltese Cross was a familiar sight on ambulances at the scene of many infamous atrocities.

Chapter 6

The Field: The Field refers to the destination for Orange Lodges that march on 12 July. The parade usually begins at an Orange Hall and proceeds to a large park or field where the marchers, their friends and family, and the general public gather to eat, drink and listen to speeches by clergymen, politicians and senior members of the Order.

Apprentice Boys: The Apprentice Boys of Derry was founded to commemorate the 1689 Siege of Derry when the Catholic James II laid siege to the walled city, which was at the time a Protestant stronghold.

Unity Flats: Unity Flats was a Catholic development that stretched from the Loyalist Peter's Hill at the city end of the Shankill Road to the Nationalist Clifton Street and New Lodge areas. It consisted of 20 blocks of flats and two-storey maisonettes built in the 1960s. In 1969, when it came under fierce attack from Loyalists, it comprised 200 dwellings and provided housing for about 1,000 men, women and children.

City of Culture: Using the joint names Derry/Londonderry, the city became the first ever UK City of Culture in 2013. The UK City of Culture title brought many social and economic benefits to the area.

Europa Hotel: A four-star hotel in Great Victoria Street, Belfast. Opened in 1971, it has hosted presidents, prime ministers and celebrities. It became known as the 'most bombed hotel in Europe' and the 'most bombed hotel in the world' after suffering 36 bomb attacks during the Troubles.

Chapter 7

The Bone Heights: An area located between Ardoyne and the Oldpark areas that was a very popular location for children and adults for recreation and football. The Bone Heights provide an ideal viewing point across most of the Ardoyne district.

Chapter 8

Millie Dam: An area to the back of Holy Cross Boys' School in Butler Street and Brompton Park. It was a favourite play place for children in Ardoyne, surrounded by broken railings and visited by swans every year.

Canary Wharf: The IRA agreed to a ceasefire in August 1994 on the understanding that Sinn Féin would be allowed to take part in peace negotiations. When the British Government then demanded a full IRA disarmament as a precondition for peace talks, the IRA resumed its campaign. The Canary Wharf bombing occurred on 9 February 1996 when the IRA detonated a powerful truck bomb in South Quay (which is actually outside Canary Wharf). The blast killed two people and devastated a wide area, causing an estimated £150 million worth of damage.

Chapter 9

New Ireland Society: The New Ireland Society was a student debating society at Queen's University Belfast. Its purpose was to give a platform to students of a Nationalist frame of mind. There was also a Unionist Society and a Labour Society. They held regular debates attended by students of all persuasions. This was before the Civil Rights Movement got off the ground and People's Democracy came to the fore. The New Ireland Society's main motivator was Ciarán McKeown, who was subsequently one of the founders of the Peace People in 1976.

Literific Society: The Literific (Literary and Scientific) Society attracted the bulk of students across the religious divide. It was the main debating society at Queen's University Belfast.

Chapter 10

Edel Quinn: Edel Quinn was born in County Cork in 1907. She played a prominent role in the Legion of Mary and established the organisation in Africa in 1937. She died from tuberculosis in 1944 at 36 years of age. The process for her canonisation was opened in 1963.

Association for Legal Justice: The Association for Legal Justice (ALJ) was set up in 1970 by people such as Fr Denis Faul, Fr Raymond Murray, Fr Brian Brady, Anne Murray and Clara Reilly. The ALJ recorded by hand thousands of accounts of arrest and torture of detainees. The ALJ was instrumental in convincing the Irish Government to take the British Government to the European Court of Human Rights, where it was found guilty of degrading political detainees known as the 'hooded men'.

Chapter 11

CS gas: CS gas was used extensively in Derry and Belfast from 1969 to 1972. During a two-day riot in the Bogside in August 1969, over 1,000 canisters were released in the densely populated residential area, while the following year, the Army fired up to 1,600 canisters into the densely populated Falls Road area in an attempt to quell rioting during what became known as the Falls Curfew.

Fianna: Na Fianna Éireann, known as the Fianna, was 'the junior wing' of the IRA for boys up to sixteen years of age. At the age of seventeen a boy was eligible to join the main IRA.

Wimpeys: Small armoured cars that were used by the British Army on the streets of Belfast.

Chapter 12

Free State Army: The Free State, or National Army, sometimes referred to as the **Regulars**, was the Army of the Irish Free State from January 1922 until October 1924. Its first troops were volunteers of the Irish Republican Army (IRA) who supported the Anglo-Irish Treaty. Michael Collins was the Army's first Chief of Staff from its formation until his death in August 1922. The term 'National Army' was superseded by the legal establishment of the Defence Forces for the then Irish Free State.

Irregulars: Following the signing of the Anglo-Irish Treaty there was a split between members within both Sinn Féin and the IRA. IRA Volunteers faced the dilemma of choosing the side to which they give their allegiance. This choice was based not only on political considerations, but also often on the personality of individual leaders at local level. The same dynamic could be identified following the split in Sinn Féin at the 1969 Ard Fhéis that led to the formation of the Official and Provisional IRA.

The International Brigade: The Spanish Civil War lasted from 17 July 1936 to 1 April 1939, and while both sides attracted participants from Ireland, the majority sided with the Nationalist (Francoist) faction. The Irish bishops issued a pastoral letter that firmly supported Franco, and, encouraged by the attitude of the Church hierarchy, Eoin O'Duffy started to recruit a brigade of Irish volunteers to fight in

Spain in defence of the Church. By November 1936 about 700 men were selected and sailed to Spain, where they became known as the 'Irish Brigade'.

Active Service Unit: In 1977, both in an attempt to become more effective and due to fears around the ability of the security forces to gain information through informers, the Provisional IRA started to move away from the larger conventional military structure. A system of two parallel types of unit within an IRA brigade was introduced in place of the battalion structures. Firstly, the old 'company' structures were used for support activities such as 'policing' Nationalist areas, intelligence-gathering, and hiding weapons, while the majority of actual attacks were the responsibility of what became known as an Active Service Unit (ASU). These were smaller, tight-knit cells, usually consisting of four to eight members.

Cumann na mBan: The Irish Republican women's organisation founded in April 1914 in response to the all-male Irish Volunteers. The Republican women played their role in the Easter Rising of 1916, although active involvement in the fighting was prohibited for Cumann na mBan. In response, some of its members joined James Connolly's Irish Citizen Army. When the Republican movement split at the Ard Fhéis of 1969, the majority of Cumann na mBan pledged their allegiance to the newly formed Provisional Army Council in spring 1970 while others joined the Official Republican movement. Instead of forming their own Official Cumann na mBan these women were absorbed into the Official IRA. In September 1970, the Provisionals followed their example and also accepted women Volunteers into the IRA.

National Archives, Kew: The National Archives is the official archive and publisher for the UK Government and for England and Wales. It contains national documents dating back over 1,000 years, including military records relating to the role of the British Army in the Troubles.

Chapter 14

Proxy bomb: The **proxy bomb**, also known as a **human bomb**, was a tactic used mainly by the Provisional IRA during the Troubles. It involved forcing civilians or off-duty members of the security forces to drive car bombs to British military targets after placing them or their families under some kind of threat.

Bayardo Bar: The mid-1970s saw a series of retaliatory attacks by Loyalists and the IRA. In July 1975, the Miami Showband was ambushed by the UVF outside

Banbridge in an incident which saw two bombers and three members of the band perish when a bomb exploded prematurely. A fortnight later the IRA mounted a gun and bomb attack on the Bayardo Bar on the Shankill Road, killing five and injuring more than forty people.

Introduction

Ardoyne is my home. It is where I was born, received my primary education and currently work. It is an area of approximately one square mile that grew up around the linen and flax industries of the nineteenth century. Despite its size it is also one of the best-known districts in Belfast, but unfortunately that reputation comes from being at the heart of so much conflict and trauma over the course of the recent Troubles. Ninety-nine people from this small community lost their lives as result of conflict, in a population that fluctuated around 6,000 people. Few families escaped the impact of violence that had been simmering under the surface with sporadic unrest taking place before eventually erupting in brutal violence in August 1969.

Over a period of some three years, I collected the stories of individuals who had direct experience of the events of August 1969 in Ardoyne. In doing so, I was anxious to discover how people from the same community, who experienced the same event, remember and tell the story differently, and how their subsequent life experiences brought them down many different and contrasting paths. As so many participants reflected, it is the story of ordinary people caught up in extraordinary circumstances, and their heroic struggle to find hope and meaning in the midst of struggle and suffering.

This book does not set out to make political or moral judgement; in fact it fights strongly to resist any temptation to do so, either on the people from within this community, or upon those who carried out actions that impacted upon this community. The book aims rather to create a space for ordinary people to tell their story. While the common thread may be the three days of 14–16 August 1969, when the experience of this community was changed utterly, it situates those three days within the personal life experiences of the individuals who generously shared their stories with me.

My original plan for this book was to invite people to share their memories of the specific days of 14–16 August, and to subsequently collate these stories into a chronological record of events. I was already conscious of the power behind stories, particularly stories of struggle and of hope, but people having the trust to share their story with me was both a privilege and an intensely emotional experience that caused me to rethink my original plan, and rather than present a chronological record, I now share the stories of these fourteen individuals in their own right, each one a privileged insight into the lives of individuals and into the life of this proud community. The horrific events of these three days, people's reactions to them and the decisions they made in their aftermath did not come out of the blue. This book is an attempt to explore the wider context within which the three days were situated, but also the wider life experience of individuals that influenced subsequent decisions they made in response to the awful events taking place around them.

In this book you will encounter the stories of people who experienced three traumatic days in the history of this proud community. One went on to become President of Ireland, one became the Officer in Command of IRA prisoners during the Long Kesh Hunger Strike in 1981, while another joined the RUC just one year after being on the barricades in August 1969. Some of these individuals stayed in Ardoyne, while others moved away, but all share a deep love and respect for the place and the people from which they were carved. One thing they share in common is that each and every one is fiercely proud of the fact that they come from Ardoyne. Through their stories we are introduced not only to the Troubles, but also to the social realities of the life of this community at that time, with all its humour and all its struggles.

A crucial factor that the reader needs to be conscious of in order to understand both the reaction of the Ardoyne community to the initial violence, as well as the depth of the trauma endured, is that such raw, sectarian violence was not new to this community. Ardoyne had been the setting for trouble between the Nationalist and Unionist communities since the 1920s and 30s. The civil disturbances in 1921 had an effect on the life of Ardoyne. Present-day Ladbrook Drive was used as a firing range by the 'B' Specials, and in May of that year the procession in honour of Our Lady held each year within the parish was cancelled. The daily chronicles kept by the Passionist community who served the people of the parish records:

Owing to the unsettled state of the district the usual processions throughout the month of May have not been held. We cannot fail to notice the ever decreasing congregations at the Sunday Masses and evening Devotions. Many of our best city friends who rarely failed in their appearing here on Sunday, are too timorous (and with good reason) to venture up the Crumlin Road.

The effects of civil disorder were even more keenly felt by the same Passionist community in Holy Cross Retreat when on Easter Monday 1922 a group of postulants (students) took a late evening walk in the gardens of the Retreat House and were fired upon from a passing military car. One of the students was severely wounded in the leg. In a further incident a bullet pierced a window and ripped through the fifth Station of the Cross that hung in the church.

In 1926, a general strike occurred in England, but its impact was soon felt in Ardoyne. One consequence of the strike was that coal became very scarce, and as coal was needed to run the mills that provided the bulk of employment in Ardoyne, they partly closed and many workers were laid off. The growing unemployment and poverty led to the Andrews Estate, situated at the edge of Ardoyne, being broken into by local residents, who cut down the trees in the estate to use as firewood. This practice went on for a few years and soon the previously heavily wooded area became quite open and bare. Ten years later, part of the area was bought by the estate agents McKibben and Company, to build a new housing estate at Ardoyne, to be called Glenard. During the 12 July celebrations of 1926, Loyalists attacked Catholic homes in the Little Italy area of Belfast (York Street, Lancaster Street, around the Docks area) and the Crumlin Road areas. The rioting soon spread across Belfast and hundreds of Catholics fled to the relative safety of the still uncompleted Glenard. Approximately 144 displaced families squatted in many of the newly built and half-built houses that were lying empty in the Glenard area. The Protestant residents of Glenard attempted to block off the 'Gutthery Gap' (now known as the 'Brompton Gap' or 'the Stumps') to prevent the Catholics from Ardoyne entering Glenard. In order to bring resolution to the growing tension in the area, the Bishop of Down and Connor purchased many of these houses so that the families were able to stay. One of the conditions imposed by the land owner was that, due to the bad reputation now associated with Glenard, the name was not to be used for this new estate. So, when sectarian violence erupted in the summer of 1969, old wounds and fears were brought to the surface again.

I am conscious that I am sharing the story of Ardoyne through the lenses of people who lived within that community. Others will have a different perspective. My invitation to you is to read these stories not as those of victims or perpetrators, or as a way of searching out evidence of who was right or who was wrong, but as a channel through which you can listen to the lived experience of a community that, despite the struggles they went through, never gave up hope. So many communities on both sides of divided society could share similar stories. I hope they will.

1

Brian McKee

ention of 'the summer of 69' will bring a smile to the faces of many people who lived through those sultry summer days. It is one of those periods in time that somehow is captured within the collective memory of those who lived through the iconic events of that summer. For some, those memories almost instinctively trigger an inner rendition of Bryan Adams' song with its message of carefree living and summer sunshine. Many others will recall sitting up late at night, watching in amazement at the black-and-white film of men in white space suits bobbing up and down on the surface of the moon. They will smile at recalling people debating as to whether these incredible scenes were real, or if they were part of an extensive plot by the American Secret Service in its quest to keep ahead of the Russian space programme. However, behind the arguments as to merits of the glorious summer of 1969 being enshrined as being the best year of their lives or not, one thing is certain – for people living in the North of Ireland, the humdrum ordinariness of everyday living was shattered during those summer days, and the scourge of many long years of violence and fear was unleashed.

I was ten years of age in the summer of 1969, about to start my final year in primary school and due to sit the dreaded 11+ examination. I had started completing 'test papers' in the final term of Primary 6, and in a strange way I was both dreading and looking forward to that rite of transition, which would eventually force separation on friends who together had shared the formative years of childhood.

On 12 July, along with a few friends, I had walked alongside supporters of the Orange Parade down the Crumlin Road. I was struck by the manner in which the music dramatically increased in volume and the drummers became more energetic as the bands reached the roundabout at Twaddell Avenue and came within sight of Holy Cross Church. It was as if the drummer was determined to beat a hole in his drum, with the full-throttled encouragement of onlookers and fellow bandsmen.

We walked past the front gates of the church, following the colourful banners with their strange blend of battle scenes and churches, oblivious to the triumphalist message behind the loud music blasted out by the 'kick the Pope bands'. We were so caught up in the ritual, that we probably would have kicked the Pope ourselves had he dared join us for the occasion!

We passed streets that were as yet unaware of the menace and notoriety that was about to be thrust upon them over the course of coming weeks: Butler Street, Hooker Street, Chief Street, Disraeli Street, Brookfield Street among others. While passing Palmer Street, on the Loyalist side of the road, a pole thrown high into the air by the band major went astray and punctured the thigh of an elderly lady spectator as it came down to land. Like a ten-year-old from the pages of *Tom Sawyer*, I joined the crowd of curious onlookers as we gathered round and watched with innocent excitement as the blood soaked onto the pavement as she lay propped against a wall – an omen of darker days to come.

Growing Civil Unrest

News coverage over that summer became increasingly focused on the 'civil unrest' that seemed to breaking out at regular intervals. While then unaware of the deeper story unfolding in front of me, I had already been introduced to new phrases and concepts during the early months of that year. I heard about 'civil rights'. I became aware of the deep resentment around these men called the 'B' Specials. For some reason a man called Paisley always seemed to be angry when he appeared on the television, and older relatives were using words that children really ought not to hear when they saw him. The ambush at Burntollet Bridge and rioting in Derry had filled the same screens of the black-and-white television sets on which we had seen men dressed in white break the barriers of time and space as they walked on the surface of the moon.

While the rest of the world could debate as to whether these men had indeed conquered space, or if we had all been the victims of a massive hoax, a match had been put to the fuse paper on the streets of Belfast and Derry. Angry voices had been raised, the first missiles had been thrown, and batons had come down on the skulls of protestors, breaking open years of built-up frustration and anger. Ten years of age, and growing into a society of increasing hostility and fear.

In the months leading up to August 1969, tension was growing in Ardoyne. A new Loyalist paramilitary group, called the Woodvale Defence Association (the WDA), had been ordering local Catholic families to leave the Woodvale area, situated at the very edge of the Ardoyne district. These families sought refuge in Ardoyne, while Protestant families who had lived in Ardoyne for generations moved to the houses vacated by Catholics in the Woodvale area. Homes being 'swapped' was the polite way to describe this intimidation, and the previous blurred lines of division were becoming increasingly clear. People were retreating back to 'their own side' of the community divide, with a number of furniture vans operating in the Crumlin Road area as Catholic and Protestant families switched homes on both sides of the road. Local MP Gerry Fitt, said:

This was by a mutual agreement. It was pathetic to see innocent people subjected to this type of treatment, regardless of their religion. I trust that there will be no repetition of this cruel and un-Christian behaviour (Irish News, *Monday 4 August*).

As August progressed, we witnessed a community becoming increasingly divided as long-held but sleeping sectarian attitudes awakened, and found violent expression as old political and sectarian sores reopened in a new context. It seemed that our future was in real danger of being created by our past. The possibility of martial law as a response to the escalating violence was headlines in the *Irish News* on Monday 4 August as it reported:

Dozens of Catholic families have been forced out of their homes in the Crumlin Road area of Belfast. A group of about 100 Paisleyites toured the Leopold Street, Palmer Street, Oregon Street, Ottawa Street, Columbia Street and part of Chief Street, all inter-denominational areas, warning Catholics to 'Get out or be burned out'.

The ferocity of the violence was seen in a report in the same newspaper on rioting in the Crumlin Road area:

...trouble flared just after midnight. Several petrol bombs were thrown in the Hooker Street and Herbert Street area. One of them hit a policeman and his

topcoat caught fire. His colleagues immediately rolled him on the ground and extinguished the flames.

Hot Summer – Darkening Clouds

August 1969 saw a dramatic escalation of violence and intimidation, but a report in the *Irish News* on Monday 4 August spoke of the optimism of Mr Paddy Devlin MP (West Belfast) that this displacement of families could be contained:

It is imperative in the interests of people of different denominations that the situation should be confined entirely to what has happened tonight and that no further escalation occurs.

Although the present position is very dangerous and tragically reminiscent of the troubled years of 1922–35 when thousands of innocent people suffered in this way, I have sufficient confidence in all sections of the community when I appeal to them to desist. The position is not yet irretrievable.

However, such words of cautious optimism were very quickly proven misplaced. As soon as the very next morning, the same newspaper reported of a dramatic increase in tension and violence:

More trouble flared in battered Belfast last night. This time it was mainly centred in the Crumlin Road area where large police enforcements were rushed to keep rioters in Hooker Street and Disraeli Street – on the opposite side – apart.... At the height of the disturbances a wine store in Disraeli Street was set alight and burned furiously. A house, a bookmaker's office and a butcher's shop on Crumlin Road were also damaged by petrol bombs.

A lorry, placed before barricades in Hooker Street, was burned out. Several of the petrol bombs exploded only yards away from the strong police cordon, which was contending with a fusillade of stones hurled out of Disraeli Street.

The front page contained reference to injuries received by individuals in the rioting:

Two youths who were injured during the disturbances in Butler Street late last night were anointed by Fr. Marcellus C.P., as they were being taken to hospital. One was anointed in the ambulance and the other as he was being taken from a police Land Rover.

Neil Summers (18), of 21 Dunblaine Avenue, Oldpark Road, is understood to have been knocked down by a jeep during the riots and dragged part way up the street. The other, Martin Meekin (24), of 183 Alliance Avenue, whose wife is expecting a baby, is said to have been struck by a club.

Martin Meehan's name would not be misspelt in newspapers again over the ensuing years as he went on to become a prominent leader of the Provisional IRA in Ardoyne, and later a key supporter of the Good Friday Agreement.

Rioting sparked on 14 August saw events reach breaking point. From early morning on 14 August, I was conscious of a menace and tension in the air. The Scarman Tribunal (p177) describes the scene well:

On Thursday, 14 August, there was considerable tension and apprehension among the residents of the Crumlin Road; in the words of one witness 'everybody seemed to think that something was going to happen.'

I have a memory of adults standing around in small groups on the street and talking about riots on the Falls Road. Hundreds of Loyalists had assembled on the Crumlin Road that afternoon facing Brookfield and Hooker Streets. People were talking openly about how the district was 'going to be defended' when the Orangemen attacked that evening. Residents began to erect hastily-made barricades. Men were knocking on doors asking for anything that could be used as a weapon. Milk bottles and hammers, hurling sticks and garden tools were being handed over. In the concrete jungle that was Ardoyne though, it was clear that there was no point depending upon the scarce collection of garden scythes and hedge-cutters that were being gathered for the defence of the district!

I heard a soon-to-be familiar word for the first time that day. There was talk of building 'barricades'. It is a word that was to be part and parcel of our everyday vocabulary over the next few months and subsequent years. Ardoyne bus depot had been broken into and up to 50 buses had been hijacked. Yes, another new word!

The noise of metal being trailed along the road and being thrown on to the concrete streets became louder as the day went on and the barricades became bigger and stronger at the end of every street in the district. Observers in later years would often make similar statements along the lines of, 'It must have been terrifying to live through that as a child.' It was, but it was also strangely exciting. It was like Hollywood had come to our street to make a real-life war film, in contrast to the make-believe war game of 'Japs and Germans' that we had often played during lunchtime in the playground of Holy Cross Boys' School.

Although at ten years of age I was not aware of the full dimensions of what was unfolding on the streets which up to then had been our playground, I was conscious of the tension and confusion that was growing as the days progressed. The main topic of conversation among adults was of how to defend the district to stop the 'Orangemen breaking through'. Men had emptied petrol all along the street in front of our house from the large drums 'liberated' from the bus depot. Apparently it was to give time for 'the men from the Falls' to get across to save the district once it had been over-run by the Loyalists. There seemed to be little doubt that Ardoyne was about to be invaded.

I was conscious of the sense of confusion as men were caught in the dilemma as to whether they would get involved in the unfolding events on the streets or just stay away from the trouble. Moral dilemmas were settled when word went round that Fr Marcellus Gillespie, one of the Passionist community living in Holy Cross Monastery, was spotted on one of the hijacked buses that were being used to build makeshift barricades to block access to Ardoyne.

While my dad was out making barricades with the other men of the district, my mum had brought mattresses down from the upstairs bedrooms and placed them in our back living room. She was helped by my Aunt Patricia, who lived with my grandparents further down Brompton Park, but who had stayed in our house to support my mum that night. It was deemed too dangerous for us to sleep in the upstairs rooms for fear of bullets penetrating the house. Such fear was proven appropriate that same night when a nine-year-old boy, Patrick Rooney, was killed by machine-gun fire from an RUC Shortland armoured vehicle that opened fire at Divis Flats, and the high-velocity bullets penetrated the walls of the flats and killed Patrick as he lay in his bed.

Local clergymen had met at 5 p.m. on the Crumlin Road near the Hooker Street junction to try to placate local residents. The Scarman Tribunal (p177) describes the events of that evening:

Fr. (Ailbe) Delaney was asked to investigate a rumour that petrol bombs were being stored on the roof of the Edenderry Inn. He carried out a partial search but discovered nothing.

On the streets around us the scene was being set for the events that were to subsequently unfold that evening:

By 8pm the building of a barricade in Hooker Street about 100 yards from the Crumlin Road was already in progress. An hour later a second barricade near the junction with Chatham Street was in course of construction. By 9pm, or shortly after, two parties of police had arrived to reinforce the patrols on Crumlin Road.

Finally, the anticipated attack took place. An RUC armoured vehicle smashed down the Hooker Street barricade and Loyalists charged into the district, wrecking homes and setting fire to Catholic-owned shops and pubs:

After the police moved into Hooker Street they were followed by a number of people from the Disraeli Street side of the road, some of whom were wearing helmets and armbands. It appears that no police had been left behind on the Crumlin Road to control this crowd.

There are different accounts as to the number of Loyalists who followed the RUC and the 'B' Specials into Ardoyne that evening. RUC accounts (p180) range from 'a few' to 'some 20–30.' However, another witness, Mr McMullan, told the Scarman Tribunal that:

He saw between 200 and 300 civilians enter Hooker Street immediately behind the police. This estimate is supported by the witness of Mr. Walsh, a staff reporter with the Irish Times. *We [the Scarman Tribunal] believe the number was substantial, certainly no less than 100.*

As local people attempted to defend their properties, the heavily armed RUC fired indiscriminately into peoples' homes. Accounts of who threw the first petrol bomb or stone will be forever debated and will never be agreed, but there can be no doubt of the mayhem that took place that evening. By 11 p.m., events had escalated out of control:

The missiles and later petrol bombs thrown from the Disraeli Street crowd followed shortly after the first petrol bomb came from that street. When DI Gilchrist arrived he saw hand to hand fighting in the Crumlin Road and HC Kyle described the scene he saw as a pitched battle (Scarman Tribunal, p180).

First Deaths

Death followed closely. Sammy McLarnon, a father of two, was shot through the window of his home. His wife, Ann, later recalled the events that night in the book *Ardoyne: The Untold Truth* (p32):

Sammy had been up the street helping to put out a fire at a house just before he was shot. The Protestants had come across the Crumlin Road and attacked three Catholic houses... There was a number of shots fired from the Protestant side of the Crumlin Road. So everybody went back into their homes and Sammy came into our house. At about 11pm I heard shooting, but I thought it was blanks. Sammy said to me, 'We'll take the kids over to your mammy's.' I said, 'But it could start in your mammy's street tonight.'... Then Sammy and me were standing at the right hand side of the window. I remember there was an awful bright light... We saw these two fellas kneeling down in the street... Then the RUC went over to talk to them... and the two fellas and the RUC went away. I walked away to go into the working kitchen. I came back into the living room and then the shots came in through the window. There were three bullets, very close together. The RUC tried to say that they were ricochets, but they were head high. They were obviously intended to kill. He was shot through the window. He was pulling down the blind because he must have seen something. The glass actually hit me in the face. I ran back into the working kitchen again. When I came out Sammy was on the ground of the living room. I thought he had dived to the ground. But then I realised he had been shot and I just screamed, 'My husband's shot, my husband's shot.'

Another local man, Michael Lynch, was also shot dead by the RUC as he walked home from the cinema. Mrs McAfee, an eyewitness, stated (*Ardoyne: The Untold Truth*, p36):

The men all ran towards the Crumlin Road and there was a lot of noise. My children were in bed but all the doors of the house were open and people were coming and going. Hannah McCallum and Geraldine Smart were in the house when a man I did not recognise stumbled into the living room. He collapsed on the floor. We put a pillow under his head and a blanket round him. His skin was cold and clammy and he was only semi-conscious. There was very little blood. There was just a small hole in the front of his shirt. We tried to keep him awake but he only said that his name was Michael Lynch. We knew he was badly hurt.

The role of the 'B' Specials was highlighted in a report in the *Irish News* on Friday 15 August that explicitly identified the role of members of the police, and in particular the 'B' Specials, in the escalating violence:

'B' Specials were reported to have handed out arms to civilians on the Shankill Road, where women and children were building up stocks of petrol bombs

quite openly on the road. Mr Paddy Devlin, Labour MP for Falls, Belfast was at the Royal Victoria Hospital this morning comforting the injured. He said he had lodged a protest with the City Commissioner for Police. 'I told the Commissioner,' said Mr Devlin, 'that these armoured cars were running up and down streets in Catholic areas shooting indiscriminately. I urged him to put an immediate stop to it.'

The following morning, the same newspaper ran the chilling headline '**BELFAST – A CITY CONVULSED**'. The opening paragraphs then proceeded to describe the rising tension behind the headline:

British troops went into action in Belfast last night against a background of further killings, heavy casualties, sniping in many areas into Catholic quarters and a total casualty list of 178 injured.

And early this morning 'B' Specials have gone on a terror rampage in the Ardoyne district where houses in Butler Street and Brookfield Street were ablaze. Wounded were taken to a first-aid post in Havana Street… men injured in the Specials rampage were Samuel Graham (24) of Hooker Street, Gerard Gillespie, Etna Drive and Eddie Campbell (25) of Brookfield Street.

The newspaper went on to report that it had:

… received phone calls from Ardoyne early today asking: 'For God's sake get the police or the military or we will all be slaughtered.' The callers said the Specials had been sniping from a nearby mill and were firing in all directions. Other 'B' men using an RUC armoured car drove up the Crumlin Road and fired indiscriminately into Hooker Street and Butler Street.

As the rioting raged outside our home at the top of Brompton Park, rumours spread that the UVF had broken into the monastery and were about to shoot the priests. My father and a number of other men ran across the Crumlin Road and into the grounds of Holy Cross, which at the time were covered in bushes and large trees. As they made their way up the avenue, Loyalists who had been hiding in the shrubbery came out of the darkness and attacked them. My father was hurt but was lifted by 'Big John' Kelly onto his shoulders, who then fought his way back to Brompton Park. My father was brought to the Mater Hospital as a result of his injuries. Next morning he woke to find himself lying in a bed that was placed between two Loyalists who had been injured as they attacked Ardoyne the previous evening. Needless to say, my father didn't hang around too long before making his way back to Ardoyne!

I clearly remember the sounds from that night: the sound of gunfire in the air, the squeal of the steel from the barricades being trailed across the street, the smell of smoke from burning houses, the sound of sirens and men shouting as fighting broke out in the streets around us. As we lay on the mattresses in our back kitchen I remember my older sister shouting, 'There's a sniper on our back wall!' – as a black cat slouched on its way, seeming oblivious to the mayhem erupting around it.

I also vividly remember the thought that just seems so ridiculous for a child of ten years of age: 'If I go asleep, I won't feel it when those men shoot me.' It is a memory that is still accompanied by the emotion, dented but not healed by the passing of years. The innocence of childhood shattered.

Political Background

The brutal outbreak of violence occurred against the background of a political system that was creaking at its foundations. The Nationalist community had commemorated the 50th anniversary of the Easter Rising in 1966. The associated events had kept brought the prospect of reunification back into the consciousness of Nationalism, but this had not been matched by any notable resurgence in the activities of the IRA, which had been damaged by the Border Campaign of the late 1950s and early 1960s. The Nationalist community had instead found a focus in the growth of the campaign for civil rights for Catholics in the Northern State. This campaign had also found common ground with many people from within the Protestant community who played a significant role in the growth of the Civil Rights Movement and of the People's Democracy organisation.

Unionism was feeling nervous as the voice and demands of the Catholic community became louder. Perhaps one of the failures of Unionism though was its failure to distinguish this fresh campaign for civil rights from the older struggle for Irish freedom. On 25 November 1968, Albert Kennedy, the Inspector General of the RUC, wrote a letter to the Home Minister, Bill Craig, in which he stated that:

'In my opinion, a number of people on what I call the loyalist side are confused and not making any distinction between the IRA and Civil Rights marchers... This is resulting in opposition to peaceful marches, demonstrations and meetings of such a nature as could lead to armed conflict, with the IRA stepping in to take advantage of the situation... it seems to me that not enough is being done by responsible people who should, I suggest, be busy pointing out the differences between the two kinds of activity... Police information indicates

that many professing Unionists support the protestors, and the trouble emanates from a comparatively small minority of people holding extremist views who, quite sincerely I feel, see a danger to the constitution which, as I have said above, does not exist.'

Unionism was confused in its approach to the growth in support for the Civil Rights Movement. While members of the Protestant community recognised that reform was both desirable and inevitable, the push for reform was matched by a growing opposition from within hard-line Loyalism towards any reform that would threaten the inbuilt superiority of the Protestant community. Tensions rose within Unionism to such an extent that the Prime Minister, Terence O'Neill, appeared on Northern Ireland television on 9 December 1968 and delivered his famous 'Ulster Stands at the Crossroads' speech, in which he both appealed for unity and gave an ominous warning about what could be facing the North:

'Ulster stands at the crossroads. I believe you know me well enough to appreciate that I am not a man given to extravagant language. But I must say to you this evening that our conduct over the coming days and weeks will decide our future. As we face this situation, I would be failing in my duty, to you as your prime minister, if I did not put the issues calmly and clearly before you all.

These issues are far too serious to be determined behind closed doors, or left to noisy minorities. The time has come for the people as a whole to speak in a clear voice.

For more than six years now I have tried to heal some of the deep divisions in our communities. I did so because I could not see how an Ulster divided against itself could hope to stand. I made it clear that a Northern Ireland based on the interests of any one section, rather than on the interests of all, could have no long term future...

What kind of Ulster do you want? A happy and respected province, in good standing with the rest of the United Kingdom? Or a place continually torn apart by riots and demonstrations, regarded by the rest of Britain as a political outcast? As always in a democracy, the choice is yours.

I will accept whatever your verdict may be. If it is your decision to live up to the words "Ulster is British", which is part of our creed, then my services will be at your disposal to do what I can. But if you want a separate inward-looking, selfish and divided Ulster, then you must seek for others to lead you along that road. For I cannot and will not do it.

Please weigh well all that is at stake and make your voice heard in whatever way you think best, so that we may know the views not of the few, but of the many.'

Events moved quickly within Unionism as O'Neill was encouraged by the initial positive reaction to his statement. In spite of opposition from within his own cabinet, O'Neill announced a reform package, in which five of the Civil Rights Association's demands were met – including the introduction of a points system to ensure fairer allocation of council houses, parts of the 1922 Special Powers Act were removed and an ombudsman was appointed to examine complaints. O'Neill then sacked his hard-line Home Affairs Minister, William Craig, two days later. Events on the streets, though, began to interfere with his path towards reform. On Wednesday 1 January, approximately 40 members of People's Democracy began a four-day march from Belfast to Derry. As it made its way across the North towards Derry, the numbers participating increased to several hundred. Along with increasing numbers, the march also witnessed increased violence from within extreme Loyalism, facilitated by the RUC and 'B' Specials. The violence came to a head on 4 January when the march saw a sustained attack from Loyalists, the RUC and 'B' Specials at Burntollet Bridge. The attacks on the march saw opinions strongly polarised and hopes of an agreed settlement were quickly disappearing.

On 24 January 1969 Brian Faulkner, Deputy Prime Minister and Minister of Commerce, resigned from the Unionist Government in opposition to O'Neill's policies and the lack of 'strong government'. Two days later William Morgan, then Minister of Health and Social Services, also resigned from the Government. Less than a week later twelve backbench Unionist MPs called for O'Neill's removal in order to maintain party unity. O'Neill announced the dissolution of the Stormont Parliament and the holding of a general election on 24 February 1969.

O'Neill won the election, but he would eventually lose the argument. For the first time, the Ulster Unionist Party had been put under pressure. Its vote split between those who supported Prime Minister Terence O'Neill's package of reforms and those opposed to them. Unable to see off the opposition, both from within his party and from outside, O'Neill resigned on 28 April 1969. He was replaced by James Chichester-Clark, who, in an attempt to bring unity to the Unionist party, brought Faulkner and two other critics of O'Neill into his Government, while at the same time committing to continue O'Neill's policies, including changes to the local government election franchise, and agreeing that local government boundaries would be re-drawn by an independent commission.

The challenges facing the Catholic community in its campaign for equal rights, though, was emphasised by O'Neill himself in an interview with the *Belfast Telegraph* on 10 May, just a few weeks after his resignation as Prime Minister, in which he outlined his motivation for reform:

> *'It is frightfully hard to explain to Protestants that if you give Roman Catholics a good job and a good house they will live like Protestants because they will see neighbours with cars and television sets; they will refuse to have eighteen children. But if a Roman Catholic is jobless, and lives in the most ghastly hovel, he will rear eighteen children on National Assistance. If you treat Roman Catholics with due consider and kindness, they will live like Protestants in spite of the authoritative nature of their Church...'*

Stormont

It was against this background of internal division and suspicion around civil rights and the Catholic community that the Stormont administration faced up to the outbreak of street violence. Its instability was reinforced as the violence escalated throughout the summer period. Meanwhile the Dublin Government was coming under increased pressure to intervene. The events in Belfast and Derry in the week of 9–16 August resulted in the Taoiseach, Jack Lynch, making a crucial intervention. Referring specifically to events in Derry, he said:

> *'It is evident that the Stormont Government is no longer in control of the situation. Indeed the present situation is the inevitable outcome of the policies pursued for decades by successive Stormont Governments. It is clear, also, that the Irish Government can no longer stand by and see innocent people injured and perhaps worse'* (Irish Times, 14 August 1969).

Lynch called for United Nations troops to be sent to Northern Ireland and also ordered that a number of Irish Army field hospitals be set up along the border. This appeared to many Unionists to confirm their fears of an imminent invasion by the Irish Army. Chichester-Clark called Lynch's remarks 'inflammatory and ill-considered', and said that he would hold Lynch personally responsible for any worsening of feeling. Lynch opposed the idea of British troops being sent into places like Ardoyne and Derry, and argued instead for a United Nations force to go in. Then he announced that only re-unification could provide a solution and that his Government would be entering into negotiations with the British Government on the matter. The speech seemed to confirm the rumours of a general Republican offensive to take over the North.

The next day James Chichester-Clark responded to Lynch, stating what he believed to be the true motivation for those Catholics pushing for reform:

> *'This is not the agitation of a minority seeking by lawful means the assertion of political rights. It is the conspiracy of forces seeking to overthrow a Government democratically elected by a large majority. What the teenage hooligans seek beyond cheap kicks I do not know. But of this I am quite certain – they are being manipulated and encouraged by those who seek to discredit and overthrow this Government.'*

It was clear that the then Prime Minister, James Chichester-Clark, was trying to explain the violence being witnessed in places such as Ardoyne as part of a larger IRA plot, in which they had hijacked the growing Civil Rights Movement.

Church Response

Local Catholic Church leaders were quick to respond to the unfolding events on the streets and to Chichester-Clark's statement. Cardinal Conway made an appeal for Catholics to avoid anything that might lead to further escalation of violence. On 15 August he issued a strong statement in the *Irish News* that:

> *'An extension of the present trouble would play into the hands of those who resent the very presence of Catholics in the community.'*

In a direct appeal to the Catholic community, he said:

> *'I appeal to them not to allow themselves to be swept away by emotion – however natural and understandable such emotion may be – but to keep cool heads and realize that a general eruption of violence would seriously weaken the Civil Rights Movement.'*

He also made a less-than-subtle reference to where he believed blame might eventually be laid for such violence:

> *'This is not the time to apportion precise responsibility for what has happened, but certainly a heavy burden rests on those who remained silent for over 40 years in the face of manifest injustice.'*

In that same newspaper on Monday 18 August, the Bishop of Down and Connor, Most Rev Dr Philbin, wrote of his experience of visiting Ardoyne:

'We are experiencing an outbreak of bitter and sustained attack on sections of the population which is continuing and which is producing the most disastrous results... Everywhere I have gone, I have heard the Catholic population tell of their fears for the future in terms which suggest a word I dare not use lest I be accused of exaggeration.

The bishop said he had that day appealed to the Prime Minister as a matter of the most immediate urgency for the posting of troops in the Ardoyne area "where the population is terrified at the prospect of another night such as those they have been enduring since Thursday last."'

Bishop Philbin went on:

'I have also made it clear to the Prime Minister that the Catholic community cannot accept the implication of his recent statement that the origin of the present disturbance lies in a conspiracy on their side "to subvert a democratically elected government".

I have made the widest enquiries and can hear of nobody who was even approached by anyone organizing such a conspiracy. On the contrary, Catholics have been the victims of what bears all the signs of being a widespread, sudden and fully equipped assault.

There is no Catholic sectarian armed-force.'

In a television interview on RTE following the outbreak of violence, the rector and parish priest of Holy Cross Church, Fr Columb Devine CP, stated:

'Several Catholic families were intimidated and told to leave their homes. 184 homes from the parish were burned to the ground. An attack had been made by the Protestants, and I am sad to say aided and abetted by the police and by the Ulster Special Constabulary ('B' Specials), but the Army intervened and peace was brought to the area. A very uneasy one it was...'

Despite continuing efforts by the Stormont regime to pin the blame for the emerging violence on the rebirth of the IRA, the Catholic bishops rejected any idea of armed insurrection by the IRA. On 23 August, the *Irish News* carried a statement from Cardinal William Conway, together with the Bishops of Derry, Clogher, Dromore, Kilmore, and Down & Connor, that stated:

> *'The fact is that on Thursday and Friday of last week the Catholic districts of Falls and Ardoyne were invaded by mobs equipped with machine-guns and other firearms. A community that was virtually defenceless was swept by gunfire and streets of Catholic homes were systematically set on fire. We entirely reject the hypothesis that the origin of last week's tragedy was an armed insurrection.'*

As reported on the front page of the *Irish News* on Monday 25 August, these statements from Church leaders received a warm welcome from within the Nationalist community as they had reinforced statements from Opposition MPs and other groups that the full facts relating to the outbreak of violence had not been admitted to by the Stormont Government. Ivan Cooper, Independent MP for Mid-Derry, said that the statements have shown:

> *'... only too clearly to the world at large the fact that many of the things that happened in Ardoyne in Belfast and in Bogside in Derry have not been exposed and a full inquiry is absolutely necessary... I was particularly impressed by the fact that the Cardinal and the Bishops reiterated that this was not a sectarian fight and that the Protestant community is a community to be respected. For my part, I do not believe that the full facts about the B Specials have been made known. If they were, Harold Wilson would not talk of phasing them out. He would talk of blotting them out immediately.'*

The *Irish News* highlighted the opinion of John Hume, Independent MP for Foyle, that following the bishops' statements:

> *'No-one could now doubt the argument put forward for a long time about the forces of law and order in the North. The bishops had put their finger upon the reason for recent events... All other attempts to whitewash or talk about Red plots or IRA plots were as nothing compared to this reason.'*

Perhaps the most strongly worded support for the Church leaders' statements came from Paddy Devlin, MP for Falls, who was unequivocal in his condemnation of the Stormont Government's explanation of the violence as supported by the majority of mainstream media outlets:

'Everyone of us who witnessed the attacks by the bloodthirsty mobs who murdered, looted and burned the homes of Catholic families know that fair, balanced and objective coverage was not given by the majority of the news media in Northern Ireland. Every single syllable uttered by the Government news agency was accepted without question by journalists of certain newspapers and the local TV... Neither Paddy Kennedy MP for Central nor I – both MPs for the areas involved – were invited to comment or challenge the so-called facts issued by the Government in spite of the fact that we were both on the spot throughout the time of the violence.

We could have told them that some members of the RUC using armoured vehicles and supported by the 'B' Specials and UVF were responsible for those dastardly attacks.

We could have told them that young Patrick Rooney, aged nine, was not shot by a stray bullet but by a fusilade of shots that tore through his home in Divis Towers.

We could have told them that the reason for these attacks were not IRA inspired but were directly related to the struggle for leadership within the Unionist Party between Chichester-Clark and the hard-liners led by William Craig, MP, who are seeking his overthrow.

We could have told them that the invented terror similar to that which led to extremist mobs attacking the inhabitants of Unity Walk was the weapon used throughout by Government spokesmen.

Finally, we could have told them that we will not go back to the Stormont Parliament until the maniacs responsible for these crimes are brought to justice.'

Whatever the story behind later conflict in the district, claims that the trouble in Ardoyne in August 1969 was orchestrated by Republicans, or was part of a larger Republican plot, were widely rejected by the local community. Before the riots had broken out, the International Commission of Jurists (ICJ) had already published a highly critical report on the British Government's policy in Northern Ireland. *The Times* wrote that this report

> *...criticised the Northern Ireland Government for police brutality, religious discrimination [against Catholics] and gerrymandering in politics.*

The *Belfast Telegraph* reported that the ICJ had added Northern Ireland to the list of states/jurisdictions *'where the protection of human rights is inadequately assured'.* An editorial in the *Irish News* on Monday 18 August could hardly have been more condemnatory of the attempt to apportion blame for the outbreak of violence on the Catholic community. Under the headline **'Contemptuous Statement'**, the paper stated:

> *We are visited, as we write this, by feelings of contempt for the Prime Minister of Stormont who, in his statement to the Press yesterday, adopted the peculiar posture of ignoring the evil deeds perpetrated by his supporters in Belfast, and of trying to enforce on incredulous newspapermen, not to speak of the world at large, the proposition that an IRA conspiracy was the real cause of the disorder.*

> *The impression was not merely given; it was clearly offered for acceptance that the organised assault on the homes of Catholic people, the violence and death in the streets, was somehow brought about by this conspiracy.*

> *This is hard to take.*

> *There is enough trouble in the community, one would think, without Mr Chichester-Clark inciting the long-suffering members of the Catholic community to rise up in bloody vindication of what their co-religionists in the Falls and Crumlin areas have suffered at the hands of police, of trigger-happy 'B' men (Protestant and Orange to a man); and of the armed Protestant extremists, unquestionably members of the UVF...*

> *It is intolerable, too, to find a Prime Minister with so little sympathy for the victims of the madness which we have seen unleashed by the 'B' men; and a Minister of Home Affairs, a decent, liberal man, so plainly out of his depth who, having left the Bar for the murk of Unionist politics, has now been made unhappily aware that even in this age of supposed enlightenment, that there are vast reservoirs of hate, bigotry and evil that can no longer be held back in certain areas...*

> *Mr Chichester-Clark's statement yesterday was, in the words of the Taoiseach, deplorable and tailor-made to inflame opinion. It was a statement of incredible*

clumsiness and ineptitude. And, after the foul work of the 'B' Specials, how squalid was the Prime Minister's reference to them as an extremely valuable reserve force and that their use in the present situation was right.

His statement, and the contemptuous ignoring of the facts, adds to the picture of the infinite capacity for folly of all those who traded the milder O'Neill for the hard-liner Chichester-Clark.

Underlining the human impact of the onslaught on Ardoyne, a two-column appeal is placed above this same editorial. It was headlined *'Holy Cross Ardoyne Relief Fund.'* The advert makes *'an urgent appeal for funds to aid the hundreds of homeless families in our district, and those in need of food and shelter',* and asks for all donations to be sent to the rector of Holy Cross Retreat.

On Wednesday 20 August 1969, an article appeared in the *Irish News* entitled *'Ardoyne: Fears that things will never be the same again'.* The writer was identified as 'An Ardoyne Resident'. The opening paragraph painted a sad picture of the desolation experienced by local people:

'While the troops removed the buses used as barricades and replaced them with barbed-wire fences around the Ardoyne area, I took a long walk through the district where I was born and reared and in which I hope to raise my family in peace. The sight which I beheld brought the tears to my eyes as I stood outside the gutted homes of many of my friends.'

The article paints a sad picture of what people in the district were experiencing and, unknowingly at the time, presents us with a scene that was soon to take a life and direction that was to lead to long years of conflict and heartbreak:

Desolation has indeed come to Ardoyne. One feels that things could never return to normal as people still roamed about in a dazed fashion. Many homes in the older part of the district were still empty as the occupants are staying in safer places with relatives...

The British troops when they arrived on Saturday were given a splendid welcome and the residents of Ardoyne felt relief at the sight of them and relationships with these soldiers has been tremendous up to now.

Let us hope that this will continue to be the case despite the odd rumour that petitions are being got out to get rid of the troops from Ardoyne.

Aftermath

When I returned to school in September 1969, my new classroom was on the top floor of Holy Cross Boys' School in Butler Street. We looked out classroom windows upon what could only be described as the set from a disaster movie in Hollywood. Huge cranes with swinging metal balls had moved in to demolish the charred remains of the burned-out houses in Brookfield and Hooker Streets. Dust seemed to be constantly in the air, as our streets were transformed into what seemed to be a scene from one of those war movies that we used to act out in the school playground. We didn't need make-believe anymore though, as no matter where we went in the district, soldiers and guns were always to be seen, and the sound of gunfire seemed to be constantly in the air.

The mills in Flax Street that overlooked the school were turned into military barracks. The noise and sight of helicopters flying in and out of the barracks were a constant distraction. In the innocence of those early childhood days, each time a helicopter appeared outside the windows of the classroom, our chairs became Browning machine guns, placed on the tops of our desks as we took on the might of the British Army from behind our schoolboy desks. We created our own fantasy world where nobody got hurt when they were shot, no blood was spilled when people died, and no families mourned when they came home in coffins. As we walked down the back stairs of the school, we watched the giant crane 'Goliath' being constructed in the distant world of Harland and Wolff shipyard as Ardoyne was in flames. This abnormality was to become the daily normality for life in Ardoyne over the next 40 years.

Those three days of 14–16 August saw the unleashing of unadulterated mayhem and savagery, inflicted upon this community by a combination of both State and Loyalist forces. In the subsequent years, this community was not a passive victim though, and it must be acknowledged that many lives were scarred forever by wounds afflicted from within this community, both internally and also on those perceived to be 'the enemy'.

As noted above, those days did not suddenly appear out of the blue, but were a result of almost fifty years of Unionist misrule embedded within blatant sectarianism and a misguided sense of superiority. However, perhaps underpinning that surface-level expression of superiority within Unionism there was an underlying fear of embracing equality and diversity. Whatever your political ideology, or however you make sense of the events of August 1969, one thing cannot be disputed: those three days changed forever the lives of the people of Ardoyne.

2

Brendan McFarlane

Home

I was born in 1951, and my family moved to Ardoyne in 1952. I lived in Estoril Park until I was twelve years of age, when we moved to Balholm Drive, not far from where the Crumlin Star Social Club is now situated. Growing up in Ardoyne was a fantastic experience. Just recently, I was talking to friends about one particular memory, and that was 'the Big Snow' of 1963. There was easily about three foot of snow lying on the ground. If we get two inches of snow these days you hear about it on the radio, schools get closed, and transport is brought to a standstill. This was not the attitude in 1963! My mother parcelled me out the door to school with my waterboots, jerkin, cap, and schoolbag. I then waded my way down through the snow-covered streets to school in Butler Street. When I reached the school, the first person I met was Billy Toal, the school caretaker. Billy immediately handed me a shovel to clear a pathway into the school for the rest of the boys. This memory sticks with me as something fantastic when compared with attitudes today.

Early Interests

I was an altar boy with the Passionists in Holy Cross Monastery from when I was ten years old up to when I was about fifteen. My nickname 'Bik' comes from the time I was an altar boy. Alongside the beautiful coffee that we were introduced to in the monastery, the priests also kept a supply of MacFarlane Lang biscuits. It didn't take much imagination on the part of my contemporaries for me to get the original nickname of 'Biscuit.' However, Ardoyne people are very sophisticated, and rather than talk about 'biscuits', they used the term 'bikkie', and so I eventually ended up with the nickname 'Bik'. I made lots of great friends there. In Holy Cross we had a lot of facilities that other altar servers didn't get. We had what was like a club based in an old coal cellar that had been converted into a games room. It had been baptised with the appropriate name of 'Australia'. We were also able to go for walks around the beautiful grounds and make tree huts as we had the grounds of Holy Cross Monastery as our playground. Fantastic.

Then there was the local GAA club, Ardoyne Kickhams. Our clubrooms were initially at the top of Butler Street, and then transferred to what was known as 'the Old Man's Hut' down beside a local community centre called Toby's Hall. I have great memories of growing up playing underage football with the club all during the 1960s.

Ballysillan Playing Fields was our home pitch, although it belonged to the City Council. To get to Ballysillan Playing Fields you had to walk up the Ardoyne Road past the mostly Protestant area of the Glenbryn estate. Ballysillan was a favourite pitch for many teams in Belfast. It was very level (unusual for many Gaelic pitches at that time), with sloping sides where people could sit around watching the game. We had some fantastic games there; not only underage games but the senior team also played their matches on the Ballysillan pitch.

During this time though we never had any difficulty or bother going up the Ardoyne Road to play hurling or football in Ballysillan. Two or three lads could have gone up and trained there, and then walked about the playing fields with Loyalist lads standing about, and nobody passed any remarks. There didn't seem to be an issue up until 1969/70, when it became a bit 'tetchy', for want of a better word. It became common for young lads to be challenged, stopped and chastised. I was just coming out of minor football (under-18) when the Gaelic posts were eventually sawn down by the local Loyalists, which then meant we had no home pitch for our games, but I still have some great, great memories of Ballysillan.

Family Background

My mother and father were both from the Falls Road. My father was a great footballer. We just recently discovered that during the 1941–43 period he played for Cork United (winning the League and Cup double), Distillery (the Whites), Belfast Celtic and Dundalk. He was also previously named as having played for Glentoran, but he must have been 15 or 16 at the time. His favourite position was the old number 8 position, inside right. According to the write-ups a journalist got me when I was in gaol, he was a bit of a star. We have just discovered recently, through my brother, that he played for Shelbourne during the war years, when there was no football in Britain or up here in the North.

My grandfather was the groundsman for the Distillery team, and from about four or five years of age, my da used to bring me to all the games over in Distillery's ground, Grosvenor Park. The ground was regularly packed for matches, absolutely packed solid. At half-time I would be brought into the changing rooms. The players got tea and a plain biscuit, so my granda would get me my tea and biscuit, and then I was out again for the second half. That fantastic time lasted until I decided at about ten years of age, after my da bringing me to all these soccer matches for years, that I was going to play Gaelic. I think he nearly had a heart attack, 'What! What!'

Carefree Living

Along with my mum and dad at home, I had my sister, Marian, three years younger than me, and my brother, Gerard, again three years younger than Marian. Marian was into Irish dancing and music. In fact, one of her contemporaries in St Dominic's Grammar School, and on the same badminton team, was Mary McAleese. They became great friends and they both played for the badminton team started in Ardoyne by Charlie Delaney down in Toby's Hall. To the amusement of some friends, I also joined the badminton team for a while. 'Badminton? Badminton? I thought you played Gaelic and hurling.' 'I do, but I am playing badminton as well.' They would then use some terminology that would have to be crossed out of a respectable book!

Early Heartbreak

Getting back to Gaelic football with the Ardoyne Kickhams and in school, I remember some great games at the back of St Gabriel's School. I have an abiding memory around Fred Heatley, Nick Mulholland, and myself. Both Fred and Nick are now dead, but Nick was from Newbridge, in south Derry, and he died young. He arrived into Belfast when he was fourteen years old and he automatically got onto the Gaelic team in St Gabriel's School. Nick, Fred and myself also played together for Ardoyne. I remember the three of us were selected for the Antrim Vocational Schools team, which was made up of the best players from across the secondary schools in the county. It was the first time Antrim were entering the Vocational

Schools competition. However, during the previous summer I had left school and had started an apprentice engineering course in Felden House, and while I am not saying I was guaranteed my position, they had me marked down as right half-back on the Antrim team. The trainer came up to me at training and said, 'Bik, I can't use you. You need to be registered at school to play for this team.'

So I couldn't play, and Antrim won the All-Ireland Final. The first All-Ireland title, apart from camogie, that any Antrim team had won, and it could have been me! I cried my eyes out. Within the next three years, the Antrim under-21s went on the win the All-Ireland Final in Croke Park. Mickey Cuthbert, Andy McCallan, the Hamills, Martin McAleese. I actually played minor football against Martin McAleese, Mary's husband. Some great memories!

Ardoyne Kickhams, though, was not just a football club. It was a genuinely family-orientated club, with old stalwarts like Jimmy Fennell, Dessie Smart, Seamy White, and all those guys who looked after us when there was no money around. Their dedication to that area and to that club was absolutely phenomenal. Rain, hail, sleet or snow, they made sure we got to the games, that we had full teams, that the kits were cleaned and that everybody was provided for. What an absolute gift to this community! When Jimmy Fennel died, he had become such a legend in the GAA world that his name went up on the big screen in Croke Park in tribute to him.

Thoughts of Priesthood

Growing up in the 1960s, people didn't have their lives planned out the way kids seem to have today. Life was just too enjoyable for forward-planning! Times were financially difficult and you had to fight to get a job, which were few and far between in our areas. It was only through education that people were able to move on. As the 1960s progressed, we saw attempts to correct the inherent imbalance that was structured into the institutions of the State. Catholics got an education and could eventually say, 'We can now get to university.' Young people today would be jealous, because you got a grant, not a loan! You got paid to go to university! So it is just crazy stuff altogether.

I came from a very Catholic background; my mother and father were pretty religious and regular attenders at Mass. My experience of growing up at four to five years of age was one of kneeling down to say the Rosary, and of serving Mass as an altar boy. All that was undoubtedly an influence at the back of my head, so when I started thinking about my future life the possibility of the priesthood seemed an obvious option. I found myself attracted to the Divine Word Missionaries. It is a missionary order and, if I remember correctly, a very radical order for the time. It had not been long since Vatican II had taken place, described by Pope John XXIII as like 'opening the windows of the Vatican' and letting in a bit of fresh air in order to deal with things on a global scale. We had issues like *Humanae Vitae* on birth control, changing the Mass to be celebrated in English, and all the other reforms that came with it.

The Attraction of Radicalism

I was 15/16 years old and at St Gabriel's at the time, just getting ready to make decisions about leaving school. The 'recruiting sergeant' for the Divine Word Missionaries arrived into our class and showed us what they did and told us their reasons for doing it. It seemed to me that the Divine Word Missionaries were rooted in that new vision of Church talked about in Vatican II. It is a German order with its headquarters in Germany, but they were in places like Brazil, Nicaragua, the Philippines, Papua New Guinea. All hard, difficult places, where people were poor and were fighting against unjust systems of oppression. So when he sold this way of life to us, I thought, 'Yea, I will give it a week's trial.'

I remember Winker Watson from the Bone had gone for a week's trial to an English First Division club. A fellow altar boy, Seamie O'Neill, had also gone for a week's trial with Leeds United, so I thought that I would go for a week's trial to the Divine Word Missionaries! Along with Francie Murphy from Ladbrook Drive, we parcelled up our gear and headed off for a week. I hadn't known that Francie had applied, but we both ended up going for a week's trial to see how we shaped up.

First Impressions of Religious Life

I was fascinated by the week. First of all, by Donamon Castle itself. The Divine Word Missionaries bought the castle when they came to Ireland in 1939. It is one of the oldest inhabited buildings in Ireland, overlooking the River Suck in County Roscommon. Ironically, given later developments in my life, it had been taken over by the IRA in late 1932 to set up an IRA training camp!

There was something about that place. I met some great people who shared their lifestyle with me and spoke of their work in Third World countries, describing how they were helping people. So when I reflected on the best way that I could help people, I thought, 'Maybe this is something for me to consider.' However, I left school and had gone into apprentice engineering, but this idea was still niggling away in the background. I finally decided that I was going to give it a go. I needed to go back to college to complete my 'O' levels, so that I could get into university. So in September 1968, I was parcelled off to Wales to complete my studies with the Divine Word Missionaries, along with Tommy Morrison, also from Ardoyne, who ended up being ordained a priest. Tommy died a number of years later in Sao Paulo, Brazil.

Trouble at Home

Getting information about what was happening in the outside world was difficult. If something major happened when I was in college in Wales, I would have heard about it. However, the outlets for getting information were limited. The only television channels then were BBC1, BBC2 and ITV. That was the sum total of what was available! The newspapers we got in the seminary were *The Times*, *The Telegraph* and *The Guardian*, so there wasn't a big focus on developments in Belfast. However, people were writing me letters, and telling me about the Civil Rights campaign, and when I came home on holidays I was seeing and being told about the protests going on with the Civil Rights Movement, People's Democracy and so on.

I was aware of the Civil Rights Movement in the United States that was making world headlines, but I then slowly began to become aware of the parades at home, the demonstrations, the demand for 'one man, one vote', and the rest. I saw people standing up and looking for a better deal, for equality of opportunity, for employment and housing, and for being treated with respect in what had been a one-party State for fifty years, and in which discrimination was inherent.

While I wasn't obviously aware of all that on a day-to-day basis, I knew that when my father was going for a job he was getting second choice. All the shipyard workers were from East Belfast or from other Unionist areas. I think even at the height of the shipbuilding industry and when Harland and Wolff was the second biggest ship building industry in Europe with about 15,000 workers, only about 500 were from the Catholic community.

We also had a police force that was always pretty aggressive towards us as kids. I remember the 'B' Specials in uniform as we went to Ballysillan Playing Fields along the Ardoyne Road. The RUC wasn't your friendly 'bobby' on the corner, or the kindly peeler you asked directions from. We knew that if we went to kick a football against the depot wall, you had to run when the cops came. It was always that awareness that you cannot do anything but that the RUC would be down on top of you, or the 'B' Specials would be there moving you round.

Home for Holidays

In 1969 I came home from college in Wales on holidays. Believe it or not, I got off the boat on the morning of 12 July, and my father had come down to pick me up to bring me home. I had previously been writing to the lads from the Gaelic club, and we had arranged to drive around Ireland in a minibus with big Dennis McMullan driving. I wasn't at home for more than two hours before I was away again, with the voice of my mum in my ears saying, 'You are only home two hours and you are away again!' Then she gave me a few pounds to send me off.

As we left Belfast, I was aware that things were very tense. There was fear associated with the marches and the demonstrations, and temperatures were certainly on the rise, but we were young and carefree: 'Let's go and tour Ireland!' So we all headed off to tour Ireland, but the further we toured down round Waterford, Cork, Kerry, people were saying to us, 'Are you from Belfast? What about the trouble up there? What's happening?' We heard about the rioting in the places we visited and people kept asking everywhere we went, 'It must be tight up there. It must be hard.'

To be honest though, I didn't have any real sense yet of what was happening. We got back to Ardoyne towards the end of July, with the marching season in full flow, and the temperature was rising dramatically. This increased dramatically as entered into August.

Violence Erupts

In August, rioting erupted in Derry. I recall constantly looking at it on the news every day during that week, as the people defended the Bogside against the RUC and the 'B' Specials. Then Belfast erupted with the attacks on Bombay Street, and the attacks on Ardoyne. The attacks on Ardoyne started further down along the front of the Crumlin Road: Herbert Street, Brookfield Street, Hooker Street. The family of one of my friends, Terry Fagan, owned a house on the front of the Crumlin Road, just across from Bray Street. Tessy Donegan's shop was on the same block as their home, just below Herbert Street.

When I heard about the trouble breaking out, I went down to see what was happening, and people were really fearful about the houses getting attacked. There was anything from 1,000 to 2,000 Loyalists on the road. I noticed that some had armbands on, that later transpired to be the WDA, John McKeague's Woodvale Defence Association. What puzzled me a bit was that there were all sorts of police jeeps coming out of the streets on to the Crumlin Road, and the Loyalists were in the midst of them. It wasn't as if the jeeps were trying to hem them in.

We were in Terry Fagan's front porch, which had a small garden area in front of it. His mum and dad along with some relatives were also there. Everybody was really on edge, so they went down to remonstrate with the sergeant of the RUC. He was sitting in the jeep, but some of the Loyalists had unscrewed a petrol cap, and he was panicking about a rag going into it. They shouted, 'You have to hold these people back.' He replied, 'We are trying, we are trying,' but the jeeps were just driving around and didn't go into a formation to block the front of the road to keep the Loyalists back.

I got fearful at that time that the Loyalists were going to come in on top of us, and within a minute petrol bombs starting to come flying over along with a frenzy of bricks and bottles. We tried to defend the house for about thirty seconds, but his mum and dad were shouting, 'Get in. Get in. Get in', so we went into the house and closed the doors, but the Loyalists came streaming across the road, joined by the RUC and the 'B' Specials. We got everybody firstly to the back of the house, and then out into Herbert Street. We bolted out the back of the house into Herbert Street, and decided to run up Chatham Street towards Kerrera Street. Just as we got the family away, and as we were getting ourselves out the back of the house, the Loyalists came through the windows and the front door. The RUC had driven into Herbert Street, and the same thing was happening in Hooker Street. The Loyalists were in the police jeeps, running between the jeeps, and they just came flying into the district.

Luckily we were fit and fast from playing minor football. I remember Brian Quinn ran all the way down Herbert Street towards Brompton Park, and the next thing the shooting started. Brian got shot in the back, just above the hip. When I heard the gunfire I was away like a whippet until I got past Butler Street, and further on up to Kerrera Street. The Loyalists came flying up in their droves through the streets and banging doors as they went. Shotguns were getting fired. Machine guns were getting fired. They were armed to the teeth.

There was a whippet armoured car that came driving in firing one of those .30 calibre machine guns. Everybody just bolted up out of the way of it. By now there were quite a considerable amount of lads down round Herbert/Brookfield and Hooker Streets in an attempt to defend the area, but they were really up against it that night against the full military array of the State. The full force of Loyalists, RUC, and 'B' Specials were in on top of them.

I remember at one stage the houses were going on fire across from Bray Street and the fire engine came down the Crumlin Road from where the Ardoyne ambulance station is now situated. I was standing at Frank the barber's and Paddy Cassidy's shop, just across from the gate of the church at the top of Butler Street. I watched the cops and the Loyalists stop the fire engine and wouldn't let it down past Chief Street.

The firemen were remonstrating with the Loyalist crowd and with the cops, 'We need to put the fire out. We need to put the fire out.' They wouldn't let them through. Firemen were frustrated and then someone started throwing bricks at the firemen, 'Take yourselves off.' The firemen were of course fearful of the crowd confronting them, and they had to reverse. I then spotted someone in the chapel grounds. I ran across to see who it was. Someone shouted, 'Don't! It might be a Loyalist.' I said, 'No, they are all down the road.' It turned out to be a cameraman. There was a guy with me as we ran across the road, and when we got up the steps of the church we shouted, 'What are you doing here?' It turned out he was a cameraman from ITN, kneeling there with a big state-of-the-art camera! 'I want to film this,' he said. 'Go ahead,' I said, 'but I am going with you.'

He then came out into the middle of the Crumlin Road, and was filming what was happening further down the road. The Loyalists by now had moved in from the Crumlin Road, down along Herbert Street, and were making their way up through the district. We were at the top section of Chatham Street and Butler Street, and he was filming away. I was with Terry Fagan, Mickey McKervey and I think Malachy McRoberts, but the Loyalists were coming and coming. I kept saying to this camera man, 'Come on! Let's get out of here!'

'No, I want to get more,' he kept replying! He wanted to get every last detail, but the Loyalists were no more than 20 yards away, and he was still filming. At that stage I said to him: 'I'm away', and bolted up Chatham Street. I have never seen any of that film on any news reel or anything like that. Whether or not the RUC took him in, I will never know, but he got incredible footage and there is a good possibility they seized it.

At this stage, we could hear the gunfire down in Herbert Street and up in Chatham Street. We ran round into Balholm Drive. The cops followed us to the top of Brompton Park, but they would not come in any further. They stood out opposite Holy Cross Hall and looked down. I think they were fearful of what might have been there, as there were the barricades erected in their path.

The night of 14–15 August was when it all went up in smoke. The Loyalists, police and 'B' Specials had burned their way through Hooker Street, Brookfield Street and the top end of Herbert Street, all the way down in front of the Crumlin Road. Once the flames had taken up you couldn't come in or go out. It was just an inferno. They just flattened it, so we just had to come back up into the district. Men from the district had gathered all along Butler Street at the back of Herbert Street to hold them back. It levelled off in the early part of the Friday morning.

At one stage I heard that there was a Mills bomb going off at the front of the Crumlin Road. Somebody threw it at the Loyalists to hold them back, but there was precious little weaponry in the area to hold these people back. I remember Dessie Carmichael, God rest him, he was at the back end of the area. I remember talking to him on the Saturday. He wouldn't have known me, but I knew who he was and he was around looking for Martin Meehan or one of the Larkins. He said we only have a .303 with so many rounds of ammunition. Strangely nothing happened over at Alliance or Jamaica Street. The Loyalists were there but they didn't encroach at that end, whether they were fearful that people there had weapons or what. Of course, the famous Fr Marcellus was in the midst of it all. I remember him saying to me, 'Can you drive?' He knew I was home from the seminary. I said 'No.'

'Well,' he said, 'we need somebody to drive this bus.'

I asked, 'What bus?'

It was then that I realised the men from the district had opened Ardoyne bus station and had taken out every single bus. The men drove them down through the district. I saw guys driving buses down the Crumlin Road who couldn't even drive a car. I was going to say 'parking them', but they practically crashed them into the corner of Butler Street and Kerrera Street in order to stop them. They put the buses all round Glenard as well, blocking off every single street. The cops must have thought that people in the district were well-prepared, so they were cautious about coming in. Consequently it was 'Old Ardoyne' that took the brunt of the attack. The devastation was awful.

Death Comes to the Parish

Michael Lynch and Sammy McLarnon were killed that night. To best of my knowledge, Neil Summers was deliberately run over by an armoured car and lost his leg. The driver in later years gave evidence that he was ordered to drive over him by the sergeant in charge. There was something in the region of ninety people treated for those type of injuries and gunshot wounds over those couple of nights. It was horrendous, and everybody thought that this is the end, and that Ardoyne was going to be overrun by the Loyalists and the police.

I think the Loyalists were trying to get in the back of the Grove beside the chapel, and there were patrols of men there keeping an eye on things, but the main thrust of the attack was on the Crumlin Road. They burnt Logue's pub and the Wheatfield Inn. The Wheatfield Inn was one of the most famous pubs in Belfast. The Dubliners had just played at its reopening a few months beforehand.

Role of the IRA

There were IRA people in the area, but there was no organised structure. Martin Meehan was in the midst of it, and there was a collection of IRA people, but they were so poorly equipped. There were shotguns, but these were almost legally held weapons from men who used to go over the hills hunting for the foxes, etc. The people who were there though, fought to a standstill and put their lives on the line to defend the area.

On Saturday 16 August I walked down past the GAA in Butler Street as far as Oakfield Street and Fairfield Street. All the lads were gathering at this stage, and I knew a number of them to be IRA people I had grown up with. I was going in and out of some of these houses with them, but some of the women who were there knew that I was going away studying to be a priest, and they shouted over, 'Keep him out of trouble. He has to go back to the seminary!' The lads shouted back, 'Never mind, we will get him into the pulpit and he can recruit for us from there!'

Martin Meehan, in his early twenties, was one of the older ones involved in preparing to defend the area. He was standing there wearing a big military jacket with a pair of binoculars round his neck and a shotgun over his shoulder. I was saying, 'Defend the area? Against that! Martin – you have a shotgun!' There were a few other guys about, but few weapons. I think I saw someone with a .22 rifle. It was about 5 p.m. on the Saturday afternoon, and I heard Meehan shout, 'Oh Jesus, look at that!'

The 'B' Specials were climbing up the roof of the mill and were erecting a machine post. I thought, 'We are going to get slaughtered here.' As we were watching them setting up this post, some of the lads were discussing how to sort this situation out. Next thing, we see the 'B' Specials scampering off the roof and down a ladder. Then we found out why. Someone shouted, 'The Army are coming into Chief Street!'

They must have come into the district from the Falls Road direction. Some of them had green vegetation in their helmets, but they all had bayonets fixed. We ran out to see them arrive, as they took up position on the Crumlin Road, lying down on the road facing us with rifles and bayonets and helmets. My immediate reaction was 'Good grief!', and a sense that the immediate mayhem had been brought to a close.

The Army moved in and took over all the vantage points around the area. They sealed off the edges of the district with their blockades, their 'P' Checks and all the rest of it. The next couple of weeks were a relief for many people in a sense, and you could feel that sense of relief that we were not going to be overrun.

When I walked down to Hooker Street, Herbert Street, the front of the Crumlin Road – the devastation was horrendous. People had lost homes. These were poor working-class parishioners and they were dealing with the aftermath of the onslaught: getting people rehoused, dealing with death and funerals. There was a harsh, heavy atmosphere mixed with the relief that to some extent that was an end to the physical attacks. The question now was how to rebuild from what the district had gone through.

The Army arriving had created a buffer zone, but now people had to work out what was going to happen next. However, a number of weeks later I was away back to seminary and in the time that followed so much change had happened regarding the IRA. The split had occurred at the Ard Fhéis, and, with that, real recruitment had begun within local areas. When I came back home for Christmas 1969, people had started re-arming, the CDC was formed, and defence mechanisms had been put in place in Ardoyne, the Falls and other areas. A lot of my friends had already joined up and when I came home for holidays, they were asking me, 'What are you going to do?'

When I was home on holidays again the following Easter, I was in wee Mary Mullan's house in Jamaica Street. I knocked about with her son, Brian, and later on, Jimmy. We played Gaelic together and I would have gone in and out of their house from a very young age. So I called into her house during that Easter period and there is a large group of local IRA gathered in the house, obviously having some kind of meeting. They showed me a tea chest with so many weapons in it that there wasn't space to get a water pistol in. People didn't mind showing you what they were doing. There were hand guns, heavy machine guns, rifles... and I was going back to seminary! I diplomatically said, 'I will come back later.'

Mary replied, 'Come you on in here and sit down.'

Some of those present are saying, 'He's the one away studying to be a priest!' One of them shouted out, 'That's great! You keep at that. See when you get into that pulpit you will be able to encourage people to join the IRA!'

At the same time I can hear Mary shouting out of the kitchen, 'Leave him alone! He is going back to college. Keep your hands off him!'

The message though was very clear, 'We are going to defend this area. Come hell or high water this will never happen again!' It was obvious that the district was being well organised. People like Martin Meehan and Barney McKenna leading the armed response, while other people like Tom Fleming, Paddy McArdle and his wife took on the 'relief' aspect of it. Everybody was rowing in together to make a defensive package for the area that involved the IRA, the CCDC, first aid, welfare, outreach to the people. From the mayhem and despair of 1969, there was this build-up of confidence and a real commitment that was encapsulated in the often-used sentence of the time, 'This is never going to happen again.'

Impact of the Violence on Life Plans

The events I witnessed in August 1969 had a major impact upon me, but it was the same for others who were about at that time, from the youngest to the oldest. It was a turning point. A turning point in the history of the conflict here, but also in the lives of individuals in terms of how it changed their perception of things, their manner of doing things, and ultimately upon the course of their lives.

For me personally, I was away over in the seminary at St David's in north Wales, coming home on holidays and having an absolutely fantastic year over there. I am not boasting, but I was doing very well in my studies. I took to it all like a duck to water. The student life was great for me in every way. I came home on holidays and ended up in the midst of all this turmoil in 1969 and the pogroms. I had first-hand experience of being in Terry Fagan's house when it got attacked, and we were lucky to get out the back of the house that Friday night before it was burned down.

The next morning had a major impact upon me, when Terry and I went back down to his house. There was no house. Only rubble. Terry almost physically crumbled. He uttered this loud audible sigh. His home was all gone. I could feel that. He was one of my best mates. We knocked about together around the GAA club. We grew up together, but I still had my house while Terry had just had the life-changing experience of losing his home.

Heading Back to Seminary

I actually went back to the seminary over a day late. I had got my dates mixed up. I arrived on 18 September, but should have been there on 17 September. There was no way of communication other than someone writing a letter. I got the boat, the train and the buses, and ended up walking back into the college, where everyone had already been there since the previous day.

I was to do two years in Wales before transferring down to the house in Dunamon in Roscommon for further studies. Even though I was one of the youngest, I had been made a prefect in the college during my first year. I had been a good student. Academically I was doing the business, but I dropped off a wee bit in that second year. I don't know what it was, but there were a mixture of things that led to me not applying myself as I had done during my first year.

I cannot put my finger on it, or say 'Here's why I packed it in', because I had been home on holidays, going out with girls, and that all had to come to an end at some stage. (Well, in modern days you never know!) I remember getting slide lectures from some of the Divine Word Missionaries, home on a break from maybe Central America, and there is a picture of one of the missionaries coming out of a church in Amsterdam. He is holding hands with an absolutely delectable-looking 26-year-old woman, and I was asking, 'Is that his sister? Father, who is that?' The priest, a Dubliner, replied, 'No, some of the fathers have a "wider view on life" and are inclined to step outside the mould! That would be his girlfriend.'

We were going, 'What!' Of course, Vatican II was in the middle of changing things and we were sitting there thinking, 'Well, you never know!' I remember that incident distinctly and can still see that guy and the young woman in the slide.

Anyway, issues are building up for me at college. I had similar issues in the first year as well, and I ended up in a couple of fisticuffs, primarily on the football pitch. That is very excusable of course for a GAA player, because if you go through your life as a GAA player and don't lift your hands at some stage, there is something wrong! In my first year though, these confrontations quickly fizzled out, but in the second year, I ended up in a couple of tight situations and I know that I went a little bit overboard.

Maybe I was getting to the realisation that this was just not for me, but I didn't settle in the same way, or apply myself to my studies in the same way. I was focused on what was happening at home. I was coming home at Christmas for holidays. I was coming home at Easter, but psychologically I think I was bringing a heavy presence with me. It was always in the back of my head. I can look back and ask if I was the kind of person who was cut out for the long haul of heading off to be a missionary, maybe it just wasn't for me, but certainly the experience of 1969 had a huge impact. It was an awakening to many people.

Discernment

Keeping up to date with developments at home when I was back in the seminary became difficult as the coverage slowly began to dwindle until it was off the broadsheets. Coming home at Christmas I noticed the physical changes to the area; the watchtowers had gone up all around our area, and I was asking, 'Why are all the watchtowers up?'

My friends were saying to me, 'Well, this is the way the British have done it. They have set up their base in the mill.' There were 24-hour checkpoints set up all around the district to get in and out of Ardoyne. I thought, 'But we didn't attack anybody. It wasn't the people of Ardoyne who crossed that road to attack people! The attack came from the Loyalist side of the road, helped by the State forces of the RUC and the 'B' Specials!'

I had seen McKeague's WDA with their armbands on the other side of the road before they attacked. It was all hand-in-glove between the State and the Loyalists, and I thought, 'Why have they not gone in to search for those weapons? The weapons are on the other side of the road.' Then I realised that the honeymoon period at the start was starting to disappear. People used to talk to the Brits, give them tea. Then the searches started, because the State knew that the IRA were re-forming, recruiting and building up armaments. All the talk in the district was about the IRA re-arming with weapons coming in from the United States. People knew that the arms dumps were being built up in preparation for further attacks from the Loyalists, and so many people were saying, 'This is not going to happen again.' I was getting a growing awareness that these are changed circumstances. This is not what I grew up in. 1969 had changed everything.

Rebirth of the IRA

When I moved back home after eventually leaving the seminary, I went straight back into the GAA club. I was back to training and playing right away. Some of the lads were asking what I was going to do with myself. I told them I was finished with the studies. 'Do you want to come in with us? We could use more people to help.'

'Absolutely', I replied. 'No problem.'

This happened right after 27 June 1970. It was in the aftermath of a prohibited Orange march on Workman Avenue on the Springfield Road. Republicans had declared that the parade would not get up the road following the damage caused by them the previous year in Bombay Street. British troops had moved in to block the Loyalist march going through, but to be able to do that the Army had taken reinforcements from all over the city. When the Loyalists couldn't get through the Springfield, they did an about-turn and moved across to Ardoyne. There was about 2,000–3,000 in the crowd. The Short Strand got attacked that same day in what became known as The Battle of the Short Strand.

There was a skeleton crew of Brits left at vantage points in Ardoyne, totally incapable of preventing any kind of organised attack like that. So the alarm went up that Ardoyne was being attacked by Loyalists. We had just come off training at the Ballysillan Playing Fields, and as we were coming down the road, someone shouted to us, 'You have to help here!' So a couple of us ran down. I remember Paul Shevlin being with me. We ran down the front of the road into Hooker Street. There was hand-to-hand fighting at Hooker Street. The next thing I heard the gunfire from the top of Logue's roof at the corner of Bray Street. It was a battle royal. The Loyalists had produced rifles and pistols and were firing into the district. We were out of their sights from where they were on the top of Logue's roof, as they had to shoot straight down into the street. So there were people 50 yards behind me getting hit – Mrs Fennell got hit in her throat or shoulder – and different people got injured, but they were all away behind us due to the angle at which this guy was shooting.

Once the gunfire started, people moved back a bit to try to see where it was coming from. Next thing, I saw a car pulling up. Out got Martin Meehan and other local IRA men. The boot of the car opened, and out came machine guns, rifles, the whole heap. The gunfire started, and they were rattling like blue blazes against the Loyalists who had been firing into the district.

In the meantime the Brits arrived back and got into positions all over the place. I thought it was time for us to move off the front of the road. I looked from the corner of Hooker Street up towards Holy Cross Church. There must have been about 200 people standing in the driveway in front of it, out of the line of gunfire, looking down from the church steps towards what had been happening. I just thought, 'This is mad!'

That day, both in Ardoyne and in the Short Strand, marked a rebirth of the IRA. The IRA was able to demonstrate that Loyalist attacks were not going to happen again without the appropriate response.

Hard Choices

That particular day wasn't so much the turning point for me regarding getting involved, but it struck home to me that we needed to be able to defend our area. A couple of mates said to me after this incident, 'Where were you?'

'On the front of the Crumlin Road,' I told them. I was explaining to them what had happened and, at that time, you wouldn't have thought twice about mentioning the names of the people who were involved, because the security aspect just didn't come into your mind then. I was only 18 at this time, and I was mesmerised by what I had seen. It was a significant day in the Troubles in Ardoyne, because it showed that there were now people with the ability to defend the area.

On the back of that, young people were being recruited and trained. Right after that the barriers were built right down both sides of the Crumlin Road. The streets were now permanently blocked off. Ardoyne quickly became totally sealed off, with only three ways in and out: Flax Street, Alliance Avenue and Estoril Park. These were the only streets where you could drive in and out, with the 'dragons' teeth' barriers put up by the Army in every other street.

People asked me if I would become part of the defence structures in the district and by 1970 I was playing my part in defending the district, particularly around Farringdon/Eskdale and down as far as Jamaica Street. I was of course around in Old Ardoyne on lots of occasions, but that's for another day! I also had my day job. So I went to work every day and remained off the radar as far as the Brits were concerned, whereas the Martin Meehans and the Dutch Dohertys of this world were hunted every day of the week.

My involvement with the Republican movement was a slow integration. Coming home from college on holidays, getting introduced to various people, people asking if I would get involved, when at home attempting in some small way to defend the area, and then 27 June 1970 was a landmark day. By the time of internment being introduced I was regularly engaged in defensive action. I was well off the radar of the cops though: off to work, playing football and hurling regularly for the club. So if the Brits came into the club they would see me there in the table-tennis room. My name might have come up somewhere as a potential suspect for involvement, but after internment, when the Brits realised that the information that the RUC and the Special Branch had was absolutely useless, they then started building up their own intelligence. I would have been on their radar as I knocked about with the Mullans, and they all ended up interned or in gaol.

Priesthood/IRA – Contradiction?

I have often been asked in interviews how I reconcile studying for the priesthood with joining the IRA, particularly with students from the United States. It is usually the lecturers who raise it as a question if I haven't mentioned it: 'So you were away studying to be a priest...'. You can see the reaction of the students: 'What? Where does this come from?' Priesthood is presented as a good choice, while joining the IRA is obviously seen by them as being a bad choice, but that's not how I look at it. It's more complicated than that.

Different expressions have been used to describe that transfer from one to another. The Order I had chosen to join was a missionary order, and I know some of the places they were in: Central America, the Philippines, South America, Nicaragua, El Salvador. They had people living in conflict zones and they got involved with the indigenous population. People like Tommy Morrison. He was in Brazil. An absolute gem of a guy. He was a saint. Tommy wasn't a violent person and would not have resorted to arms, but I remember him being home on holidays and telling me about the struggle against the rubber plantation owners, who were armed to the teeth against the local peasantry with whom he lived and worked. He told me how they fought in terms of getting union rights, and trying to get bishops on their side to support the battle for rights for indigenous communities.

I had been reading about all this when I was studying with the Divine Word Order. So I was conscious of this Order going out to help the underprivileged, downtrodden, oppressed people because that was the big need. This was something that been instilled in us that we were preparing to get involved in – going out to help people who are underprivileged, downtrodden and oppressed. Our commitment was to do this through non-violent means, but when I came back home to Ardoyne there was the realisation, that I suppose I always had, that we were being treated as second-class citizens and were suffering from oppression at home.

However having witnessed the full onslaught of the State against peaceful democratic demonstrations and protests, I knew that this was like an apartheid regime. So from being a student and aiming towards helping other people, I thought that it was a natural progression to move into being involved in defending people, not in

El Salvador, Papua New Guinea or Nicaragua, but in my local community that was underprivileged, with little employment and facing vast discrimination. For me, it wasn't as much a big jump as more a natural move from one set of circumstances in another part of the world to circumstances where violence was visited by the State upon my community at home. That's where the seeming contradictions sit together for me. It was a natural development from seeing people getting battened off the streets to the situation where I saw no alternative to physical force.

Arrest and Long Kesh

I lost count of the number of occasions on which I was arrested. I did one stint right after internment, in October 1971. I got battered from the Monday until the Wednesday by the screws. Without going into all the details, I will say it was a hard time. I was 19 at the time, playing football and as a result was extremely physically fit. If it were now, I would end up in the hospital. I came through it, and got out the other end. On other occasions I was arrested and brought to Flax Street, or arrested around the Border, but the interrogation was nowhere near as bad as that occasion.

When I went to prison, the system was regimented and we had political status. You get sentenced; the screws bring you up to the Cages; they locked your door, woke you up, brought you to your visitor or to court, but all the time we had our own clothes. It was regimented, but under the IRA structures. The only time you saw a guard was when they came in for a search, when you walked round the yard or when you went for a visit.

The IRA set the rules for those inside. Everyone has to get up and get showered. Everybody has to parade on the ground. There was no lying in your bed all day. It was a regimented system put into place by the IRA to instil a bit of discipline, but I found that easy. I guess that was because I had spent two years in the seminary, getting up at 7 a.m. every morning and going to bed at 10 p.m. every night. The regimentation of the life did not impinge upon me whatsoever because I was used to living in a community, getting up and interacting in a community context.

Apart from the fact that I had lost my liberty, I just worked my way through it. The whole concentration was on escape and I got involved in all that. That's all a big buzz. Although I was doing an inordinate amount of time, the focus was on the need to dig a tunnel; the need to cut a fence; the need to swop a visit; the need to get to court, and escape, escape, escape!

Escape was just ingrained in me, but I also had my music, my instruments, my sport. We played Gaelic and soccer. We had our own education classes. We learned Irish, politics, history, all of which was decided by us. For me, probably the first six months I spent in Cage 11 was a political awakening in terms of reading and studying, and discussing what the Brits were at in terms of their strategy in Ireland. In my first six months in Cage 11, I learned more than I had done in the previous twenty years! I was in the company of people like Gerry Adams, 'the Dark' (Brendan Hughes) and Big Cleaky (Clarke). They were all in that Cage with me. Just fascinating.

Hunger Strike

I was heavily involved in education in the Cages, and then, of course, in cutting fences and digging tunnels. Eventually I got caught, and they transferred Larry Marley, Pat McGeown and myself straight to the H-Blocks. We were first put on 'the Boards', (punishment for disobeying orders of the screws), and then transferred straight to the H-Blocks. They took away our political status. People can romanticise what we were doing, but I can tell you that the first three weeks that I was on that 'blanket' I was crawling up the walls. The psychological impact of trying to come to terms with being in a cell 24/7, with no clothes and with the door locked, was very difficult. I had to come to terms with it though, as I was probably more aware than most others of what the Brits were trying to achieve through this tactic, as I had been typing up all Gerry Adams' (Brownie) articles. I had been reading Frank Kitson's *Low Intensity Operations*, in which he had outlined how the British Army would respond to civil disorder. We had been studying these in the Cages as we were helping to highlight and get the right propaganda around the whole thing. We knew that this was not a three-month wonder, and the political ramifications of what we had embarked on were massive. I was now thrown right into the midst of it due to trying to escape.

I recall the No. 1 governor at the time, Hilditch, saying straight into our faces, 'I will put the escapes out of you guys!' In fairness he did, until you fast-forward a number of years. So I ended up in the H-Blocks in 1978, and that was horrendous. For me, I just felt tremendous pressure. It was such a depressing situation. You could read your Bible. You could learn Irish. Sing-songs were going on at night as you stood at your door after the screws had gone, but it probably took me about three weeks to get myself up off my arse and focused. I knew that I would be in for a protracted period unless something major occurred to change things. This would really be for life as I knew it!

At this stage I did not hold any positions of responsibility in the H-Blocks. People like 'the Dark', Joe Barnes, Big Cleaky and all those guys had been moved over. I was in H4, and Bobby Sands was in H5. These guys were the camp staff. Larry Marley and Pat McGeown were with me. Larry ended up as OC of H-Block C, but at this stage I didn't hold any position, and just got on with writing letters and whatever else I was asked to do.

Then thirty of us, including most of the IRA leadership in the gaol, got shifted to H-Block 6 in January. We thought that this meant a hardening of the regime for us, but to be honest they went to town in brutalising people in H-Block 3 and H-Block 4, more than they did to us in H-Block 6. We maybe got disorientated by the shifting about every five or six days, but it ended up that most of the leadership in the camp were in H-Block 6. The authorities then split that wing up in August, and spread us around the other blocks. I ended up in a cell with Jake Jackson in H-Block 3 alongside 'the Dark' and Bobby Sands. Thomas McIlwee was next door.

The brutality at that stage was severe. A couple of decisions were made to try to make things a bit easier for boys going in and out of visits. Eventually the discussion turned as to how we were going to get out of this situation, as there now over 300 prisoners engaged in the protest, and it was beginning to have its toll. Some guys were having psychological or psychiatric treatment, and were transferred to the prison hospital. There was, of course, a lot of resistance to the brutality of the prison authorities, but we needed to get out of this situation.

The 'No Wash' protest had reached its peak in late 1978, when Cardinal O'Fiaich had released his statement following a visit to the Blocks saying that the prisoners were living in conditions akin to the sewer-pipe dwellings in Calcutta. That was the pinnacle of the public outrage, and received massive media attention, both at home and at international level. When even that didn't force the Brits into a position to lessen the impact of the harshness of the regime we knew that they were not going to move at all. This was their opportunity to defeat the IRA, and their criminalisation policy and their 'Ulsterisation' policy (pushing local troops to the fore and getting less casualties among the Brits themselves), led to us discussing the possibility of hunger strike.

Officer in Command during the Hunger Strike

To understand the background to the hunger strike, we need to go to the end of the first hunger strike in 1980. There had been an expectation that something was in the air and that reform would take place. I remember Bobby Sands going out and dealing with the prison governor, and Hilditch said to him, 'The bottom line is this. You are not getting out of the cells until your men put on that uniform and do precisely what my officers tell them to do.' That was the end of any hope of a resolution. We were then into the second hunger strike. When Hilditch made that statement, Republican prisoners entered into a fierce argument with the IRA outside the prison. The IRA had already opposed the first hunger strike on all logical bases, and because the first had ended the way it did they were adamantly opposed to a second hunger strike. They believed that somebody was going to die and, in their words, 'We cannot allow you to put the integrity of the struggle on your shoulders.'

There ensued a 'battle' between the prisoners and the IRA. Bobby was back and forward on visits and having arguments, and eventually the prisoners asked the IRA to give them an alternative way to get out of this situation that did not involve a surrender. The IRA said that was 'not possible', as they did not have an alternative. Reluctantly, they consequently agreed to the second hunger strike going ahead.

Inside the prison, we made the decision to use a staggered strategy of intermittent hunger strikers. Bobby Sands made the decision that he would be the first prisoner to embark on the hunger strike. By that stage of the game I was like a PR person, pretty much down the wage scale when it comes to priority. My role was to help people write or structure their smuggled letters. I would be giving target lists to prisoners in the various wings to target academics, sports personalities, celebrities. People like Jane Fonda responded. Danny Morrison wrote to inform me that the Dean of St Paul's Cathedral, London, had put one of my 'coms' (short notes to people outside Long Kesh on developments inside) on display in the main aisle of the cathedral. It wasn't heavy-hitting, just a short one asking for justice and for our demands to be met. This was my role at this stage, but it soon changed drastically.

Bobby Sands called me in to his cell and said to me, '[Danny] Morrison was up on a visit there. I told him to tell the boys that as and from this hunger strike starting next week, you are "it".' I said, 'I am what?' He said, 'You'll be doing OC. You need to take over.' I replied, 'I will not be doing OC.' We had an argument in Gaelic that people could hear from outside the door. I was adamant that there was no way I would be OC. Finally he said, 'This is it. You are doing the job. I need you in that position.'

We had been together for the few years during the whole of the previous protests, and he knew that I got all the ins and outs of it. I also knew that we already had in the camp the OC; the vice OC; the adjutant; the education officer; the intelligence officer. We were so organised we even had a TO (technical officer for training in weapons/explosives), but that was an honorary title in prison! We used to make a joke that the Loyalists also had a TO – a 'Telligence Officer'! I was PR officer, which was mostly about writing letters. It wasn't that it was unimportant but I was well down the feeding order.

I said to Bobby, 'I am well down the chain of command here. I am over in H5. You have two people at least who are more senior to me and longer on the blanket than me. They have been through the entire process with us. Séanna Walsh is the next man down in command.'

He said, 'Stop. Séanna Walsh is my best mate.'

I said, 'And?'

He said, 'Well, if he is in this position and this hunger strike runs to a crisis and I am in a condition where I have no ability to negotiate between camp staff and the hunger strikers, then he will not let me die.'

I said, 'So what do you mean? And I will?'

He said, 'Yes.' He just simply said 'Yes.'

I said, 'Well thanks very fucking much for your confidence in my abilities. So that's what you think of me.'

He said, 'That's the way it is. If there is an offer put down and I am not in a position to negotiate it, and it isn't what we want, then you have to say, "No thank you." Hopefully it doesn't come to that, but I need you there. You have to do it, and I know that you will do it.'

I said, 'You know more than I do.'

He was going on hunger strike, so how could I refuse to do the easier job.

The Weight of Responsibility

I never ultimately had to make a decision to as to whether we accepted or rejected what was negotiated. That decision ended up as a collective decision of the hunger strikers themselves. It didn't end up with just Bobby. If you move forward to when the hunger strike ended, it was discovered that there were interventions during the course of the hunger strike by families to take their sons off because they were in a coma. After the families take the decision, you know you are not going anywhere as nobody has control of it. You, as a hunger striker don't have control, no matter what you say.

So I went into the prison hospital towards the end of the hunger strike to emphasise this point of who had control. One guy had been on hunger strike for a week. Pat Sheehan had been on it for 54 days. We were all in the hospital, and the Brits probably had the place wired. I said to them, 'Here is the craic. All your families bar one are all going to intervene if you go into a coma. To be straight I don't know which one it is, I haven't been told. To me, that renders the hunger strike totally and absolutely null and void. You guys need to think, and need to make a decision in relation to this. Do we continue? How do we continue? What is the situation?'

They discussed it and decided that they were all agreed that there was no point. Believe it or not, somebody made the proposal that they were going to get the lawyer in to sign power of attorney for their lives over to me. I said, 'That ain't going to happen! For starters, it will not hold up. Secondly, it is the wrong thing to do. You will be throwing power for your life over to the IRA. Do you think if you go into a coma that the doctors are going to say: "I am sorry, the IRA have made the decision." If your wife or your mother, or somebody close, makes an intervention, it's not going to work.' These were some of the issues they were discussing before they eventually ended it. Collectively.

When the Red Cross and the Irish Commission for Justice and Peace were in, they first dealt with the prisoners collectively and then they came to me. The Red Cross were straight up about it. They told me, 'The British are not going to move. You have no chance of getting this.' I said, 'Thank you for your time.' They then went about their business.

The Irish Commission for Justice and Peace tried to play the ball out by saying that they had negotiated certain things, which later turned out to be inaccurate. In the aftermath, it was proven that the British had slapped them in the face. In a documentary some 20 years later, Fr Crilly, a member of the Commission, actually stated that he would never trust the British Government again. The reason he gave was that the Government had undermined and told lies about the Commission, and had told them things that were not right. Basically, the Government had led them up the garden path, as we had told them at the time.

I got fired into the cauldron during that whole hunger strike period. It wasn't comfortable. Things weren't comfortable either during the blanket protest or again when I was doing the PR stuff during the hunger strikes. I remember the day that Bobby Sands announced I was taking over as OC. I felt like the roof had moved in on me, and the pressure was sitting on my shoulders. It was almost a physical sensation. Its impact was massive on me and I had to work my way through it. People have often asked me, 'How did you manage to get through that? How did you survive?'

One of the key things was that I was dealing with hunger strikers, so you are not in the same league as them. I was dealing with people who were focused, determined, and who had a vision of precisely what road they are taking, and how they are going to take it. My role was to support that.

Of course there was pressure. One of the telling factors was that everybody ends up with walls coming in on them at the worst possible time, but then I look at the photograph of Bobby Sands' son, eight years old when he walked behind his father's coffin. Joe McDonald's son was also behind his father's coffin. I see their families, Mrs Sands at the back of the van talking about her son dying, and I am telling myself, 'That is pressure! What I feel is not in the same league as what I am seeing, hearing and witnessing from these families.' I had to almost admonish myself for daring to feel that everything was on top of me. The pressure was on the men lying in the prison hospital and on their families, so I need to do better tomorrow than I have done today!

Faith and Prison Life

I remember Fr Murphy (the prison chaplain) talking about so many people gravitating on a Sunday morning to Mass in the prison. Now first of all, on a Sunday morning if you put on a pair of gaol trousers you got out of your cell to get to the canteen for Mass. Everybody went. Apart from one or two who would be hard-nosed about it, as in we are not putting those prison clothes on so we are not going to Mass.

There was a variety of reasons for going to Mass. Firstly, it was your opportunity to get tobacco. It was also your opportunity to get a yarn with somebody, an opportunity for engagement with other men and to get smuggled stuff, like notes or possibly even a Parker pen. We were curious about the priest. 'I wonder what priest is in today? If it's one of those monks from Portglenone [Abbey], Jesus, let me up to confession to him.' They were brilliant! They even gave us some tobacco and polo mints. Tobacco was the big thing.

A lot of guys also wanted to go to confession. The upsurge in Catholicism in terms of people genuinely wanting to be involved, as in an expression of their faith, was great. Lots of people were focused on the Mass. So whoever was at the back had to be quiet and keep their distractions down low. If the camp staff had a wireless in the corner, or people who were not Catholic orientated were talking they would be told, 'Keep it down boys! Go to the back out of the room', because there were priests who would just stop the Mass and glare at you. I used to look behind and see lots of guys whom you would never see at church now, except for maybe a funeral.

The severity of the protest against isolation and the brutality of the regime gave a context for this expression of faith. The rosary was a big thing. In every wing in the gaol, bar one, once the screws went off duty at 7.30, the first item on the agenda was the rosary. Lots of guys would take a turn at doing the various Mysteries. Guys were focused on reading the Bible. Religion took an upsurge, and I think it was probably this pull towards something that gave relief. Pray to God that we will get through this. Pray to God and His Holy Mother, etc. that we will get through this, and there was a comfort in that. So faith, for a lot of the prisoners, was immensely important, and that was manifested with people going to Mass on a Sunday or going to Confession.

When the protests all finished in the late 1980s the numbers began to drop off, and as things were heading towards ceasefires, there were very few prisoners going to Mass on a Sunday morning. Was faith a crutch for people? Yes, probably, but there were people there who were genuine Catholics. There were also some who I would have referred to as fundamentalists, or zealots. You have them in every church, but faith played a big role for many men in the prisons.

My Relationship with Faith

I had dispensed with faith at one stage, though I can't remember exactly when it was. There were times when I went up and sat at Mass with the guys, or if a certain priest was in who was a friend of mine, I would sit and tell people to quieten down. I would have sat many times, just quietly going through the Mass. I used to read the Bible. I found some of it fascinating. I loved reading through the psalms. In a sense though, for me, even prior to being in the Blocks during the hunger strikes, I had drifted off from religion, and the Church didn't really mean anything to me. Belief in the Catholic Church no longer meant anything to me, but occasionally in the Cages I would have gone to sit at Mass, maybe to hear a sermon of a certain priest.

Faith was certainly important for many people though, and it certainly helped people get through the darkest days. No question about that. Those days were undoubtedly the darkest days that many men had faced in their lives to date, and I know that some people are still suffering some form of psychological impact having gone through all that. I also am sure that many have still to face up to that. When people look at the minutiae of what they experienced, and begin to talk about the Blanket Protest and the Hunger Strike, it becomes highly charged. It's not like the Cages. The Cages were a different ball game. For many people, once they sit down and begin to unravel the Blanket Protest and the Hunger Strike experience, it becomes highly emotional and many just don't want to talk about it.

Guys got out of gaol, went on with their lives and got married. They moved to different areas and didn't get involved in the IRA campaign after their release, which is fine, but their children or grandchildren will say, 'I never knew my da (or granda) was on the Blanket Protest!' The guys didn't talk about it. 'We thought he was only interned.' Many of the men don't talk about their experience on the blanket, unless they get involved in some conversation where it comes up and they can say that they were there.

Looking Back...

I don't think anybody can look back on their life and say they are the perfect person and that they have done everything right. We certainly didn't do everything right in terms of struggle and conflict, and I was part of a particular squad of people who didn't do everything right. We were involved in horrendous struggle, and some of my regrets are that some things were not done differently. Some of those things should have been done differently. Certain people didn't have to suffer because of actions we took. Could we have done it better? Yes, we probably could have, but retrospective analysis is always on the mark. Nobody is ever wrong with retrospective analysis.

People say to me, 'You came out of college and almost went straight into conflict.' I would jokingly say to them, 'Yea. I could have been a brilliant footballer!' I would never have been a soccer player, although I was a decent Gaelic player. I could have been a musician, and I know that would have been a real possibility had I concentrated on the music in different circumstances. If I had taken an extra step regarding the music and not got involved in the conflict, things might well have gone further than they did in the music field. Gaol put a hold on that and I never really got back into it until I got out of gaol.

I could have travelled. Being away in college in Wales, a different environment, a different set of circumstances, I was able to get the freedom to go out walking, unlike the insular experience of living in Ardoyne. Ardoyne was completely closed in on itself, and then post-1969 it just became what in reality was a large prison camp for so many people. Nobody left it to go anywhere to do anything. I knew there was more to life than that.

I sometimes thought that I should have travelled more. What brought that to mind was the time I was 'on the run' on the continent. I was all over the continent and I realised, 'My God, life is massive! There's a whole world out here.' Yet in Ardoyne the conversations were, 'Where are you going?'

'Down to the Star and round to the League afterwards.' And that was your weekend.

Whereas when I was on the run over on the continent, the conversation was different, 'Where are you going?'

'Oh I think I will walk down to the Louvre today!'

'No – let's go to Brittany!' I got that wider perspective, and I certainly regret not doing a lot of travelling.

When asked about what it means to me to come from Ardoyne, I think about the *True North* (BBC) documentary made about the altar boys in 1969 who all followed very different paths in life. Ardoyne was so important to us. It shaped us.

The altar boys and the GAA club were the two mainstays for me in growing up in Ardoyne, and both were fantastic experiences. The two things went in tandem for me. I joined both around ten or eleven years of age, and those few years I spent in them were fantastic parts of my growing up.

When I look at Ardoyne, I am conscious of the people who came out of the area. Even from within the altar boys alone, there is such an array of people at the pinnacle of so many fields in life. Out of those few small streets in Ardoyne you have the likes of Freddie Gilroy (World Champion boxer), Cathal Goan (Director General, RTE), Seamie O'Neill (professional footballer), Mary McAleese (President of Ireland). The personalities, the different individuals, the sports stars, the academics – all coming out of those few small streets. It is fascinating for me to think of where people from Ardoyne went to in their lives. So to me, coming out of Ardoyne is hugely important. A small, tight area, with no facilities. I loved it.

Ardoyne was a vibrant community, and then post-1969 you had the resilience, the resistance, the comradery as the people came together to support each other and to defend their area. It was brilliant just to be part of that. It has obviously had its mark on me. It shaped me. The 'Westies' (West Belfast people) always slag me: 'An Ardoyne man – watch those boys!'

I would retort, 'Yes, sure we needed visas to get through Castle Street to get into West Belfast!'

I have no doubt that the area you grow up in is hugely important. I loved Ardoyne. Wonderful memories. Growing up there has just all these beautiful memories. The crazy memories obviously hit when 1969 came in. That's when it all changes, but Ardoyne is still a great community. Like everywhere else it has its difficulties, its head cases, but there are loads of great people in there. So many unknown heroes about Ardoyne, so many good people who underpinned the defence and the resistance within that community. Nobody knows them. Nobody ever speaks their names. The unsung heroes.

3

Brian McCargo

Hard Beginnings

I am a retired police officer who was born and reared in Ardoyne. Like a lot of other people in Ardoyne during and after the Second World War, I grew up in poor circumstances. I was born in Dunedin Park in 1942, but at the age of three, as a result of my mother and father splitting up, I moved with my brother, Pat, to Brompton Park to live with my grandmother. We lived beside what was to become known locally as 'the Stumps', or 'the Brompton Gap'. It was an entry that led from Brompton Park in Glenard into Herbert Street in Old Ardoyne, and was to have a pivotal role in the Troubles starting in 1969. Growing up in Ardoyne, I moved back and forward between Brompton Park and my paternal grandparents' house in Elmfield Street, in what was known as 'Old Ardoyne'.

I attended Holy Cross Boys' Primary School, with Miss Farrell as my first teacher. Our classroom was a wooden structure known as the Annex, and was by an old mill stream at the bottom of Butler Street. We then moved further up Butler Street to old Nissen huts which, because they had a playground, appeared to be quite modern. My teacher there was Mr Devlin. From there we moved further up Butler Street onto the Crumlin Road to spend some time in the old boys' school on the Crumlin Road, before eventually ending up in Wheatfield, the old seminary for the

Passionist Fathers. After primary school, I went from Holy Cross Boys' School to Hardinge Street Christian Brothers in North Queen Street.

This was a time without television or cars and, as a young boy, I got involved in things like youth clubs, various Church activities, handball, Ardoyne GAC, and local soccer teams. I was very keen on sport and played a lot of soccer, but my favourite sports were Gaelic football and hurling. I also boxed for the St John Bosco Boxing Club in Lower Donegall Street and was a member of St Patrick's Boys Scouts.

Sporting Interests

My father's side of the family were sporty people. My father played for the Ardoyne Gaelic team, as did my uncles Joe and Bobby. Both Joe and Bobby played in goals for Ardoyne. Uncle Billy was a great footballer and played for Belfast Celtic. I had a big interest in Gaelic football when I attended Holy Cross Bovs' School in Wheatfield, where our teacher was Brian Moore, who eventually became the vice-principal of the new St Gabriel's Intermediate School.

Brian was very strict, but a great teacher and very much an Irish Nationalist. He taught us Irish, which I really enjoyed. At that time, Holy Cross Boys' School probably had the best school soccer team in the whole of Northern Ireland. We could beat everybody at soccer, but we didn't have a Gaelic team. Brian Moore changed that when he started the school's first ever Gaelic team, with all the players coming out of the one class. That got me started in Gaelic football and I was relatively good at it. I went on to play for the school, and because of Brian Moore's influence in GAA circles Holy Cross School actually played at the opening of Casement Park in 1952.

Along with my brother, Pat, I went on to play for Ardoyne Kickhams at both minor and senior level. Pat played both hurling and football for the county, while I played at minor and junior levels, as well as playing in a number of senior games with Antrim. Over the years, both of us won quite a few trophies.

I was no shrinking violet. I boxed for St John Bosco and was well able to defend myself. I never looked for trouble, but I never ran away from it either. I was one those people who if I hit you hard and you hit me hard on a Gaelic pitch, that was fine. If you wanted to get nasty, well that was a different thing. I was known for being a hard but fair player.

America Calling

My closest friend, Tommy Brown, got married and I found myself at a loose end, so I decided to go to America at the end of 1962. I was to go earlier, except that the Cuban Missile Crisis was ongoing and my mother didn't want me to go at that time. After a few months I ended up playing Gaelic football in Gaelic Park, New York, for the Offaly Association team. During my time there a few people worked hard to get an Ulster side together, and I ended up playing for the Tyrone Association. I also played soccer for a team in New York called Yonkers Celtic.

Playing Gaelic was very different in New York. When I played for Ardoyne I didn't get paid and that was fine, but when I played football in Gaelic Park they would put money in my pocket and even bought me boots and any other kit that I needed. However, homesickness became a real problem for me. My mother would send me out the *Irish News* and *Ireland's Saturday Night* (sports results on a Saturday night), and they would arrive a week after she posted them. I would go straight to the write-ups about Ardoyne, or the 'North Enders', as they were referred to. I would have looked up the results and read the reports about the guys I grew up playing with. Reading all the match reports, I often felt the loss when Ardoyne lost a great match, and I would wonder whether I would have made a difference had I been there, especially when they were playing Pearses in a local derby. I missed that. That was the GAA! Your friends, your local community, your parish.

Lucky Escape

An injury I received training with Ardoyne in 1958 had a big influence in shaping my life in New York though. One night when I was training up at the Ballysillan Playing Fields, Danny McLaughlin and I were running for a ball up a verge at the side of the pitch. Danny nudged me in the back and I fell over. It was nothing malicious but I fell onto a broken bottle and ended up with gangrene in my knee. I was in a bad way and it took a while for me to get over it. At one stage it was feared I could lose my leg. I was only sixteen and was on the panel for the Antrim minor team, so that knocked me back a bit. Thanks to the Mater Hospital I made a good recovery and was able to play again. The impact of that one incident, though, was about to play a big role in regarding my future in the United States.

My plans were to stay in America and I was called up to do my medical for the Army draft and was likely to go to Vietnam. As a result of my earlier leg injury, the Army medical people said that I hadn't enough mobility in my leg, and because of that my entry into the United States Army was deferred. What the medical people did not know was that a few days earlier I had run, and won, a mile race on a track beside Yankee Stadium. My time was 4 minutes 22 seconds, which was a very good time in those days!

I had a good job in New York. I worked on Park Avenue, which was a great business address to have, but my homesickness wouldn't go away. Following my experience at the draft medical, I realised that I needed to go home. I spent my 21st birthday in America, but decided that I wasn't going to spend my 22nd birthday there. I travelled home on the last voyage of the *Mauretania* and arrived home on my birthday. Shortly after I got home, I went to Romano's Ballroom on King Street. There I met a girl called Mary. I asked her out and she is now my wife of 50 years. We have two daughters and three grandsons.

The company I had been working for prior to going to America gave me my old job back immediately. I went back to playing Gaelic football and hurling for Ardoyne, and that settled me back to life in Belfast. Six months later, I got a letter to report to the Draft Office in New York. I informed them that it was my intention to remain at home, but if I returned to America I would happily complete my military service. Little did anyone know that Vietnam was to become America's nightmare. Little did I know that at that time that Northern Ireland would soon face its own nightmare.

The Unfolding Nightmare

Like everyone who goes away to America or other foreign fields, I longed for home, and often talked about it to anyone who would listen. I worked with a guy who had been born in Germany, but who eventually worked for the American Army Intelligence during the Second World War. I remember we were going up to a place in upstate New York, called Poughkeepsie, where IBM had a large plant. On the journey up we were chatting, and I was singing the praises of home as usual. I will never forget what happened shortly after that. We went into our hotel and the next thing I heard him shout, 'Brian, come in here quick. Is this the great place you are effing talking about?' I looked at the television and the riots were going on in Divis Street involving the police and a crowd of Paisleyites. It was over a tricolour flying at the Ard Scoil. 'Yes', I said, 'but that is not the normal.' Unfortunately, it became the normal, and that's why I will never forgive Paisley and others, who despite indulging in the worst aspects of sectarianism ended up getting lordships, or were elevated to some higher authority, despite the devastation they helped to bring about.

On another occasion in early 1969, I was driving up the M1 motorway in England, working for the company I had been with in America. There was a discussion on the radio regarding riots in Ardoyne and throughout Northern Ireland. I couldn't really understand why the riots were happening, but obviously something had caused them and I tried to make sense of what was developing.

Discrimination existed in Northern Ireland and no one could deny it but unfortunately it was something that people had largely accepted up to this stage. As a young Catholic, you learned to keep your horizons low and hoped that you might get a job in the post office as a telegram boy or, if you were fortunate, an opportunity to serve your time as an apprentice at some trade. If you set your sights too high you would only face disappointment. That attitude seemed to be the order of the day, but that attitude was now beginning to change.

Suddenly People's Democracy came along with the vision of 'one man, one vote'. Austin Currie, a Nationalist MP at Stormont, and two local men had occupied a house in Caledon, Tyrone on 20 June 1968. This was in protest against the allocation of the house by the local council to a nineteen-year-old unmarried Protestant, Emily Beattie, who was secretary of a local Unionist politician. A Catholic family with three young children had recently been evicted from the house next door.

Gerrymandering was clearly going on in Derry. Four electoral seats had been allocated to Queen's University, with three of them guaranteed to be Unionist, just an example of how Unionists dominated politics. From a position of seeing all these things going on in everyday life and accepting them, suddenly there were people standing up and saying, 'We are not accepting this anymore, and we need to do something about it.'

Influence of Paddy Devlin

I had a growing realisation that there was something wrong here, and it made me think back to some key influences upon me as a young boy. My uncle Joe had been a supervisor in Kennedy's Milk Company, based in Tate's Avenue. Uncle Joe had given a job of driving a milk vehicle to a man who had been interned with Uncle Bobby during the 1940s. That man was Paddy Devlin. Paddy was a Belfast socialist who had been interned for IRA membership during the Second World War, but had latterly turned his back on violence and became a founder member of the Social Democratic Labour Party in 1970. As a four-year-old boy I helped Paddy with his milk round. I would stand outside what became Mary McAleese's home behind Holy Cross Church on the Woodvale Road. I got 4d at the weekend – you might say child labour! 4d! But I just loved doing it, and Paddy Devlin was good to me. It was amazing what you could get for 4d just after the war. More importantly though, that early encounter with Paddy Devlin later encouraged me to think Labour. He became an influential trade unionist, and so as I grew up I became interested in the Northern Ireland Labour Party. However, I found it to be too pro-communist, and a little bit too much to the left for me.

I left school at fourteen, and went on to serve my time as a weighbridge engineer in Smithfield, and as part of my work I regularly visited Andrews Flour and Animal Feed Mills in Percy Street. Who did I meet up with again? The general manager was none other than Paddy Devlin. He went into Andrews Mills to find work and ended up running the place.

He asked me, 'What are you doing with yourself? Have you left school?' I told him I had no option but to leave school. I had to earn something. £2 a week was my pay at that stage, and out of that they took my National Insurance stamp of six shillings a week. Whatever was left was handed to my mother out of necessity. He said to me, 'I told you to educate yourself. Right, are you in the trade union?' I belonged to a trade union as an apprentice, the Amalgamated Engineering Union. He said, 'Well get yourself into the TUC, and get on to a correspondence course.'

That's exactly what I did. In addition, I started night school and I never looked back. At one stage, I was earmarked for Ruskin College, Oxford. I wasn't necessarily going to go, but because I was getting good results from my correspondence courses a pathway was created. I was studying English, Physics, Commerce and Economics. One thing I was never good at though, simply because I was lazy, was Maths. I was very good at English, which got me into Hardinge Street Christian Brothers, and into night school at the Belfast Technical College. 'O' levels and 'A' levels followed, but ultimately it was through the police that I eventually got a university education and obtained my degrees. Eventually, I even took over that academic side of policing, and acted as liaison officer between the police and the universities. I also lectured on a number of subjects at the University of Ulster, Jordanstown. In 1989 I was made an honorary teacher by the university and was presented with a certificate to mark the occasion. It is something I am very proud of.

Growing Fear

At the start of the summer of 1969 there was a growing fear in the air. I will always remember that, but how do you understand it unless you were there? There was a tense atmosphere hanging over Ardoyne. It was an atmosphere of fear, and people were just waiting for something to happen. The question was, when?

There was talk and rumours of Loyalists gangs going to invade Ardoyne from the other side of the Crumlin Road. At the same time, riots were happening up in Derry. I heard people refer to starting riots in West Belfast and Ardoyne in order to 'take the heat off Derry'. I don't know how much truth there was in that, but I was certainly never aware of anyone coming around and encouraging people to get out and riot. Many people though were in fear of their lives.

This was a very different experience for me. When I was growing up, I had a lot of good friends from the Shankill Road area. I worked with great people from the Shankill in Brookfield Mill and they had been kind and had treated me very well. My friends and I would have gone down the Shankill on the 11th Night to see the bonfires and to enjoy ourselves. Never a word was said to us. In Hooker Street, which at that time was known as the 'Protestant Street' in Old Ardoyne, they put up buntings and flags to celebrate the 'Twelfth'. When you went down Butler Street from Holy Cross Church, there was a patch of waste ground between Herbert Street and Holyrood Hall at the corner of Brookfield Street. We would gather wood and placed it there for the bonfire on the 11th Night. That's how Ardoyne was.

Then things started to change. One of the incidents that I remember as sparking off the Troubles in Ardoyne was in Hooker Street, at the junction with Chatham Street, involving a character known as Skinny Lizzy. She had a shop just at the corner of the street, and every 12 July she put the Union Jack out at the corner facing the Edenderry Inn, just across the road. We used to go in and out of her shop to buy sweets as kids but when the Twelfth came along, out went the Union Jack. An individual from Brookfield Street tried to remove the flag, and rumour had it that Lizzy dispatched him after threatening to bury a hatchet in his head. This incident had the effect of raising tensions. As tension increased, people reacted. I remember the buses being brought out of the Ardoyne bus depot and being placed at the end of most streets in the district. The fear factor was heightened with the talk that the Loyalists were going to invade Ardoyne, and that all hell was going to break loose.

I remember wondering to myself, 'What am I supposed to do?' Then other things happened. I remember the Protestants in Hooker Street having to move out of their homes. I will never forget that. It was like a scene from *Fiddler on the Roof*. The Protestants had to get out of Hooker Street, because the Catholics were being put out of their homes on the other side of the Crumlin Road. I knew a lot of those people having to leave Ardoyne. It was absolutely heart-breaking watching as they loaded vans, hand carts and horse-drawn carts with their possessions and move to the other side of the road. I don't know if those scenes were ever captured on camera but it was a very sad day for Ardoyne.

Outbreak of Violence

I remember the build-up of fear, buses being taken out of the depot, trouble breaking out in Derry, people being forced to leave their homes. I was left wondering when all hell was going to break loose. From where I lived at the Stumps I could see up the Berwick Road from the front of the house, and from the back I could see right down Herbert and Butler Streets. It was a great vantage point.

I will never forget the scenes of the real trouble breaking out around me. I thought that World War III had started: the shooting, the loud bangs, fire, sand, the smell of burning all over the place. I couldn't sleep in our house. It was too dangerous. A very kind neighbour, Mrs Sarah Brown, came down to me from three doors above us. Her oldest son, Joe, had been a petty officer in the Royal Navy. 'Brian,' she said, 'come on up and lie on our floor.' I went up and managed to get a few hours' sleep.

There was shooting going on throughout the night. Sammy McLarnon was shot dead. Sammy was a classmate of mine, and he was shot dead looking out the window of his living room in Herbert Street. The one thing that I didn't see, nor was I aware of, was the IRA. I did hear people ask, 'Where the fuck are they? I thought they were supposed to protect the people here.' There were some ex-Army guys in Ardoyne and a number of legally owned shotguns, but the people were terrorised that night, and were left wondering about what was going to happen next. The whole feeling in the district was that we were going to be overrun by Loyalist gangs. I certainly wasn't aware of the presence of the IRA.

At about 6.30 in the morning of 15 August, a beautiful morning, I met up with a friend of mine and we walked up to the top of Brompton Park and turned left down towards the chapel. I couldn't believe what I was looking at. I just couldn't believe it. I was astonished. I had heard about the Blitz and the bombs. That couldn't have been any worse than what we witnessed as we walked down towards Brookfield Street. The houses were gutted. The Edenderry Inn was burnt out. There were other businesses along the road that were burnt to the ground.

One of the sights that really saddened me was the home of Tess Donegan. Sadly today kids don't read comics, but when I was growing up Tess's shop was where we went to get the *Dandy*, the *Beano*, the *Eagle*. Tess was not only who we got our comics from but she organised a wee savings club for Christmas. We may not have saved very much but maybe enough for the *Dandy* or *Beano* Christmas annual.

Tess lived in the back of the house and her shop was in the front room. She sold all kinds of religious regalia. As we walked down the road we saw Tess's house – totally gutted! Tess. In the name of God, what had Tess ever done to upset anyone? You could not have met a nicer person, or one less able to defend herself. Such an innocent wee woman to become a victim of all this mayhem. Sadly, she was only one of many.

Shops were also burned on the other side of the road. Paddy O'Hara's Wheatfield Bar got a touch, along with the Brookfield Mill. The police couldn't cope with the mayhem. Having been in the job, I can now understand that. The police were undermanned. There were only 3,000–4,000 police officers across the North. Many were also doing the desk jobs, as there were very few civilians working in police establishments at that time. They were then expected to cope with the public order situation on the streets. Officers were out on the streets who had not been trained for that kind of policing, but they were ordered into action.

There were rumours of impending carnage in the aftermath of those days of August 1969. Many people were moving across the border in fear of their lives. I remember going up to see my uncle Joe and aunt Meg, who were living in Glenbank at the time, a staunchly Loyalist area close to Ardoyne, and I was worried about them. Joe was a good golfer, and a lot of police officers with whom he played golf used to come into their house. Their son was in the Army, like so many other young men in Ardoyne who were in the Forces. It would have amazed you. In Brompton Park alone you could have put your own company together! I was one of the few who never had any ambitions to join any of the armed services, mostly due to the influence of my mother, a very strong Republican. As I walked up towards Glenbank, I could see that some parts of the city were covered in smoke. What really struck me though was the very obvious sense of fear.

The Violence Hits Home

I can't remember exactly when it happened, but Joe and Meg had a knock on the door and were told, 'You are going to have to move out of here.'

Aunt Meg asked, 'What are we going to do?' They were given two alternatives, a house on the Shore Road, which as a Loyalist area was not an option for them, and the other was in Lenadoon. They chose Lenadoon. I witnessed my uncle and aunt being told to get out, and suddenly all that was happening around me started to hit home.

Fear was rampant on both sides of the community. The Loyalists were afraid of the IRA and of the people over in Ardoyne, and it was the opposite story in Ardoyne. I just couldn't believe that this had happened in the area I had grown up in. An area in which I had friends in Chief Street and Bray Street on the opposite side of the road. A Protestant was shot dead in Palmer Street. Who did it was another thing but, of course, the people in Ardoyne got the blame. The finger-pointing and blaming each other was rife. There was talk around the district that Loyalists were coming across the road again to finish off the job. The fear was palpable. It was so bad I remember all the talk was about the need for the Army to come in.

The Army arrived some time on the Saturday afternoon. I ran out to Herbert Street with others, and the Army was coming down along the front of Holy Cross Church. They were wearing NATO-style helmets, and were carrying rifles in front of them. I have the memory of a banner that said, 'Disperse or be shot'. I am sure I saw this, but I haven't seen anything referring to it in the archives. The arrival of the Army eventually brought a calmness to the district but unfortunately that did not last for long.

Buses erected as a barricade at the top of Brompton Park (above) and Kerrera Street (below) (© Hugh McKeown)

Homes and McManus' hairdressers (Mary McAleese's aunt) burnt out on the main Crumlin Road (© Hugh McKeown)

Paddy Harkey and Gerard Murphy playing in the driving seat of a burnt-out bus (© Hugh McKeown)

Ordnance survey map showing both sides of interface on the Crumlin Road

The aftermath of the night's rioting in an area known as 'the Pad' (Butler Street)
(© Hugh McKeown) (above and below)

People attending the funeral of Sammy McLarnon (first victim of the Troubles in Ardoyne) (© Hugh McKeown)

Chatham Street littered with debris in the aftermath of violence (© Jim Moreland)

Holy Cross Church as seen from Butler Street (© Hugh McKeown)

Scenes from Hooker Street as (above) the remnants of buses smoulder outside
'Paddy the Barbers' and (below) children watch on as a family is helped to remove
their possessions and flee to safety (© Jim Moreland)

Playing 'war games' – a young boy wears the helmet of a British soldier facing into Ardoyne (© Jim Moreland)

Advert in the *Irish News* seeking donations for food and shelter for Ardoyne families (courtesy of the *Irish News*) (below left)

Scene of devastation looking up main Crumlin Road from Hooker Street (© Jim Moreland) (below right)

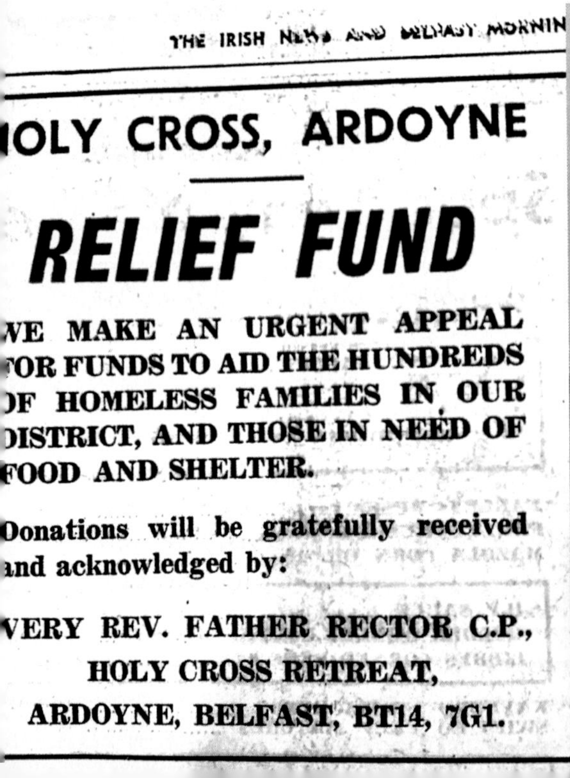

THE IRISH NEWS AND BELFAST MORNIN

HOLY CROSS, ARDOYNE

RELIEF FUND

WE MAKE AN URGENT APPEAL FOR FUNDS TO AID THE HUNDREDS OF HOMELESS FAMILIES IN OUR DISTRICT, AND THOSE IN NEED OF FOOD AND SHELTER.

Donations will be gratefully received and acknowledged by:

VERY REV. FATHER RECTOR C.P.,
HOLY CROSS RETREAT,
ARDOYNE, BELFAST, BT14, 7G1.

One thing needs to be stated. The police had been well accepted in Ardoyne prior to the Troubles breaking out. The people had welcomed them. The police were doing a good job as far as the community was concerned. There was no one throwing stones at them or calling them names. People had a fear of the police, but for no other reason than out of respect for the law. If you played football in the street and the police came around the corner you thought, 'I better run.' I couldn't see too many young people running today!

Defending My Community

I was waiting for a reaction to the violence inflicted upon Ardoyne. I wondered when it would happen. Then the reaction came. The people in Ardoyne formed the ad-hoc Ardoyne Citizens' Defence Committee. This group organised people from the district going out at night, standing at the gable walls and street corners to alert the district to further attacks. I was out at night with the other men at the gable walls at Berwick Road and Brompton Park, using small do-it-yourself huts as a base. The whole idea was that if something happened at night, we would be in a position to raise the alarm, and I did my bit. I took my turn out on the streets for a few hours each night keeping watch. I didn't know what we going to do if something did happen, but we were out there! The violence had occurred outside my home so what else was I supposed to do?

There were a lot of good guys in the CDC, but there were some others who in my mind were thugs. Prior to this, they had been running about the district like loose cannons, and if you didn't agree with them you got a difficult time, but suddenly the situation gave them a degree of legitimacy and they saw themselves as 'protectors'.

There was a strong feeling that Ardoyne had been left to defend itself, while West Belfast had been protected by the IRA. There was a lot of talk about what was happening on the streets in front of us and how we could confront it. Then there was talk of well-known Republicans coming over from West Belfast to speak to the residents. If I said they were coming to form the PIRA I would be telling lies, but they were coming over to talk to people anyway.

Joining the Police

I have to say that as a young person I had always wanted to be a police officer and it wasn't that I was suddenly struck by the idea. I didn't want to be in the Gardaí or in the Metropolitan Police. I just wanted to be a police officer within my own community. Those early aspirations I had as a child had been buried, given that I was living in Ardoyne and becoming a police officer would not have been something that was encouraged in young people within the district at the time.

Following the rioting of 1969, the Hunt Report was published following an inquiry into the RUC and the 'B' Specials. It recommended the demilitarisation of the RUC and the disbandment of the 'B' Specials. There was also clear encouragement from members of the Catholic Church and from Nationalist politicians, such as Eddie McAteer in Derry, that young Catholics should join the police. That was being talked about openly and I agreed with what they were saying.

Anyway, those thoughts were floating around in my mind as I tried to make sense of it all. One afternoon, not unusually it has to be said, trouble was taking place right outside our house. I went out the front door, walked towards the Stumps and found myself in the middle of a large crowd. One guy, from Lower Chatham Street, was pointing his finger vigorously into the face of one of our local priests, who was trying to calm the situation and shouted, 'Fuck away off back to your chapel! What would you know about what's going on?'

I had never witnessed a priest being treated like that. At that moment, something just clicked inside me and I thought, 'That's it. I am a Catholic, and I am joining the police.'

As soon as I made that decision I knew there was no going back. I was aware in my own mind that there were various ways of dealing with this madness we were living in. I decided to join the police. As a young lad from Ardoyne with a Gaelic footballing background I was going to get in there and do my best in everything I did. I didn't think that I was going to change the police, but I did believe that the more Catholics who joined the better understanding the police would have of the people in Ardoyne and other similar areas. I wouldn't have been the first Catholic in the RUC though. In those days there were quite a few Catholics in the force. Percentage wise it was about 10 per cent, but when you say 10 per cent of 3,000 or 4,000, that was larger than some of the smaller police forces in England and Scotland at the time.

I was, however, probably the first person from Ardoyne to join the police. I knew what I was doing. I first joined the RUC Reserve, and after my initial training I was on the streets by 1 July 1970. I wasn't the only Catholic who joined the Reserve, although I was probably more prominent because I was playing Gaelic football and was fairly well known in sporting circles. I was joined by other young Catholics who also saw it as a better way to deal with the problems arising within communities.

I joined the RUC, an organisation which Nationalist people had criticised for years. I soon found that my fellow officers were mostly ordinary working-class guys like myself. You can't expect someone to be brought up in Ardoyne or on the Shankill Road and not have some sort of views, but we wanted to create a climate of respect for each other. My view was simple: 'I will lead and others can follow. I will let them see what a man from Ardoyne can do when he is given an opportunity.'

I went into the RUC Training Centre, Enniskillen and was determined to do my very best. I was awarded the Baton of Honour, awarded to the most outstanding recruit each year at training school. I was aware of my Catholic/Nationalist background, and I didn't want to let anyone down. Not only did I get the Baton of Honour, but I went up through the ranks very quickly and was a sergeant within three years, and an inspector in five. That put me on a career path to academic and university attainment. I was about to get married at the time I decided to join the RUC Reserve. I was married by the time I was sworn in, but I was still turning up to play Gaelic football for Ardoyne.

Meanwhile, the *Belfast Telegraph* had a whole feature article about me being a young Catholic from Ardoyne who had joined the police. It was an attempt to encourage more Catholics to join. I was attached to Willowfield RUC station at the time, and there were a number of photographs along with the article, including one of me getting into a police car with my sergeant.

The Tide Turns

Until the newspaper article was issued, nobody in Ardoyne had said anything to me about joining the Police Reserve. The night after it appeared I went up to St Gabriel's School to train with the Ardoyne team, and I noticed copies of the article posted along the corridors. I continued into the training session. More than half the boys were delighted that I was in the Reserve. There were no issues with them. Some others had misgivings.

The following Sunday we were due to play Lamh Dhearg in a league match. My brother and I were good players and we were both due to play on the team. Pat was on the county hurling and Gaelic teams, and I had made a few appearances for the county after returning home from America. After the incident at training I turned up to the clubrooms in Butler Street down beside Holyrood Hall. I could sense a tense atmosphere. I was directed to stand at one side of the hall. I will always remember the individuals who came across to me and said, 'Brian, you know that under Rule 21 you are not welcome here anymore.' I was devastated. Rule 21 banned members of the British Armed Forces from being members of the GAA. Although it was in place at the time, I believed that there was a new dispensation, and that things were about to change for the better. I was wrong.

I was told to leave Ardoyne Gaelic Club by these people, but clearly not everyone was in agreement. Many players contacted me and gave me their support, but sadly there were the hard-liners as well and they were unforgiving. The club was divided on it. Many of the guys did not want me to go, but I always remember the ones who showed me the door. When I went out the door my brother, Pat, came with me and he said to them, 'If that is what you are going to do to him after what he has done for this club, I am away too.' That was the moment when all my bridges with the club were burned and I found myself in a whole new environment.

Facing the Consequences

My mother had died earlier in March 1969, and that was devastating for me. I can honestly say that the second most devastating thing to ever happen to me was being told that I was no longer welcome at the Ardoyne Gaelic Club. I remember going home and just crying my eyes out. I had given so much to Ardoyne over the years and was left with the question 'Why can someone not understand that what I am trying to achieve is, for me, the right way forward? Why can they not see that?'

As the saying goes though, 'As one door closes, another one opens.' Days after being asked to leave Ardoyne Gaelic Club I went into Willowfield police station and there on the notice board was a message from the RUC Rugby Club looking for players. I went along to the training sessions at Newforge and have never looked back since. I became captain, secretary and eventually chairman, and had the honour of captaining the RUC at a cup final in Ravenhill.

My interest in Gaelic football never went away though. For years I campaigned to get rid of the GAA's Rule 21, and had great support from people throughout Ireland, including many All-Ireland winners. I was amazed how few people in the Republic had even heard of the rule, and that was because it didn't apply south of the border. The rule was eventually removed from the GAA rule book in 2001, and then I founded the PSNI Gaelic Football Club. We played our first official game against the Gardaí in 2002. Shortly after that I retired from the police.

Those were hard days. They were hard for me, but I was determined that I wanted to see things change in Northern Ireland, and to do what I could to improve them. I saw the best of both worlds in terms of Catholics and Protestants when I was growing up and when I was working with them. I saw joining the police as an opportunity to move forward. I knew what I was doing, and whatever the reaction I wasn't going to be stopped. I hoped that people would see things differently, but as time moved on I realised that wasn't the case, and I had to burn my bridges.

When I was growing up, my mother was a big trade unionist, and she taught me to believe that people are basically good. I grew up with that belief. When I went into the police, I never forgot that. The guys I served with were just like me. We struggled when things were difficult and I made many good friends. When you think of the Americans at the end of the Pacific War, some were in favour of dropping the atomic bomb, while others were against it, but all were basically good people making the decision they thought was best. Why did I join the police? Because I grew up thinking that there must be better ways of doing things.

Exiled

The real difficulties with joining the police came with the realisation that I couldn't go home. I couldn't go back to Ardoyne to visit relatives. I couldn't go to funerals. I couldn't go to baptisms. I couldn't go to weddings. Attempting to go home would probably end in death or injury, not just for myself but for relatives and friends as well. I didn't want that. I made a big decision not to go back, and it broke my heart. It was thirty years later before I next visited Holy Cross Church, when my uncle Charlie, my mother's brother, died in 2001. That was very emotional. Fr Kenneth, the parish priest, phoned me and asked, 'Will you read a lesson?' I said that I would.

I was going back to Ardoyne following the Good Friday Agreement. I was a chief superintendent in charge of RUC Community Affairs, and my colleagues said they would make sure there was plenty of protection for me when I went back. I said, 'No. Absolutely not. There is to be no protection. If I know the people of Ardoyne whom I grew up with and played Gaelic football with, there will be no issues. I don't want to see a Land Rover, or police of any nature, anywhere near the funeral.'

I made my way up to Ardoyne. When I went into the church, there were so many people there whom I knew. Many of them came over to talk to me when we left the church. People like Seán Brown, whom I boxed with in the St John Bosco Club, and Malachy McLaughlin, whom I played with on the Ardoyne Gaelic team, served communion. There were so many people I once knew so well. It was very emotional as I was walking down the aisle.

When my uncle's coffin was being taken out of the church and down towards the church gate, we stopped to put it in the hearse. Three or four guys then approached me, and one of them asked, 'You are Brian, aren't you?'

'Yes,' I replied.

'Brian,' he said, 'we want you to have this.' He then put his hand into his pocket, and I thought, 'No! Not at my uncle Charlie's funeral!' I really thought that I was about to be shot. What followed next highlights the people of Ardoyne as I knew them. He pulled out a brown envelope and said, 'That is to help bury your uncle Charlie. It is from his friends in the Crumlin Star Club, and we want you to have it.' There was £350 in the envelope which I handed to my aunt Agnes. That incident just summed up for me the people of Ardoyne.

Lives Changed Forever

When I think back to those days of 14–16 August and to the people I knew – Bikkie McFarlane, Cleakey Clarke (RIP), Terry Toolan (RIP), Frank Corr (RIP), Ted McQuaid (RIP) and others – these were some of the people who played for Ardoyne and were killed in the Troubles or who had an impact on the Troubles. We were all friends who grew up together and played football and hurling together or social-ised together. Then along comes this one weekend in August 1969, and our lives were changed forever.

I believe in the old saying, 'There but for the grace of God go I.' I chose my path, others chose theirs. I am always sympathetic to those who experienced the awful events over thirty years and who lived through the violence. They were good guys. If the Troubles hadn't come along it is possible we would all have been on different paths somewhere else, but that weekend changed things, and I have accepted that.

Confronted by My Past

I have helped a lot of people from Ardoyne in my career as a police officer. People would come up to me and say, 'It's great to see you.' There are also others who would have happily spat in my eye.

Bik McFarland was involved in the Great Escape from the Maze with Gerry Kelly, but he was involved long before that in another attempted escape from the same location. Around 1978 he dressed up as a prison warder with Larry Marley and one other guy from Beechmount in an escape attempt. They almost made it, except that the prison pass they were using was out of date, and this was spotted by a prison warden.

This is where you get back to your grassroots. Although I was stationed in Lisburn at the time, I was the inspector with responsibility for Hillsborough and the Maze Prison. If anything happened at the prison I had to respond to it. When the court case came up for Bikkie attempting this first escape from the Maze Prison, I remember my colleagues from Lisburn saying, 'Bikkie McFarlane is up.' I was duty inspector and one of my colleagues asked, 'Do you want to do it?'

I said, 'Certainly.' I knew Bikkie from playing football and whether I went to court with him or not, it would change nothing. I had joined the police and I was not going to hide it.

Basil McIvor was the resident magistrate, and although the case was due to be heard that morning, there was confusion over the wrong papers being handed over, and Mr McIvor directed the CID to get the right papers. In the meantime, he placed the guys in the cell downstairs. It was September and the All-Ireland Final was coming up. I told the guards that I was going into the cells to talk to the prisoners. The guards were fairly surprised, as you would imagine. I sat down with Bik and asked him how he was. We had a very emotional discussion from his point of view. Along with the case he was facing, his father had died and we discussed some personal relationship issues. We also talked about better times, and I thought, 'Is this what the Troubles have done? Here am I a police officer looking after Bikkie, and there he is convicted of murder, none of which would have happened prior to 1969.'

But that's the way it was. Bik McFarlane, like so many others, would not have been where he was had the Troubles not happened. Terry Toolan would not have been killed. Frank Corr would not have been murdered. I could go on and on. You can't get rid of the emotional ties you grew up with. How can you tell a guy you grew up with and played football with, 'Well, now I hate you!'

On another occasion, I went to arrest a young man in Ardoyne. I won't give the particular details, but my boss asked me how I felt about it. I explained that I couldn't pick and choose my jobs. I had joined the police, and if I had to go into Ardoyne to arrest someone, then that was my duty. I knew the individual's family well. They were a lovely family, but I had to go in and make the arrest. The oldest boy in the family had been shot dead by the IRA, and this other son was to be arrested because he had allegedly been involved in the burning of buses. It was the early hours of the morning when we went in to arrest him. The father, for whom I had so much regard, was lying on the sofa, almost oblivious to what was going on. He said to me, 'Just take him.' The boy's mother had died recently. It was a difficult situation.

These are the kind of things I wanted to deal with personally, because I wanted them to be dealt with in a sensitive manner. When I went in through that front door I saw a lovely family destroyed. Why? Because of the Troubles. That's why! If it hadn't been for the Troubles this would never have happened. The son would never have been shot dead, and the other son would never have been arrested and charged. That was the impact of the Troubles and there are so many stories like that.

Martin Meehan

I have one particular memory of Martin Meehan that goes back to the Queen's Jubilee visit in 1977. I was a sergeant in Castlereagh on ordinary duty. There was the main station in Castlereagh that dealt with ordinary policing, and then there was 'the police office', which dealt with terrorism-related incidents. On the day of the Queen's visit a lot of IRA suspects had been brought in, as well as a load of

Loyalists, including the Shankill Butchers. Castlereagh was bursting at the seams. I was asked to go to the police office to assist. I was aware that Martin Meehan had been brought in, and sometime later he asked to see me. I went to see him and he asked, 'Brian, can you do me a favour? My wife is dying. She has cancer and is in the Royal Hospital.' I was stunned, because I knew she wasn't all that old. He asked if I could keep him informed about how she was keeping.

The police had people in all the hospitals for a variety of reasons, including hospital liaison officers. I contacted one in the Royal and told him the story. I explained, 'Look, she is in the Royal. She has cancer, and what I want you to do is to find out how she is doing.' I don't know how long it took, but he came back to me and said, 'Martin Meehan's wife has just died.'

I was absolutely stunned. Such a young woman, but I had to go down and tell Martin the sad news. From a situation of not seeing each other for years, with all that had happened in between, and I was now dealing with a very emotional situation affecting his family. I spoke to the CID and others involved and told them the story. I suggested, 'Look, if you are not going to be able to charge Martin Meehan with a crime, I think you should let him go. His wife has just died, and we are not achieving anything by holding him here.' They could have held him for up to seven days, but they agreed with me. I informed Martin of the CID decision and arranged transport for him to go home.

The story continues with Martin in 1980. He had gone on hunger strike, but although he had just come off it, he was close to death. As an inspector in the Special Patrol Group, I was directed to go up to Ward 18 in Musgrave Park Hospital, where they kept those charged with terrorist offences who were in need of medical attention. My task was to escort Martin Meehan back to the Maze Prison. I remember him coming out of the hospital. He wouldn't have recognised me as he was in an awful state. I then had to get him into the back of an ambulance and return him to the Maze.

Roll on over twenty years after that experience to the day of the result of the Good Friday Referendum. By that time I was a superintendent and deputy divisional commander of A Division, (Belfast city centre and surrounding areas). It was also the day of the Lord Mayor's Show. Alban Maginness was the Lord Mayor. He decided that for the Lord Mayor's procession he would go down the Ormeau Road, which led to us having to deal with a minor riot at the junction of Donegall Pass and the Ormeau Road. I then had to go from there to the King's Hall to see how the vote was proceeding. As soon as I walked in the front door, the Chief Executive met me and invited me for a cup of coffee.

I hadn't spoken to Martin Meehan since the incident in Castlereagh in 1977, but as I turned to go for the coffee, bear in mind the cameras of the world are on this, who is walking towards me only Martin. I was in my full RUC uniform, braid cap and accompanied by my staff officer. He walked towards me, stuck out his hand and said, 'Brian, the war is over.' Those were his exact words to me: 'Brian, the war is over.'

He said a few other things, and made some joke about becoming Minister of Justice and giving me a pay rise, but then he stopped joking and said to me, 'Brian, I haven't seen you since that day in Castlereagh when Mary was dying, and I never got the chance to thank you.'

I said, 'But I have seen you.'

He said, 'No you haven't!'

I then related to him the day he was brought out of Ward 18 following his hunger strike, and taken back to the Maze Prison.

'Well Brian,' he said, 'To be honest I have also been watching for you.' He then proceeded to tell me all the different stations in which I had been stationed!

I said, 'Martin, were you keeping an eye on me for any good reason?'

He rubbed his hands together, smiled, and replied, 'Brian, the war is over!'

Following Different Paths

I still think about the people I grew up with, and whom I went to school and played football with. It is difficult to disconnect. I never forgot about my roots in Holy Cross parish. I joined the police to help people and to do positive things. My greatest wish was to get these Troubles over and to get on with life.

The one thing that is important for me to say is that I would not have allowed my children to use the word 'hate'. Never say you hate someone. It is all-consuming. It is a destructive word and it destroys those who use it and could destroy those whom you use it against. I couldn't turn around and suddenly say that I hate those guys I grew up with because they joined the PIRA. How could I do that? However, I am in no doubt that there were people who may have hated me because I joined the police. There were a few people who let me know how they felt. That's what democracy is all about, but wherever I could have helped people I helped them irrespective of their views.

For me, a lot of the difficulty is in people's heads. For instance, the weekend Arlene Foster went down to the Ulster Final in Clones in 2018, did the ground open up? Was there a bolt of lightning from the sky? Not at all. She got a great welcome. I bet she was saying to herself, 'I should have done this earlier.' It was the same with me fighting to get Rule 21 abolished. My fight wasn't for me, as I never played Gaelic football again, but I knew that when the police played their first match the ground wouldn't open up for the GAA, and they wouldn't be struck by a bolt of lightning. I know that in the years ahead people will ask, 'What was it all about?'

Changing Times

We are getting to a stage now that my youngest daughter knows nothing about the Troubles. If I talk to her about anything connected with the Troubles she wouldn't have a clue what I was referring to. When they opened Aquinas Grammar School she was able to go there. It was different for my oldest daughter, who went to St Dominic's on the Falls Road. She had to put up with all the difficulties, like her dad not being able to leave her to school or to collect her. I would maybe drop her off at the lights at the Royal Victoria Hospital, or further down the Falls Road when I was stationed in North Queen Street.

We also lived in what would have been called a 'Protestant area', an area where she stood out because of her St Dominic's uniform, so she had to get permission to wear a different school coat to cover her uniform. When she then got to school, they would ask why she was wearing a different coat. Kate Adie did a series about 'dangerous jobs', and I was one of the people featured. It focused on my whole situation, but particularly trying to protect my family.

What difference did it make to me? I couldn't go home, couldn't do this, couldn't do that, couldn't see my daughter going to St Dominic's. I couldn't do a whole lot of things, and yet, at the end of it all, when I did go to Holy Cross, albeit for the death of my uncle, I was made welcome. It was very emotional. Then I met up with Martin Meehan, and he thanked me. I was involved in opening GAA grounds with Martin McGuinness during my time with Sport NI. The last time I was down at an All-Ireland Final, or attending the Ulster Final between Donegal and Derry, I was in the company of Martin McGuinness and President Mary McAleese.

You talk about life turning full circle. I think attending that Ulster Final was Mary McAleese's last public engagement as President. Mary knew me anyway, so it was nothing new being with her. It was different with Martin McGuinness. He and I also opened up a number of GAA grounds in south Derry, and I was left thinking, 'There is a man who at a time I probably may have had to shoot, or he would have had to shoot me.' It sounded crazy as we were now sitting down amicably, watching a Gaelic match and discussing which team we thought might win.

Forever Home

I loved Ardoyne. I have never forgotten Ardoyne to this day. Never. That is where my grounding is. Bearing in mind my grandparents, the McCargos, were from the

'Real Ardoyne'! They were from Elmfield Street. They weren't blow-ins from North Queen Street like my mother was.

We were a fairly poor family, as most families were those days, and I made great friendships. It was a great community. It is true that you left the key in your door, and that your back door was open if anyone wanted to come in. Ardoyne was a great big family. If you wanted to go to the Forum Picture House in those days it was just 4d to get in. If you hadn't got it, all your other mates would have said to their mums, 'Hey Mammy, Brian McCargo has only a penny.' We always managed to raise the necessary amount.

That's the way life was in those days. There was always good comradery around the church, like the processions in May around the church grounds, the confraternities, bulletins, everybody going to Mass on Sunday, including guys from Ardoyne who had joined the armed forces parading in military uniforms. Catholic police officers from Leopold Street station would start off early in the morning by calling in at the back of the church and attending Mass. It was all part of Holy Cross parish life.

I always went out of my way to do my best for people. In fact, a week or two before I retired, Fr Myles brought me along to the Flax Trust in the Brookfield Mill for a lunch with a number of people whom he had invited in from Ardoyne. He said, 'We just want to say thanks to you for all the work you have done for others that nobody knows anything about and without grabbing the headlines, including your work at Holy Cross Girl's School.'

Time moves on, and when my grandson asked me, 'Papa, what television programmes did you watch when you were my age?' I replied, 'Alexander, there was no television when I was your age!' He can't get that. He can't get that in to his head. Yes, time moves on and a lot of things have changed. What will never change though is that I loved Ardoyne. I loved the whole community atmosphere. The saddest thing about Ardoyne was when the Troubles hit and changed it forever, but I really believe that my experience at my uncle's funeral was typical Ardoyne at its best, and that will never change.

4

Mary McAleese

Early Days

I was born and reared in Ardoyne, although, as the family grew, we moved five times during the time we lived in the district. I was the first of nine children, and started off life in 60 Ladbrook Drive, back-to-back with my grandparents, John and Cassie McManus, who lived in 23 Dunedin Park. The lanes behind the houses (entries as they were known) were close to one another. Then we moved a few yards to Balholm Drive, where one of our neighbours, Billy Bates, ended up allegedly being fed powdered glass by his Republican comrades in Crumlin Road Gaol. When he lived next door, his biggest crime, according to my mother, was to try to teach me to curse. I was about eighteen months and he was not much older. We moved from there across the road to 23 Mountainview Gardens.

At that time there were only two streets in Mountainview, the Gardens and the Parade, which ran at right angles to one another. Mountainview Gardens ran up the back of the shops parallel to the main road while the Parade ran from the Crumlin Road at right angles from beside the fire station. I would have been maybe two or three years of age when my parents moved there. That's the place I remember best as a child because it was then a fantastic place to live.

We were the first Catholics to live in that street; all our neighbours were Protestant and many of them became great friends and are friends to this day. These were people we would have gone on holidays with, people whose churches I would go along to with them because they all went to loads of different churches, everything from gospel hall to Reverend Sydney Callaghan's church down the Shankill. Two of my sisters were bridesmaids to the daughters of Protestant neighbours.

At the bottom of our street there were fields and fields and fields, which ran all the way down to the glen. Those fields were an open playground for us. The vestiges of the Second World War were still there, because I think, if I remember rightly, there were old Nissen huts and other visible reminders of the time that soldiers, particularly American soldiers, had been billeted around there. It was a great place to grow up.

Mixed Emotions

We then moved to 142 Woodvale Road, which I didn't like at all. The house was grim. The road was grim. It was at the top of the Shankill Road and on a main thoroughfare, so gone was playing on the street or in those fields! It didn't have a big garden liked we were used to in Mountainview, just an old bit of a yard and a baked mud-patch.

Once again, we were one of very few Catholic families living on the road. The neighbours were friendly, and while the hinterland was almost entirely Protestant, we had relatives, the O'Haras, who lived a few doors up. They owned an off-licence down the lower end of Ardoyne in Crumlin Street. Mrs O'Hara (Aunt Doll) was my paternal grandmother's sister and, like my father, was from County Roscommon. There were a couple of Catholic families near us, one of whom, the O'Reillys, we were particularly friendly with. They were also in the off-licence business. There were four or five kids in the family by then. I hated that house as much as I had loved Mountainview.

A lot of the women who lived in Mountainview had worked in the flax and linen mills in Ardoyne. They were called 'millies' and 'doffers'. Some of them worked in the Beltex Mill, and because ours was a sewing and knitting household they used to bring me lovely bits of material and ribbons, ideal for baby clothes or dolls' dresses.

All my grandmother's grandchildren, particularly the girls, were good with their hands. My grandmother and mother taught us how to be good seamstresses. There were no Dunnes, Penneys or Primark then. Everything was handmade. We spent the evenings making clothes or knitting for the inevitable next baby, but when we moved to the Woodvale Road the Beltex bounty stopped.

I was miserable there, but worse was to come. It turned out that the nice lady next door was a piano teacher, and so we started music lessons – a crime against humanity! Let's just say that written theory tests presented no problem, but practicing scales and playing dull, worthy pieces soon revealed that this was not a career option for me.

Awareness of Difference

After primary school, I started St Dominic's Grammar School on the Falls Road. I was getting a bit older and starting to explore things a bit more on my own, and used to take a shortcut through Woodvale Park to get to school. I was very conscious that for the likes of me, in a Catholic school uniform, it was getting difficult, and so I carried my hurley stick, but not necessarily for the purpose for which it was intended. We knew from playing in the park that we were only safe when our Protestant friends were with us. They were our defenders. That's where I heard the word 'Fenian' first used, and I was growing in awareness that Belfast was a deeply sectarian city, and that Ardoyne had a dangerous history and undercurrent. This was mixed with the fact that I lived in a mixed area in terms of religion and politics, and many of my friends were Protestants who went to the nearby Everton Secondary School or, more rarely, Belfast Royal Academy.

My sister Nora was bridesmaid for Florence Maxwell, one of our Protestant friends who lived in Mountainview Gardens. Florence married Stuart Taylor, a serving Scottish soldier in Thiepval Barracks in Lisburn. We were all at the wedding and the officiating minister, Sydney Callaghan, one of the finest Christians I ever met, remarked that the person he knew best was me, from seeing me in his church on the Shankill Road. Engaging in such close acquaintance with British soldiers was a recipe for being seen with suspicion. If the IRA had known of this relationship we would all have been tarred and feathered by the local IRA, but somehow we escaped that fate.

Another sister, Kate, was bridesmaid for Anna Shaw, a member of a Plymouth Brethren family who lived a few doors from us on the Woodvale Road. The Brethren disapproved of alcohol, so it was notionally a dry wedding. My father wondered how he would get through the day, but it turned out that the grandfather of the groom wasn't entirely taken with this abstentionism, and he had arranged with the hotel porter that there would be a back room where a man could get a drop of whiskey to make a decent wedding out of it. So that's how mixed we were.

We had a very strong consciousness of Catholic and Protestant identities, but we also had great friendship and loyalty among our friends, alongside an undercurrent of suspicion, fear and lack of trust outside of those known circles. When we were outside these comfort zones, we didn't know who we would meet. We could be ok, we might not be ok. We might get thumped, we might not get thumped.

John Shaw, Anna's youngest brother, was in and out of our house and we ran in and out of his. His parents adored our Kate and spoilt her. John joined a Loyalist paramilitary group, and on one night alone he murdered four Catholics and a Protestant neighbour of ours whom he mistook for a Catholic. His family was torn apart by his actions. He spent years in prison. We tried to stay in contact with his parents, whom we knew to be kindly people. All our lives were frayed, fractured, ruptured by the return to Belfast of the latent and deeply embedded sectarian violence in the 1960s.

On the Move Again

Our next house move was straight up the road to 657 Crumlin Road, on the corner with Hesketh Park, next door to Everton School. Again, it was a mixed area. Four of our immediate neighbours were Protestant ministers, one of them my father's close friend the Rev Jimmy Arbuthnott. That is where I was living in August of 1969, travelling across town to St Dominic's and spending lunchtimes in my father's pub, The Long Bar on Leeson Street, close to the Grosvenor Road, and a few yards from Jimmy Arbuthnott's church.

Shortly after Loyalist paramilitaries machine-gunned us out of 657 Crumlin Road in 1973, and thankfully managed not to kill any of us, our pub was blown up by a Loyalist car bomb. Olive McConnell, a young mother, was killed. She was a sister of one of my good volunteer friends from the Saint Vincent de Paul Society, Gerry Kavanagh from Cavendish Street. The Troubles shattered the life that we had been trundling through and it became more and more obvious that despite living on superficially good terms, literally cheek-by-jowl with people of different politics and religious persuasions, there was no mutual understanding of each other's history, politics or thinking. It was such a shock and such a pity, for, in the immediate post-war years, and after the IRA campaign of the 1950s had petered out, Belfast was quietening down and people had started to create mixed streets. With O'Neill and Lemass leading the two governments, North and South respectively, it seemed to be a time when we could look forward to some peace, with new levels of mutual respect and political engagement. We were about to learn of course that life doesn't work in those linear ways.

One of the things life in Northern Ireland has taught me is that for every action there is an equal and opposite reaction. The equal and opposite reaction to the growing calm was the firebrand fundamentalism of Rev Ian Paisley, and a growing Loyalist paramilitarism, stirring up again the dozing sectarian dragon. A new generation of educated Catholics, aided by a few human-rights-minded Protestants, began to campaign for civil rights, and the coming together of these two trends demonstrated that the progress that had been made had not gone deep enough or wide enough, and the fractures in this society started to show in the mid-1960s.

Friends, Not Strangers

We lived in a Protestant area. My father was from the west of Ireland, and had his understanding of the realities of Northern politics been less naïve and trusting he probably would never have bought any of the houses he did. He might have moved us deeper into Ardoyne or into the Catholic side of Ardoyne, or deeper into Andersonstown, but my father had a great open mind to politics. He would have been a staunch Nationalist, but he hadn't a sectarian bone in his body.

When we lived on Woodvale Road, my parents advertised in the *Belfast Telegraph* for somebody to help my mother with the cleaning. My mammy had eleven difficult pregnancies and nine live children. She hadn't been all that well after each birth and that had been very tough on her. This woman came to the house in response to the advert, and as she came through the door she saw the statue of the Sacred Heart. I remember her saying at the doorway, 'I think I am in the wrong house. I live in the Hammer on the Shankill.' My father said, 'If it is a problem for you that is fine, but it wouldn't be a problem for us you know.' She said, 'Well, if it wouldn't be a problem for you, it wouldn't be a problem for me.'

She was our housekeeper for years when she was living on the Shankill. Many a story she told us about her husband teaching her grandchild to say 'F the pope', and we just accepted all that. That was life. It gave us an insight into a world that was literally a few hundred yards away, but from which we were hermetically sealed by virtue of religion and religious experience and ghettoisation.

She must have spoken well of us, because when I visited the Hammer many years later as President, one of her Loyalist neighbours from the Hammer publicly upbraided the Secretary of State, Peter Mandelson, for daring to welcome me to the event as a 'stranger', when in fact, I was her 'neighbour's child'.

A Father's Influence

My father moved us to Rostrevor after we lost our home and business. The first thing in our new home-cum-pub was to employ a local Protestant lad as a barman. He had that openness. He was also a very avid reader, and, though he had left school at fourteen, he introduced us to many of the writings on the national question, and especially that of Daniel O'Connell. I would have been aware of the two traditions, the paramilitary tradition and the O'Connellite tradition of trying to solve political problems through the use of parliamentary power. I was brought up believing, as

I do to this day, that any claims that are made by the British Parliament to democracy began with Dan O'Connell.

O'Connell introduced the British to the idea of fundamental human rights, to the idea of democracy, to egalitarianism, to equality. He did so much for Irish Catholics by the campaign for Catholic Emancipation, which he achieved in 1829, but he was also an internationally celebrated campaigner for Russian Jews, African-American slaves and Presbyterians. He believed in the equality and dignity of all human beings.

I grew up reading and being told about the great Irish leaders – O'Connell, Tone, Emmet, Pearse, Plunkett – and learning that there was a choice to be made between their philosophies. I learnt from first principles that the choice was easier for a teenage girl than a teenage boy in the maelstrom that became the Troubles. That is one of the reasons why, when the Troubles did hit, my father sent the boys of the family to boarding school for their safety, whether he could afford it or not. At home in Ardoyne they were not safe from Loyalist attacks, nor from the strong gravitational of paramilitarism and of militarism. This has always been important for me to remember: that when we talk about paramilitarism, the culture of paramilitarism was always over and against and part of a centuries-long embedded culture of militarism from Government and State forces. It was embedded too in our thinking.

1969 – 'Something in the Air'

I am a child who grew up in the aftermath of the Second World War, with the beginning of the civility that we had with Lemass and O'Neill, what I would call the politics of decency and good neighbourliness, but then came the 50th anniversary of the 1916 Rising and, simultaneously, the 50th anniversary of the Somme, which by then had become victim of a split and false history.

The whole Catholic Nationalist contribution to British success in the Great War had been conveniently overlooked, even excised, by both sides of the community. The Nationalist community was focused in 1966 on commemorating the Rising. I can still remember watching the parade coming up the Falls Road. I was standing at the gates of my father's aunt's home (Mrs Cassidy) on the front of the Falls Road opposite Beechmount Avenue. Her daughter Nora was married to Frank McAreavey, a man we all knew as Frank the Barber, for he had a barber's shop in Butler Street in Ardoyne. Frank was an old IRA man, and he was the grand marshall of the parade that day.

My great-aunt was one of four sisters, three of whom came from Country Roscommon to live in Belfast as young women. My grandmother didn't. She stayed in the west of Ireland. Mrs Cassidy, my great-aunt, was a very elegant and refined old lady who had married an RIC man. She ran a boarding house, and bad language would have been anathema to her, but I can remember her using some very unparliamentary language when she saw a man stop at the gate of the boarding house to talk to my father. The man was dressed in ordinary mufti, but he was a Catholic Special Branch man called Dunleavy who lived in Ardoyne, and my aunt could see that he was not there for the fun of it. She roared at us to, 'Get down the stairs and tell your father that if he doesn't want to be shot to move away from that man Dunleavey.' His daughter was actually at St Dominic's a couple of years ahead of me. She must have had a hard time, because when we schoolgirls assembled at the top of Twaddell Avenue to get the bus to school, there was a coldness towards her because of her father. That was the kind of sub-text to life there.

From 1966 onwards we had the mischief-making of Paisley and his Loyalist followers, with incidents such as breaking into the Sinn Féin offices, taking the Irish flag, planting bombs in order to blame the IRA – things which were nakedly sectarian. I was very aware that the tension was starting to grow and concerned about where that was going to take us to. How was that going to impact upon our lives? Certainly it made going to places around Belfast increasingly more fraught.

Key People at Key Times

1969 was the year I did 'A' Levels, in itself a big concern, and I had other preoccupations. It was also the year that my mother gave birth to her last child, my youngest brother, Clement. He was born slap bang in the middle of my mock 'A' Levels – most inconvenient! He was also a yappy wee person! My mother was very, very ill after he was born. So ill that she subsequently had a hysterectomy because she was just in an awful way. She had been advised two children earlier to have the hysterectomy, but with Catholic doctrine and Catholic priests (Fr Honorius Kelly CP was our parish priest at the time), it just didn't happen. After that child though, it became a matter of life and death. Mammy wasn't fit to get up in the night to feed him, so my sister Nora and I became the surrogate mammies. We looked after the wee ones, getting all six of them out to school in the mornings, as well as being up in the middle of the night to feed baby Clement.

I must have looked like the wreck of the *Hesperus*, for my wonderful A-level English teacher, Mrs O'Friel, despite an austere look about her that would 'frighten the melt out of you', had a gentle way of looking out for us and a great sense of humour. Out of the wide blue yonder she started to turn up at my front door in her battered Morris Minor, apparently just by accident. She said, 'I was just thinking. I go past your door in the morning and, sure, couldn't I give you a lift over to school?'

At that very time I had been thinking that maybe I should leave school and get a job. It was just too difficult trying to study and manage a house with eight other kids, all younger than me, all steps and stairs, a sick mammy and the beginnings of the Troubles. I remember seeing an advert for a job as a trainee manager in Woolworths. I had thought that maybe I would apply for that.

I had already been told by Fr Honorius, when I told him that I was thinking of going to university and would like to be a lawyer, that I couldn't do that: 'You are a woman, and you have no one belonging to you in the Law.' So I didn't have that much backing for any visions beyond school. Mrs O'Friel never said to me though, 'I know there are problems at home. I know you are having doubts about doing 'A' Levels.' She just turned up and brought me to school, which was fantastic, because it saved me two buses and, more importantly, there was something about her actions that said to me, 'She thinks I am worth something!'

She taught me English for 'A' Level, and I was good at it, for I loved the subject. She said to me, 'You know you don't have to come to every class. It must be hard enough at evenings to get the studying done. Why don't you go down to the Central Library? Don't tell anybody!'

She said this to me and a few others, and we were able to get all our work and study done in the library, so that I could come home in the evening to do whatever needed to be done in the house, including making dinner and lunches for the other children. There were a few lads from St Mary's too whom I ran into at the library, one whom I am still seeing fifty years later – my husband, Martin!

Hard to Escape!

During the summer of 1969 the 'A' Level results came out, and I got enough to get into Law in Queen's – the first of my family to go and do a degree. My mother had left school at 15, and was a hairdresser in my grand-aunt Nora (Sis) McDrury's salon on the front of the Crumlin Road, directly opposite the chapel steps. My mammy was one of eleven children, of whom one, Bernadette, died as an infant. Everywhere I looked in Ardoyne there was somebody belonging to me, either on my father or mother's side. I couldn't have done much wrong without reports getting back home! There was always an auntie or an uncle or a cousin around. Bear in mind that my mother and her siblings had sixty children between them and, while my father's side were less prolific, there was always a huge big clan around.

On the front of the Crumlin Road there was my great-aunt Sis's salon, my mother's sister Una's hairdressing salon a block further down below the chapel, and my aunt Kathleen's dress shop next door to Una. I worked in Una's and Kathleen's on Saturdays and during the holidays, as well as in my father's pub and the Top

Shop sweet shop up near the bus depot. I was a member of the Ovada badminton club and Ardoyne Kickham's camogie club, so it was a very Ardoyne-centred, busy life. My parents, both very clever, never had the chance to stay on at school or go to university, and so were thrilled that I was going to university.

Dinner with the Parish Priest

Fr Honorius, the man who had told me that I shouldn't think about university at all, was, like my parents, also delighted to hear that I had passed my exams, and on the night of 14 August 1969 he took myself and Eileen Gilmartin, a girl who lived in Mountainview Gardens and who was also going to university (UCD), out to dinner to celebrate.

Eileen's daddy was also from the west of Ireland, Geevagh in Co. Sligo, not very far from my father. He was a barman, and so our parents were great friends, and so were Eileen and I. Eileen and I had the extraordinary experience of being taken out for dinner by our parish priest! Never in my life had I ever been taken out to dinner – ever. This was an amazing thing altogether and it was our parish priest who was doing it!

Fr Honorius was held in great respect. His own name was Phelim Kelly, and I have a brother called after him. He was a Dubliner. Very grand, and a bit arch conservative, but a decent old skin! A very interesting man, he used to call into our house regularly, but, of course, our house was a publican's house, a dram or two always on the go, so you never knew if he was there for pastoral reasons or other concerns. He took Eileen and I out to the Woodburn Lodge Hotel, which later became a police barracks. We went there on the night of 14 August 1969. We left the parish happy with Fr Honorius and he brought us to dinner in a car, but when we came back – all had changed!

Violence Erupts

It was as if there had been an earthquake. That's how calamitous it was. The first thing we saw as we came up Twaddell Avenue, to the apex where Twaddell Avenue meets with Woodvale and Crumlin Road, was Eileen's daddy, Jack Gilmartin. This was late at night, probably after 11 p.m., and we saw a bunch of men with hurls and sticks and bottles. We were astounded! Absolutely astounded! What were they doing? Jack stopped our car. He was looking out for us as it turned out. He knew that we were on our way back from dinner, and there were no mobile phones at that time. He was there looking out for us and was obviously in great distress.

He said, 'You are not going to believe it. You are going to have difficulty getting up that street now.' He got Eileen safely home. Then got me safely home. He got Fr Honorius into the monastery through the back door, as there was no way he could have gone down the Crumlin Road to turn into the monastery.

We were at the top of Twaddell Avenue, looking down the Crumlin Road, and stood and watched men in uniform. There were 'B' Specials, pointing out Catholic homes and setting fire to them. I remember thinking, 'Oh my God! Nurse McBrierty's house!' That amazing woman who brought so many Ardonians into the world had to suffer an appalling attack on her house that night. We scoured our house for clothes to give her and her family for they were left with nothing.

I remember going down through the names of the houses under attack and was in complete disbelief! Bear in mind that these were the uniformed forces of law and order who were doing this, and I was about to become a law student. I went home that night and, sure, nobody slept! I don't know how my father got home from the bar that night. I had no idea, but there was this awful sense of, 'What happens next?' A sense of losing control of something – of things running out of our control now.

I walked down the road and through Ardoyne the next morning. I had so many questions stirring around in my head: Is my aunt Nora McDrury still alive? Were the McAreaveys still alive? What was the story with my cousin Paddy Cassidy, who had a newsagent shop near Sis's? What was the story with our friends the Goan family, who lived next to Paddy's shop? What was the story with all the people we knew? Was my aunt Una's shop still there? Was my aunt Kathleen's shop still there? I walked down the Crumlin Road in dread, and the first person I saw coming towards me from the monastery, wearing his big black cloak, was Fr Honorius. He saw me coming. He held out the two arms shouting, 'Mary! We were fiddling while Rome burnt!' Drama ran in his family. His nephew was the late gifted actor Frank Kelly, famous as Fr Jack in the television comedy *Father Ted*.

Ah dear Lord! The desolation of it! The realisation that something has happened here that has opened a Pandora's Box, and how would we be able to start getting things back into that box? I didn't know it was going to be 30 years and longer before we got anything into the box, but I knew that this was cataclysmic. I knew that it couldn't be easily fixed.

I also remember that night because nobody slept. People were constantly coming to our house, and to the McBrierty house, where Nurse McBrierty and her nurse daughter Annette were out around the parish helping others rather than helping themselves. I remember people coming to our house looking for clothes, and us raiding the wardrobe and getting stuff together to send down to people who had lost their homes. In the midst of it all, and this is hard to believe, I remember

Jack Gilmartin coming to our house looking for marbles! It was surreal. There were five wee boys in our house, so there were cartloads of marbles. I do remember wrecking the house looking for marbles and handing them over. They were used to bang off the chapel wall to imitate the sound of gunfire to try to frighten away those 'B' Specials and their thugs who were with them.

That's how unprepared the parish was. There were no guns. There was no IRA. There were no protectors, and over the next few days life just descended into chaos. Sectarian chaos. The fractures that had been healing were opened. The wounds were scraped open and that was the start of the horror story.

Soldiers on My Streets

I remember my parents, my mother in particular, saying, 'Dear God, will they ever send the soldiers in to sort this out?' I remember we wanted the soldiers there. I remember the welcoming they received when they came in. My younger sister Claire was the 'gofer' for them. She was the one who they would send down to get cigarettes or chocolate bars in the shop. With the result that for donkey's years after, every time I was stopped by a soldier and handed over my licence in Belfast – bear in mind I am thirteen years older than my sister Claire – almost without exception some soldier would say to me, 'Are you related to Claire?' She was their wee gofer. She was only six or seven, and she loved it! They gave her a thru'penny bit or whatever it was at the time. My mother baked for them and treated them with great kindness when they first came. But that was to change. That all evaporated eventually.

Then of course we lost our home, because we were living in a very vulnerable area, and we had quite a few really rough episodes about the house. My deaf brother John was set upon by Loyalist thugs who tried to kill him. They severed his artery and they might as well have severed his life. Nobody was ever prosecuted for that, even though we knew who it was. The father of the young man who was the ringleader was very high up in the Orange Order, and regrettably he was never prosecuted. He subsequently went on to murder a Catholic man who was the manager of an Ulster Bank not too far from where we lived.

On my very first day as a barrister, this young police officer, whom I didn't recognise because he was bearded, said to me, 'You don't know me, but I was in your house when your brother was injured. You were just starting off as a law student then.' It was the police officer who investigated John's case. He congratulated me as I had just been called to the Bar. He went on to say to me, 'That was the worst time. If only at that time we had prosecuted that young man. He is in court today and he is up on a charge of murder.'

That was life then. We were adrift. Our lives were all adrift. There was shooting from the roof of the school beside us. Our house was also right in between the Protestant Everton and Somerdale schools, and the Catholic boys' school, St Gabriel's. We had a brick wall that was literally up and down as the bricks were used to fire at each other on the way home from school.

The road in front of our home literally became a regular battlefield. After my brother John was very badly injured, my sister Kate was coming home one afternoon in her St Dominic's school uniform when she set upon by a group of Protestant girls who lived behind our house. Our parents were out and I had my mother's car. I spotted the attackers setting upon Kate just at Everton School, so raced to our door and got Nora to come and help. We did not hold back, and we won that battle on that night, but, even if we did, Kate was only eleven at the time. It was her first year at secondary school when this happened at our front door, just like the attack on John. When your front door becomes the place where you are not safe, then your life just becomes a series of fractures and questions. Some of my friends of course, at that time, when confronted with that kind of situation joined the IRA. I also had to ask myself the question, 'What do I do now?'

For me, I was lucky. I always think 'there but for the grace of God go I.' In any other circumstance, who knows what decisions would have been made? But I had the voice of Daniel O'Connell drilled into me. I had the gospel that I believed in, that love could conquer, and that forgiveness was important.

Fr Justin CP

I had another great mentor who had just died before all this nonsense started, and that was Fr Justin Coyne CP. Fr Justin was the children's priest in Ardoyne. He couldn't preach for toffee but, boy, he was a saint and a gentleman. He came to our house every Sunday evening in life after the evening Mass. Usually the film was on, and in he would come talking metaphysics. I loved the conversations with him. Fr Justin was not our parish priest. Fr Honorious was, and I think there was a bit of jealousy on Fr Honorious' part. Fr Justin had met me one Saturday coming out of confession and he said to me, 'Your face is very familiar to me. Are you anything to the McManus girls?' I answered, 'No, but I am the daughter of one of them.'

Years before he had been in the parish, he taught in the Passionist seminary that was based in the parish, and he got to know the bunch of good-looking McManus girls, and I was very like them. He said, 'I will come up to see you and the family.'

He started to come to visit our house on a Sunday evening. We would talk about God and faith, and, boy, that guy had some interesting perspectives. A great openness. The other person who came to our house every second night was the

Church of Ireland minister Jimmy Arbuthnott, whose son was studying in Trinity College. So we had this gathering that was actually an ecumenical gathering long before it became popular. So in a way, intellectually and emotionally, I had unusual resources available to me in that Ardoyne home. They kept me on the path that believed that the law was the way to go: democracy was the way to go. Discourse and dialogue, forgiveness, resistance to the temptation to meet arms with arms, but also the need to understand why people did what they did.

I was terrified that any of my own family would ever get caught up in paramilitarism, because I also knew what thuggery went on at the heart of it too. That became our hinterland from that time on. We had the rebirth and the sense of the IRA and of Loyalist paramilitarism, which was literally on our doorstep, all being worked out right outside our door, and I had friends and acquaintances in both.

Shared Experience – Different Paths

People outside the experience of living through the violence are often not able to understand the choices some people made to get involved in the conflict. They don't understand what might have pushed those choices. For example, I think of a young man whom I knew well and played badminton with. He was a really good lad: thoughtful, deeply spiritual, very religious. He left Ardoyne to start studies for the priesthood. The summer he came home from seminary, two friends of his were sitting on a bus travelling into town when Loyalist paramilitaries shot them dead. He joined the IRA and became a well-known figure in the IRA.

No, decisions are not taken coldly. Sometimes they are taken in the heat of the moment. Paramilitarism was a long-standing culture, and it has to be remembered that the people who helped to seedbed it were Loyalists. The first paramilitaries of the twentieth century in Ireland were not the Catholic Irish Volunteers but the Protestant Ulster Volunteers, who threatened civil war against the British. So we have to be careful with the facts as they are told, and how we edit or distribute history.

Tragedy across 'the Divide'

I mentioned the young man John Shaw earlier, a neighbour of ours. A fine young man. Raised in a very good and very religious Plymouth Brethren home. 'Very good living' as we used to say. He was part of a group of young Loyalists who wanted to avenge the sectarian deaths that caused grief in their community that came from the Republicans. Republicans had killed Protestants. They had killed police officers. They had killed people whom John knew, and, in his anger, as he is sitting in a Loyalist club one night, he decides that it is about time he stood up. Their hinterland tells them that you are not a man unless you go out and stand up for your neighbourhood.

They went out that night on a killing spree. They got a gun from somewhere, and they killed four Catholics, including a young girl who was just selling petrol at a petrol station. They also killed one Protestant man who was walking down past Ardoyne chapel. My cousin Paddy was first on the scene. The man was still vaguely alive at the time when, as we do in the Catholic tradition, Paddy whispered the Act of Contrition into his ear. He then died in Paddy's arms. Paddy was just distracted over that. Such events cause you grief: emotional and mental grief.

Years later, a book called *Lost Lives* was produced on the Troubles, and I was asked to talk about one of the people who appeared in that book. I knew a lot of people in that book: Margaret McCorry, Tony O'Reilly, Myles O'Reilly. I wasn't fit to talk about Tony and Myles. I still can't talk about Tony and Myles very much. They were murdered on the morning of my wedding and I was as close to them as I was to anybody growing up, so I couldn't talk about them. I thought I would talk about that Protestant man who had been murdered, and who had died in Paddy's arms.

Somewhere that talk got into a police file. Years later, the man's then eight-year-old daughter had become a woman in her 40s, and she was trying to find out information about her father. She was an only child and, of course, her mother went to pieces after the father's death, and nobody had ever talked to her about it. So often we overlook the trauma of children, thinking it passes them by – but it doesn't and it didn't.

Her mother got early Alzheimer's, so there was nobody around willing to give her the information about her father that she was looking for. From the Historical Enquiries Team she heard about my mention of her father, and she came to see me in Áras an Uachtaráin. I told her what I knew and I said, 'I probably should also tell you of my cousin's involvement.' Paddy Cassidy was dead by then. He died too young, and I don't think the stress helped him. I told her, 'I hope you don't mind. It always bothered him that he had said an Act of Contrition into your father's ear. It is a very Catholic thing to do, but he always hoped that your family wouldn't be offended.' She just started crying and said, 'I am delighted to know that.'

We live in a world that you cannot reduce to simple yes/no/black/white cold choice. Many of these choices people made were made in the hot heat of the moment, and, quite frankly, the moments we lived in were hot, white-hot. If you lived across the border at Newry, you hadn't a clue what was going on. In fact, there were parts of Belfast where you could live and you wouldn't have a clue what was going on in areas such as Ardoyne.

Threats Close to Home

Ardoyne was a cockpit. It still has the highest number, bar nowhere, of sectarian deaths of any place in Northern Ireland, and it is only a wee village! We had all those deaths and I am thinking of young people of my age whom I knew who lost their lives, such as Peter Lane and Margaret McCorry. I am just thinking of the wastefulness of it; the stupidity of it; the heartbreak of it.

I remember up the Crumlin Road from us at the junction with Ballysillan Road, there was a sweet shop where kids used to get lucky bags. A Catholic man, Paddy Wilson, ran it. He was shot dead, and as soon as they shot him dead I knew we were next. And how stupid were we? We lived in that maelstrom, and often we didn't put two and two together, but I put two and two together, and I could feel it coming our way, but there was a problem. You see, you couldn't just up and run with nine children. There were certain realities and we knew that we were probably the next family to be targeted. The Loyalists were working their way down the road.

After Paddy's murder I said to my mum, 'We are next.' We started leaving the house each night after dinner, and coming back before breakfast in the morning, distributing the kids around relations. My father couldn't come home. They had tried to attack him one night at the door of the house, and by God's grace he just managed to avoid being killed by them. So he was staying over with my great-aunt on the Falls Road rather than travel across town.

We distributed some of the kids to an aunt on the Antrim Road; others went to where my father was staying on the Falls Road. I went to friends over in the university. So we were all distributed to different parts of the city. My mammy was getting really sick of that, gathering up the children, not knowing whether they got to school or not.

On the night of 7 December 1972, we were in the house. It sounds ridiculous to say, but the night before I had a dream. I saw the gunman at the window, and I thought we just cannot stay here tonight. My mammy wanted to stay because the next day was the feast day (8 December) and she didn't want to have to gather all the children and get them up at the crack of dawn to get to Mass. So she said, 'No, we will stay here tonight and we will get Mass in the morning. We will resume normal operations.' I said, 'No, we can't do that. It's too dangerous.' So we left the house that evening and left lights on in the living room and in my sister's bedroom window upstairs, and distributed everybody around the various houses. That night, Loyalist gunmen came to our home with machine guns and shot through our windows. My sister's bed was left like a colander.

I have been able to figure out who came to our house that night with two machine guns and emptied them through our windows. Apparently the police were never able to do that, as they never prosecuted anyone for it, but simply by the benefit of hindsight, working out what team of Loyalists were active on that road, I now am pretty sure I know who they were.

How do you get over those things? The realisation that somebody hates you enough to try to kill you? At the time it was described in the papers as the worst ever attack on a Catholic family, but sure it gets lost in the telling for far worse befell others. It gets completely forgotten about now there are so many worse things that have occurred since. My father's great friends, the McGurks, were murdered in their pub, and God forgive the police and Army who, knowing it was a sectarian Loyalist attack, tried to blame the IRA. My husband, Martin's, dental nurse, Sandra, a Protestant who worked in his Bessbrook surgery, had to face the death of her father in the Kingsmill Massacre.

On the morning of our wedding, Tony and Myles O'Reilly, two phenomenal human beings who were like big brothers to me, were murdered by Loyalists in the pub restaurant my father had advised them against buying because of its vulnerable location. Years later, when we lived for a short time in Miami, Florida, we became friends with the Northern Ireland group Clubsound, who were performing there. One of their wives lost her father, who was shot by the IRA in retaliation for the deaths of Tony and Myles. Great bonding took place between us all, because we all believed passionately in the stupid wastefulness of the sectarian violence that took those precious lives.

The Insanity of Violence

One thing I never been able to reconcile is the wastefulness of violence; the sheer abject stupid waste and how much loss of decency there is. Every death pushing people into bunkers, when the gospel I believe in teaches us to 'Leave the bunkers and trust in the love.' That's the shame I feel.

The gravitational pull of paramilitarism was so strong. It was strong, and it was embedded in the communities and in the thinking of the communities where we lived. You had to have lived inside it to fully understand. I read people commenting on events during the Troubles, but commentating from a distance, and I think, 'They haven't a clue! They don't know!' This is why I think we have to fight so hard to hold on to peace. I think back to those days of 14–16 August 1969. Things got very rough, and we didn't know what was going to happen next. My father watched the 'B' Specials come up the Crumlin Road, and we knew that it could be our street next. They were targeting random Catholics, and my father literally put us into the car and ran us out of Belfast. He took us to Dublin, and we rented a house on the Upper Kilmacud Road, where nobody had a clue what was going on or even cared.

We left Belfast so quickly that we left my sister Nora behind, as she was working in the Lyric Theatre that night. My father phoned the people in the Lyric to say that Ardoyne was in such a state that Nora was not to come home under any circumstance, but that he couldn't guarantee that we would be able to get across town to pick her up. I think it was Dr O'Malley's wife (they ran the Lyric Theatre at that time), who told him, 'We will look after her. You go on and get on the way to Dublin and mind the other eight. We will look after her.' So we ran out of Belfast without one of the children.

Imagine having to leave a sixteen- or seventeen-year-old girl working as a stage hand in the theatre as we ran out of Belfast. After our money ran out in Dublin we subsequently went on to Roscommon, where my father stuck a caravan into a field beside his parents' cottage. What were the people in Dublin and the people in Roscommon thinking? 'Are they insane or what?' They had no idea of what we had come from.

A Proud Community in Conflict

I feel very protective of my memory of Ardoyne, because Ardoyne is so misunderstood. I hear people, for example, use expressions like, 'the Ardoyne' or, 'thee Ardoyne'. Something happens to me when I hear that. I could get really upset, but I then know that I am talking to people who don't know what they are talking about. I grew up in Ardoyne. I did not grow up in 'the Ardoyne', nor 'thee Ardoyne', and part of that misuse of the name is about pushing its reality away.

I think of the suffering that people endured there. Real, real suffering that was so complicated that they will do PhDs on it eventually to try to unpack what life was like there. The tautness of it. The terror of it. The things that were done to people's nerves. I know a lot of people just lived on tablets. In describing how people got through it, somebody once said to me, 'Cans and tablets.'

It was a horrific life for a lot of people, and still I look at my grandmother for example, and how she came through with such dignity. She was a very dignified countrywoman. She had eleven children. She lived in a wee two-up, two-down house in Dunedin Park. She had grown up on a farm, a substantial farm in County Down. Her husband was one of only two brothers. One of them had joined the Garda Síochana; he had joined the IRA. That sets the scene for what was never going to be a comfortable life for her.

She was one of three children who grew up in a very comfortable farm. The choices that her husband had made in his day dictated how they would live their lives. She was a woman who cooked, cleaned, sewed and knitted. Her children were turned out immaculately. She ran a frugal but a very warm and happy home. I think of people like her and her quiet dignity. I remember the time when she needed to get something done in the house and it was the IRA who had the contract. They came to her door to do something. She just took one look at them and said, 'You don't look like plumbers. Go away and send me real plumbers.'

I remember local IRA activists coming to her door one time, and suggesting that there was such a shortage of accommodation that people like her, single and living on their own, could maybe move in together. Some genius thought of that sometime in the 1970s! Well, they met people like my granny who insisted on their own rights in the middle of a fight for rights. The people who were allegedly fighting for your rights would have taken them away from you in a minute. So, it was a really complicated place to live, and sometimes neighbours couldn't trust each other either. People knew things, or were privy to things, that in a normal society could put you in gaol, but you didn't dare to say. It was a place of lives, locked into a mixture. An extraordinary place.

An outsider will never penetrate this world. There were layers and layers and layers of secrets that we all had to live with. Within families, within neighbours and across communities. We all had to live with that. Some people found that very difficult to live with. It played on nature, and it played on nurture, and not everybody was able to handle it the way some people were able to. People were suddenly thrust into positions of power who should never have been given power. It was one heck of a complicated world and the rules were being made up as we went along. To try to live comfortably in that world was extraordinarily difficult.

Gratitude

When I reflect back on Ardoyne, and the things for which I am grateful, I think of my granny's house; that oasis of peace in the heart of Dunedin Park. I am grateful for the fact that I grew up in the Protestant area of Ardoyne, and that I had this hinterland of friends, Protestant friends, who made us welcome, and who remained friends all our lives. I am grateful for Fr Justin, and I am always thankful that he died on 22 June 1969, before all this nonsense broke loose. In that same week I had my first real encounter with a young man called Martin McAleese, and I always think that Fr Justin has guided me ever since. Sometimes when I could have made rash decisions or bad decisions, he guided me.

I remember coming up from Chatham Street one day through the riots, very bad riots, and running into Ciarán Goan. The lads from our side of the road were defending the area by throwing stones and petrol bombs, but they had ran out of bottles. I was sent up to Ruby Totten's. Ruby was born and reared a Protestant, but I was going into her house to ask for bottles. 'If they want bottles I will give them bottles!' She routed her cupboards for bottles. I ran up to our house and, because there were so many of us at home, we always had a crate at our back door with about ten milk bottles sitting in it. I ran up to get the milk bottles to bring them down to give them to the lads. My father, thank God, was home for his tea. He said, 'Where are you going with those?' I replied, 'The boys need them at the barricades.' And he just said, 'Put those back young lady. I have something to tell you, and you listen well. I did not rear a rabble!' I have said this many times and some people have said that what he said was 'I did not rear a rebel!' That is not what he said! He said, 'I did not rear a rabble!'

I remember that to this day. I put those bottles down and I went into the house. That was me shut in for the evening, and every evening after that. So I never took part in a riot. I never threw a stone, but I understand the boys who did! I really understand that world because I lived in it. Families were put to making those choices and making those decisions.

Peace – A Prize Achieved at a Heavy Price

Look! It took us a long time to piece together the Good Friday Agreement and a long time after it to achieve the peace. I know so many of the people whose lives and deaths are invested in that. The very idea of throwing that away now. Throwing it away? That's why I am so protective of Ardoyne. When I think of Brexit now, the first place that comes into my mind is Ardoyne.

I don't want any children running the gauntlet like the schoolkids in Holy Cross. I don't want any children being assaulted outside her front door like my sister. I don't want a young deaf man, a profoundly deaf boy, being assaulted and left for dead like my brother was. Thank God he didn't die, but sometimes there are worse things than death, because they live with that fear. To live with that belief that you are surrounded by people who are capable of such ugly evil. It is a hard way to live.

Sometimes the older you get, memories keep coming back and haunt you. Martin and I were married 43 years on 9 March 2019. Every year for the week before our anniversary, I start to think, 'This will be the year when we go out for dinner, when we can go out and celebrate our wedding anniversary.' Then the next thing, I have dreams about Tony, dreams about Myles. I see us going into their Golden Pheasant Inn – that lovely welcoming restaurant that my father begged them not to buy – going in there and saying to them, 'We want to have our wedding reception here. We want a small wedding.' I can still hear Tony laughing heartily and saying to me, 'Your ma will never settle for a small wedding.' And us going home saying we are having our wedding in the Golden Pheasant and my mother saying, 'No way!'

Their lives ended on our wedding day. Their photos sat on my desk in Áras an Uachtarain, alongside the picture of their friend and mine, Fr Justin Coyne CP, reminding me each day of the need to build bridges of justice, equality, mutual respect, truth, understanding, friendship and peace.

5

Ciarán Goan

Family Background

It seems a long way from Ardoyne to where we are sitting now in the original home of my grandfather, James Goan, in Cloghbolie, Co. Donegal. He married a woman from across two fields, with the name of Mary Daly. In 1917, they married in St Patrick's Church, Ballyshannon, and moved to Belfast where they settled in Havana Street in Ardoyne.

My father, Seamus, his brother Manus and two sisters, Bella and Anna, were all born in Havana Street, and after some years they moved on to the front of the Crumlin Road to number 427, which was almost on the corner of Butler Street facing Holy Cross Church.

My granduncle Johnny had lived in the house in Cloghbolie all his days. My father and his siblings had always come back and forth for summer holidays with the grandparents in Kildoney and uncles here in Cloghbolie. When Johnny died in 1972, he left the Donegal house to my father. This was to prove a lifesaver for my parents as the situation in Belfast continued to worsen.

Early Life

My parents, Seamus and Ita, moved our family from Andersonstown to Ardoyne in 1963, the year of 'the Big Snow'. They moved so my mum could take care of Seamus's elderly parents. Ita never complained, despite leaving a very comfortable house in Tullymore Gardens for a rambling three-storey house that was creaking at the seams, with the toilet out the back.

I was already at St Malachy's College, having passed the 11+, but because I lived at the front of the road I was termed by my contemporaries in Ardoyne, pardon the language, 'A fucking snob!' So I got used to getting an odd hiding from the Ardoyne ones and had to shape-up fairly quick.

As I grew up, I used to do a bit of work with my father in the Clarion Bar in Gresham Street. At the time, my dad used to talk to Frank 'Bulliver' McCallan, a leading figure within Ardoyne Kickhams GAC, and he got me involved in the club.

Even though I was neither a hurler nor a footballer, I made friends in the district through the club. I was blind as a bat, but I loved the camaraderie of being there and became fairly involved with the club. I went to a lot of games, and even occasionally acted as an umpire. (I once had to be rescued after a disputed decision against O'Donnells in Shaws Road.) I also sat on some committees with people like Jimmy Fennell, Jimmy Lynch, Frank Clarke, Larry Toolan and Frank Corr.

On Saturday nights, I worked in the club bar in Toby's Hall. I have very fond memories of a great bunch of people. There were the McCargo brothers, Tommy McAuley, the Frames, Mullans, Paddy and Stevie Dobbin, Joe Lavery, Pat Murphy, the McAleer brothers (and their mother). There are too many more to mention. All tough, but really sound.

The older guys minded the young fellows, and they minded each other as well (particularly on the playing field!). Ardoyne Kickhams had many wonderful characters, like Jimmy McLaughlin, one of nature's gentlemen and a great man to sing a song. Jimmy used to wear his football shorts very long and his socks very high. Due to whatever way his knuckles were, he had a reputation that when he hit you, he split you! There was always an edge when the 'city boys' 'went to the country', and inevitably a row would break out.

We lived in a spot where Loyalists would stop to beat the shit out of their drums during the parades. From maybe the age of eight or nine I was sent every summer to my aunt and uncle who had a little farm near Cavan town.

I loved it there. I'd leave home at the end of June and be back at the end of August. I'd milk the cows, go to the creamery and feed the pigs. I was effectively a farmer for two months every year, and then, come autumn, I'd come home and pretend to do some school work!

I was fifteen when I eventually witnessed the Loyalists beating their drums in Ardoyne. I was always aware of the vitriol that was there when these guys were allowed to stop outside Holy Cross Church. The things they were saying. It was just unreal. However, as a child, I also remember when my dad was working in the Cherrymount Inn, right where the Orange parades started at Carlisle Circus. He used to open the back door for several of the Masters that he knew, and get them in for a few drinks.

I remember going to the Glentoran Supporters' Club annual Christmas party in an Orange Hall, somewhere on the Oldpark Road. They had a great Santa Claus! My father thought nothing of that because, although it was in a 'Loyalist' area, he knew and trusted the people. To be honest, they took care of us while we were there. There was never a word said against us. This was in the late fifties or early sixties, before the tension started to rise. Me and my cousin, Michael Martin, subsequently worked for the Caseys, out of the Brown Horse Bar in Library Street in the same Orange Hall at a function. Caseys also owned a bottling store nearby in Carrick Hill. Some of the family were murdered by the UVF as they worked in the bottling store during the Troubles.

Ardoyne was a strong Nationalist/Republican area. As a young fella, I recall getting the nod from a couple of lads and found myself in a known Republican family's house where recruiting was taking place. I was in my mid-teens, and I remember thinking, 'maybe this is what we should be doing.'

I won't say who brought me there, but he played for Ardoyne Kickhams, and he was the last person I would have expected to be 'that man'. Anyway, the word got out and my dad, who could sniff these things out from a hundred yards, called me in one day and had me against the wall. 'What are you doing? What are you at? Are you at this fuckology of these so-called Republicans?'

I denied it, but he said, 'I know you are, and I tell you what now Sunshine. It's over. Right?' He then took himself over to the man's house and told him what he would do to him if he ever talked to me again.

You see, my dad and his brother had been interned for four years during the war. They weren't even released to attend the funeral of their sister Anna, who died from meningitis. This should explain some of his protectiveness over me.

In the mid-sixties, Fr Myles Kavanagh arrived to work in the parish. He was soon immersed in setting up a youth sodality (Fianna Páiste) and a youth club based in St Gabriel's School on the Upper Crumlin Road. I joined the club, and that's where I met my wife, Mary. There was a great bunch of young people in our circle, many of whom subsequently married within the group.

We had a great couple of years in the youth club where there was a great range of activities from boxing to karate and drama/musical, or just hanging out. In addition, we ran a 'hop' on Saturday nights. The club fell apart when the Troubles started.

Myles started an annual youth pilgrimage to Croagh Patrick. It was a mixture of prayer on the mountain and great craic on the bus. After a couple of years, Myles was transferred and his replacement, Fr Ailbe Delaney from County Roscommon, came to the parish. Fr Ailbe was a rock for so many people. He was out in the middle of all that trouble ministering as a priest.

On the night of my parents' 25th wedding anniversary in February 1971, there was shooting and a riot on Butler Street. An armoured personnel carrier was stopped on the street, and somebody hit it directly with a petrol bomb. Once hit, the ammunition started exploding in the carrier. Then more soldiers arrived in the Grove, and they had a vantage point down Butler Street. Barney Watt walked out from behind this, and they just blew his head off. Fr Ailbe was the one who bravely went out to minister to him.

When Joe Parker was shot down in Toby's Hall, Fr Ailbe was in our house. I brought him down to the hospital and we met Joe coming out of the Emergency Room, heading to the Operating Theatre. Fr Ailbe asked him, 'Are you going to be alright?' 'Don't worry Father. I am going to be alright.' He died that night. RIP.

A man of God and peace, Fr Ailbe found this experience very hard. The same man of God was told to 'fuck off' as he tried to calm a riot situation in the area because hard men decided that it was none of his business. From our teenage years, Ailbe was a major part of our lives. He was a friend and confidante and remained so till the day he died in 2010. I am proud to say he performed our wedding ceremony, baptised our kids, performed their wedding ceremonies, and baptised our first grandchild.

There was some nasty stuff going on back then. In particular was the execution by the IRA in 1971 of three kids up in Ligoniel – three British soldiers, aged 17, 18 and 23. They were conned and brought up there. I felt revulsion for all that. Yet, at the same time, on the morning of internment I felt a deep resentment and anger towards the Paras because we knew what was going on in Ballymurphy and in Ardoyne, and the way that they treated us.

Work Life

I did a lot of part-time work in the bar trade as I was growing up and couldn't wait to get out of school and start working full-time. When I gained basic qualifications (five O-levels), I began to apply for public service jobs (permanent and pensionable). However, I quickly learned that when a young Catholic started looking for work they were very quickly introduced to the prevalent inequalities in this society. I just wanted a job, and I started sending applications for vacancies in places like the Northern Ireland civil service. I never even got an interview. In fact, I got an immediate 'Dear John' letter, as somebody had obviously looked up the files and thought, 'We'll not be having that!'

Ironically, in the same week that I was not deemed employable by the Northern Ireland civil service, the Imperial civil service offered me a job in the Foreign Office in London. I decided not to go, as I didn't want to leave Belfast. Around the same, I received an invitation to interview with the London Metropolitan Police. Eventually, I got a job in the Belfast Corporation Gas Department on Ormeau Avenue. It was in the collection office as they called it – cutting off old women's gas for not paying their bills. Well, it was a job.

When I started there, I had my first real exposure to people who had surnames for Christian names. There were very few Marys, Ciaráns, Cathals or Gráinnes. It became very apparent that I was the odd one out. There was a man who worked there from Glenbryn called George Osborough. He was very kind to me.

Confronted by Prejudice

The Civil Rights marches had started at that time. One day, students from Queen's University marched past our office, and as I overheard the loud commentaries about what should be done with them from the upstairs offices, I realised that my future in the Belfast Corporation Gas Department would be short. It was driving me mad, so one day I just handed in my resignation, saying that I was going off for further education.

I soon found out that I couldn't just walk into another office job, so I was back working in the Brown Horse Bar. After that, I worked in Paddy Cullen's bar down at the Dufferin Dock Gate and got some part-time work at Dunmore Greyhound Stadium. No matter what happened, I always had confidence in the ability to earn a shilling. I learned that from my dad. He taught me everything about the bar trade. He was, to a large degree, a perfectionist in what he did. If he wanted me to do a job for him, I had to do it better than lads who had served their time with him in the pub.

However, I continued applying for jobs that needed a suit and offered a car. I was down to the last two in an interview process with a man called George Priestly for a rep job in Belfast. He was frank with me: 'Ciarán, I have to ask you this question. You do know that if you get this job, you will be the only Catholic in the place. I am not officially allowed to say that to you. How would you feel about that?' I replied, 'I think Mr Priestley, the problem is how would they feel about it?' He just smiled.

Two days later I once again got the 'Dear John' letter. George then wrote personally, asking me to meet him for a cup of coffee. He was starting his own business and wanted me to work for him. I became very much part of that enterprise. We were pre-packing cereals and distributing canned goods in the grocery trade.

At this time, the Civil Rights protests were going on, and I was 'going steady' with Mary. I had bought myself an old Ford Anglia motor with the arse falling out of it, and we decided to go off on holidays to Kerry. While we were there, the trouble in the North was becoming increasingly fractious. People we met down south were saying, 'Oh you poor people! How do you live with all that? We will be praying for you all.'

Summer Tensions

Tension had always been around during the so-called 'marching season'. I think that during one of the early parades, either late 1968 or early 1969, the Loyalists were coming up the main Crumlin Road and somebody hung a tricolour out the window of Kilpatrick's Pub. Legend has it that it was Topper Deeds, but I don't know if that was true. Legend also has it that when the Loyalist crowds saw the flag, they were incensed. There was a 'set to', and the police came in to take it down. The cops were getting a hard time, and Topper finished up getting a baton. He was in court the next day for 'riotous behaviour'. The judge said to him, 'have you anything to say for yourself?' Topper replied, 'I was only trying to help my mate, who was getting beaten up.' The judge said, 'Very good. Six months for your courage!'

During that summer of 1969, it was clear that families were starting to move home from one side of the road to the other, particularly around the Cambrai Street area. The Toners had been living there all their lives. Charlie Toner (senior) was feeling the pinch of it, and friends for life were no longer coming into his off-licence. Then there were Protestant people living in Hooker Street who were also feeling a bit less than safe, who had come from the other side of the road due to mixed marriages or friendships – they were leaving to live in the so-called 'neutral territory'.

The tensions were all there, but we had no idea that it was going to erupt in the manner that it did, nor to the degree that it did when it finally kicked off. We never thought that we would witness invasions by civilians wearing crash helmets, carrying bludgeon batons, running down streets, all assisted by the constabulary kicking open doors and throwing in petrol bombs.

14–16 August

The parades leading up to August 1969 had been very contentious. There had been riots, and missiles had been thrown. There was certainly bad blood coming between the community and the RUC, who had previously been tolerated to some degree, but became less so when it was seen that the vibe was 'them and us'. It seemed that, as Catholics, we were on our own from this point.

Ardoyne was like a little island. It was a Catholic/Nationalist area surrounded by Protestant/Loyalist areas. There was a feeling of isolation and of being under attack from outsiders. At this stage, I was not aware of anyone from any group taking charge of how the district might defend itself.

There was spontaneity in terms of how the people went about it. As we moved into August, I remember people moving out of their homes, because they felt under threat. Houses were vacated. Our house wasn't one of them. Ted McQuaid's mother and sisters lived a few doors away, but they decided to leave, and Ted ended up staying with me in our house for a couple of nights.

For some time we resisted getting involved in the unfolding trouble. But then, we just threw the head up, thinking that we could not take any more of the pressure, and got out to join the others who were putting up the defence.

On 14 August I saw the Loyalists running across the Crumlin Road. They were not as far up as Chief Street but were near Hooker Street and Brookfield, and then ran up towards Chatham Street. I don't think they got as far as Elmfield Street, but some of them came out of Herbert Street opposite Chief Street and just at our corner of Butler Street. The police were with them at this stage. It was then that I saw guys from Ardoyne coming out onto the road at Kerrera Street, trying to force the Loyalists and the police back down the road. People were massing in and around Elmfield Street, also trying to push them back out onto the road.

When they met a bit of resistance, the police started shooting. By this stage, they had already started burning houses. I thought they had done their worst, but then I saw the cops, more than once, shooting into Butler Street, and up towards Kerrera Street.

There was one cop in particular, and even now if he was standing in front of me I could point the finger at him. He just got out, as lazy as you like, takes out this gun, points it up the street and shoots! He fired off three shots, and then casually got back into the car as somebody roared at him. Then somebody else in the car put out an automatic machine gun and fired a short burst. There was one masked civilian shoulder-to-shoulder with a policeman outside our house leading the onslaught. Father Ailbe was in our house that night.

The situation calmed and, towards dawn, we emerged onto the road and began picking up the shells from the police weapons. We picked up sixteen spent shells while others were doing the same thing. Then, the most unusual thing happened. The corporation sweeping vehicle appeared!

Most of the rioting was during the night, and the morning brought an eerie sort of calm. There was a deadly silence. There was nothing – not even the cops. They didn't go away until three or four o'clock in the morning. You could smell the burning. It wasn't until morning broke that we discovered that Sammy McLarnon and Michael Lynch had been murdered.

Once we heard that, it certainly emphasised that this was for real. The district was filled with the smell of the burning. Men were gathering in groups trying to get organised for what was going to happen next. That's when the idea of building the bigger barricades started.

During the previous night, there were no hijacked buses on the street. However, it was daylight, or maybe towards evening time on the 15th, when Fr Marcellus CP joined the local people and went up to the Ardoyne bus depot. They took the buses and put them across the mouth of the streets leading into the district from the main Crumlin Road.

The buses were used as barricades to stop the police driving in with their machine guns. They also served to obstruct the crowds of Loyalists who were trying to get into the district, thereby giving the men time to do something about it. Once the Loyalists were confronted by these barricades and could not see what was behind those buses, they were not for coming in. It seemed to me then that hijacking buses to defend our area was a perfectly legitimate thing to do.

Fear was rife in the district. The big concern was that the Loyalists, police and 'B' Specials were going to get into the district and we were all going to be destroyed. It was as blunt as that. I spent the next couple of days with a van I had from work, helping people move out of the streets that came under attack. I took people from Kerrera Street off the Crumlin Road and brought them to relatives in safe areas of Belfast. I spent hours just going back and forth. There were also jobs to get done in terms of services required for the district, like getting bread, milk, etc.

The IRA

In subsequent years, the Government tried to blame the IRA for the riots, saying that they had taken over the Civil Rights Movement. In the view of many at that stage IRA stood for 'I Ran Away'. There was nobody there.

The quietness of the IRA at the time was confirmed to me some years later by the late Oliver Kelly, who qualified as a solicitor while he was interned in Long Kesh, and later became chairman of the Antrim County Board of the GAA. I met him many years later with my father at a tearful reunion in a hotel in Malahide the night before the 1989 hurling final, when Nicky English destroyed Antrim in Croke Park. Oliver said to me that after the IRA campaign of 1956–1962 there were weapons left behind in Larry Galligan's. He could not find any known Republican who would take them off him, so they were eventually dumped into the Lagan.

While I wasn't aware of any structure for the IRA in August 1969, I became aware of it growing very quickly from late 1969 into 1970.

The defence of the district in August 1969 was largely organised by people involved with the Ardoyne Kickhams GAC. A like-minded group was formed among them to take care of things that they thought needed taking care of. Then you had other people who were also civilian in their outlook and all they wanted to do was to protect the community. If that meant bringing arms for defensive purposes only into the parish, then that's what they thought should be done. People also needed to know how to use them. Nobody knew where all this was going, but they knew that it had to be done.

When the British Army arrived, there was a palpable sense of relief that we were safe, even if only temporarily. However, we weren't convinced it would be permanent. My poor father lost his reason when the soldiers lined up with guns facing into Ardoyne, as if we were the aggressors.

The Citizens' Defence Committee

The formation of the Citizens' Defence Committee was the result of discussions in the area following the initial riots. I am not quite sure where it came from. However, I arrived into it along with Jim Wilkinson and others in Ardoyne who wanted to help out in defending the district against the Loyalist attacks.

People like Seán Cooney, Paddy McClurg, Tom Fleming, Jim Wilkinson and myself were meeting with people who were previously involved in the Republican movement, the so-called '40s men'. All kinds of comings and goings were happening in our house on Crumlin Road. At one stage there was a meeting in the back of my work van. My father was meeting with Joe Rice, Joe Cahill and Billy McKee (all known Republicans) among others. There were five or six men at this meeting, in the back of my van, parked outside Hastings Street police station, as this was reckoned to be the safest place to meet. I wasn't privy to everything that was going on, but I could hear that there was some difference being made between protection and retaliation, offensive and defensive actions. I subsequently started to attend these meetings as a representative of Ardoyne, going over to the CDC Rooms on the Falls Road. I met with Tom Conaty, Jim Sullivan, Fr Padraig Murphy – the parish priest from St Peters, Dicky Glenholmes from the Market. I don't recall any prominent names from Republicanism, but I am sure their representatives would have been there.

I do know that as things went on, the *Voice of the North* newspaper was started. Jimmy Kelly was bringing these papers to Ardoyne, and the CDC was selling them door to door to get the donations. Jimmy used to come and collect the money. Nobody ever thought about where the money was going, but I suppose it had to be to the IRA.

The CDC and the IRA

The distinction between the Citizens' Defence Committee and the local IRA was very clear to me at the beginning. But as time moved on, I noticed that the CDC was becoming less relevant, because the IRA had been reorganised. Things were becoming more militant. There was recruitment and weapons training going on, but the person who were being trained for weapons could have been the boy around the corner. People were being trained but not taking any oaths for membership of the IRA You could say they were being trained for CDC activity. I was immersed in all that. I was knocking about with fellas, going in and out of houses and on the barricades. There was an assumption that I was 'fully paid up', as in a member of the IRA! People would be asking me questions, and I would say, 'What are you asking me for?' They would then say quietly, 'Oh right, right, right...'

Close Encounters

Although not a member of the IRA, like everyone of my age at the time in Ardoyne we all knew and often were in the company of guys who had joined the IRA. This could get us into difficult situations.

Due to my working in the food business, I had a pass issued by the Third Battalion Light Infantry as an 'essential worker'. I still have it in an old drawer. So I remember going over to a house in the Lower Falls with Pat Mailey and a few others in my old Ford Anglia. I was outside with two lads when they disappeared inside. They came back out and asked, 'What way are you going to go?'

I replied, 'The way I always go. Up the Springfield and across Tennant Street.' As we drove up the Springfield on the way back, up goes the hand. It was the army. 'Hello lads.' I showed them my pass. 'Just come back from work?' asked the soldier.

'Yeah, yeah. Tough times, ain't it?' I replied.

'Yeah, on you go.' I think it was lucky for us all they didn't search the van. The magic pass had worked its wonders!

On one occasion, my car had been burnt out, but I still had to get to work. I started getting the bus across the West Circular Road. People thought I was mad, but it was one of those things you just had to do to get to your work. It became apparent that every day I got onto the bus, there was a 'gentleman' standing a few yards away from the bus stop who got on the same bus. Of course, I was being followed by some kind of military intelligence.

Changing Dynamics

It became evident to me as time passed that there was a certain manipulation of what was going on. Incidents were created on the fringes of the parish by local members of the IRA, like blowing up a petrol station or setting off a blast bomb. People came out onto the streets in their hundreds shouting, 'we're being attacked. We're being attacked!'

A few well-placed agitators would be standing there. Then the Army would arrive, and the next thing a brick would get lobbed from the back of the crowd and smack somebody in the head, and there would be blood drawn. Then the helmets would go on. Of course, the Army didn't know how to deal with that situation, and if they decided to go after the guy who had thrown a stone, they didn't care who got in their way. Then all hell would break loose. The whole thing became very obviously manipulated by the IRA.

I witnessed one such event in Alliance Avenue with the burning of the garage opposite Jamaica Street. I could see where events were leading, and I also saw that on the fringes a recruitment process was taking place. I thought, 'this is not for me.' There were a few guys getting involved who I would say were not nice people. People who would have pulled me and given me a hammering just for the sake of it – and now they were going to be freedom-fighters! So, I went and spoke to somebody pretty senior in the Republican movement. 'What are you doing? A good number of these guys are gaol bait. They were robbing gas meters last year.' One of them subsequently got arrested and refused to recognise the court. My Dad commented that it must have been painted recently!

Boiling Point

In the middle of 1970, there were Loyalist parades organised to come up the Crumlin Road. We just could not believe that this was going to be tolerated by the powers that be, including the police at Tennant Street. So we had a meeting of the CDC in St Peter's Presbytery. I was there, as was Tom Fleming and some senior British civil servants from the Northern Ireland Office. Fr Murphy and various others were there too, but no police were present.

The sentiment was clear. 'This cannot happen.' While we were still looking at the ruins of what happened in 1969, the senior civil servant told us that he had it on good advice that there was nothing to worry about, as the police were going to control it. I said, 'Yes, like the way they led it last year!'

That was not the sort of language they wanted to hear, and the meeting was cut short. 'Well, you know what's going to happen now?' I said, 'the Marine Commandos are going to ring the district off, and they will force them up the road.'

We were still working hard up to the last minute trying to get the march stopped, or at least diverted down Cambrai Street. Everyone was standing out on the streets and along the Crumlin Road. People were pleading, 'This cannot happen. This cannot happen!' Next thing, I heard this voice behind me, 'Mr Goan, get your people off the streets!'

I had no idea who he was, but he turned out to be Military Intelligence. 'If you want them off the streets, then you put them off the streets!' I replied. So we were still at the front door of our house on the Crumlin Road when the Army was deployed across the mouth of Butler Street. As Paddy McArdle used to say, 'three tonne of soldiers!' The soldiers were facing down into Butler Street, all with their helmets and riot shields. While I was talking to the man from Military Intelligence the bands and Orangemen arrived outside my front door, marking time and then giving the drums all they could.

Next thing I saw was Tom Fleming (a normally placid man), heading through the middle of them straight for the drum. He was determined to get at it! Between the soldiers and myself we managed to pull him out of it and threw him up our hallway. 'Tom! You're going to get yourself killed, or at least arrested!' At that stage, the bottles started to come across the top of the barricades. I knew that this was not going to end well.

Earlier that day, I had been on the streets, and it was like a ghost town. I was in the GAA club, where I met Bishop Philbin and Gerry Fitt, who proclaimed, 'The worst bit is over. It is all going to be alright now. Go to your homes!'

I immediately reacted, 'Gerry – fuck off! Have you any idea about what is going in here?' I left the two of them to their own devices and went home.

When the riot started, it was hell for leather! I went out the back of our house into Butler Street to see what it was like. It was the same at the top of each street. On Herbert Street, the Brits had knelt down on the ground with their shields over their heads, encouraging us that if we were going to throw bottles, to throw them high so that they didn't land on top of them!

It seemed that, for some reason, they were sympathetic to our side of the dispute! Some of them were shouting, 'throw them over the top of us!' Next thing, I see a local leading Republican throwing his bottles at the Brits, shouting, 'foreign invaders! Get them out of Ireland!' All that kind of stuff. One of his Volunteers said, 'Hey listen! That's not what's going on at the minute.' And he decked him! The guy could only see one thing – a British Army uniform. Despite that, at this stage, they were on our side, baying at us to get into the Loyalists!

One thing is for certain, that turned into an extraordinary night of rioting. The Marine Commandos came under serious pressure. The rioting was so severe that I don't think the parade actually got up the road and was eventually turned back. It was mayhem.

Final Parade

A meeting was called the next day in the monastery parlour. It was attended by Fr Columb, the rector of Holy Cross at the time, Lt. Col. Ephraim, Commander of the Marines, Jim Wilkinson, Paddy Kane, Tom Fleming, and myself. The Marine commander arrived. He divested himself of his weapons and handed them to his aide standing outside. Then he came in and sat down. He told the assembled people how disappointed he was with the behaviour of the Ardoyne people, and that he was going to impose a curfew.

Fr Columb stood up, went purple in the face, and said to him, 'curfew is it? Let me tell you that I am only short of going to my people, all of them, and taking the shortcut to the Falls Road from here! We have had enough! So take off with your curfew, we are having none of it!' The commander was perplexed, 'Oh, I say Padre!'

I was sitting thinking, 'Is this Fr Columb?' He had lost his ball and bat! He was pretty coloured at the best of times, but he laid into this soldier. I thought, 'Right – that's the end of that one!' So we went down into the parish, into the old district and got all the people out onto the street: 'Everyone out! Bring your cups, your saucers, your chairs, your tables and whatever else you can get your hands on. Sit out on the street and have your tea!' Not everybody did it, but there were enough to make it very evident that a curfew was not an acceptable proposition. That incident marked the last parade to ever come up the Crumlin Road past Holy Cross Church.

The next day, there was a parade on Springfield Road. When it was thwarted from getting up the Springfield and had to divert, serious disorder erupted on the Shankill Road. Someone there decided that they were going to open up two fronts. So, they headed for Ardoyne.

I was in Seán Cooney's house in Middle Chatham Street and his wee girl came in screaming, 'Daddy! Daddy! They're fighting!' We went down the road and there they were, dozens of Loyalists with bottles and petrol bombs, coming across the waste ground where the houses had been burned down. I just couldn't believe it. There was no Army. Nothing! So it was all hands on deck to try to defend the district.

A car suddenly came tearing up Brookfield Street, did a handbrake turn, and the next minute – rat a tat tat. The Loyalists scattered back across the Crumlin Road. It got really nasty, and there was a pitched battle across the road. People were running for their lives, and then the Army arrived.

Memories were still fresh in Ardoyne from the summer before. People were thinking that the same thing was going to happen again. It was a really distressing time and there I was evacuating people from their homes to safety again, taking my own mother and siblings away to somewhere safe. It was horrendous. Fr Ailbe was in Chief Street at the time, helping to evacuate people from their homes. Una McManus had to flee from her hairdressing salon with her niece Mary Leneghan (later President Mary McAleese).

The activity was pumping up. Army raids were becoming more frequent. There was also a rising death toll, with police, Army, and Volunteers being killed. Sectarian murders were also on the rise and no-warning bombs in the city. Mary and I had tried to get in to the Abercorn on the day of the bomb but there was no room. Mary was also injured in a bomb explosion in Queen's Arcade. Whilst her injuries weren't severe the trauma lasted a long time. That's a phone call I will never forget.

When I think about what I witnessed and lived through, there is no other way to dress this up than it was the 'put-upon' being put upon by those who were also put upon. But nobody knew it! They were all working-class people, struggling to make a living. One-half of them had been reared to think that they were 'the people', and the others were 'croppies' who had to be put in their place. These fears and prejudices were fomented by people who in the end came to the table to agree a shared future.

Here we are, all these years on, and I still have that feeling in my gut that there is a sectarianism in both communities that is never going to go away. Having said that, I have for many years done some work in Dublin for a company near Lurgan owned by two upstanding brothers who employed all classes and creeds and supported me at all times. One of the two is a member of the Orange Order, and I call him every year on 11 July to wish him a good Twelfth. I understand that it is his culture and he has every right to celebrate it like his father before him and now his son and grandson.

It seems to me that there is a difference in attitude between the urban and rural membership of the same order and those who enjoy the parades. In Donegal the Rosnowlagh parade has continued uninterrupted even through the worst of the Troubles and is a great day out for all.

Mary and I got married in June 1971 and had bought a house in Wheatfield Crescent, which was a predominantly Protestant area. We never believed that this business was going to develop the way it did. Our neighbours were mostly an older generation and were very kind to us.

Internment

I remember getting a phone call very early on the morning of internment. It was Paddy McArdle. 'You out of bed?' he asked. 'It might be an idea to get out of where you are now because it is all kicking off. Internment raids are happening here and who knows what the consequences will be. You are not in the safest place in the world up there in Wheatfield.'

It was about 6.30 in the morning. Mary and myself got into the van, and we headed down to Ardoyne. There were periods of prolonged gunfire that appeared to be coming from over at Alliance Road/Alliance Avenue but it was unclear whether it was an Army or a civilian engagement. While the gun battle was raging there were people being housed in Butler Street School due to the threat of the increasing violence. It was like a displacement camp for people intimidated from across the Crumlin Road. People like the Knights of Malta were there, and I was in there with Paddy McArdle and a few others who were 'fringe Republicans'/CDC men.

We got the news that Paddy McAdorey (a local IRA commander) had been shot. The Knights of Malta ambulance arrived at the school, and we carried Paddy's body into the school. There was a little hole in the front of his head. We decided that we better get a priest, so I ran up and got Fr Ailbe again.

I never had much interaction with Paddy, save for one time when he was talking about the need for people to see past the sectarian events that were going on. If Ian Paisley was in his sights, he said that, in conscience, he couldn't shoot him. We thought the Army would come looking for the body lying in the school and decided that we needed to get him out discreetly so his family could grieve. He was smuggled out in the back of a bread van and brought to the Falls Road. I knew the driver well.

There was also some intermittent gunfire that night up and down the streets and along Alliance Road. People were taking cover as they walked along the streets. However, we needed to get an insertion into the newspaper about the death of Paddy McAdorey. It had to be written out in Irish and in English, and then brought down to the *Irish News* offices.

So, myself and Joe Sparks were dispatched on a fairly fast drive up Jamaica Street and round into Alliance Avenue. From there we went down to the *Irish News* office. The city was like a ghost town. There was nothing moving, including the security forces.

We went into the *Irish News*, and one man was there. He looked up in some alarm at what he must have thought were these two 'hoods' coming in. I said, 'we want you to put that into the paper for tomorrow.' He read the inscription and said, 'Ok, I will do that. I don't suppose there is an invoice wanted for this?'

'No, there isn't,' was my reply, 'but will it be in the paper?'

'Oh, yes. It will be in it.'

So we headed back up, and as we swung into Jamaica Street, there was a burst of gunfire. We thought that we were under some fire but managed to get into the district safely. The next morning there were further internment raids by the Paras. I remember being shoved against a wall with a rifle stuck in my ear while being searched. In my pocket was a card issued by the Civil Rights Association which said: 'KNOW YOUR RIGHTS'. The Para with the gun pushed it straight in my face and said: 'these are your fucking rights, Paddy'.

During the raids, the Army hit Butler Street School, where displaced people were sheltering, and the Knights of Malta had set up a first-aid station. All the men were lined up, hands on the wall, and one by one were taken into a room for an ID check. In the middle of these was Fr Ailbe. I objected, and an officer arrived to apologise, saying 'sorry, I didn't know you were a Padre'. Ailbe then demanded to know why that made a difference, so he was put back against the wall to be processed with everyone else.

On 10 August 1971, the day following the introduction of internment, tension was at boiling point in Ardoyne and eventually erupted into serious violence. Protestant families who lived in the Farringon, Cranbrook and Velsheda area of Ardoyne moved out of their homes under the protection of the British Army. They set fire to their homes as they left to ensure that Catholics could not move into them. The fire spread rapidly down the terrace, and the remaining residents fled for their lives.

Personal Impact

I think that if you have ever seen somebody with the back of their head blown out from gunshot wounds, then whatever else you do you realise that the gun is not the answer. It was soul-destroying to see funerals of lads you grew up with, like Jackie Mailey, Dinny Brown and young Mulvenna, Seamie Cassidy, Ted McQuaid, Gerry Gearon, and also Paddy McKenna, Terry Toolan, Frank Corr. There are dozens: Raymond Mooney, the Crossan brothers, Ciarán Murphy, just 17 years old. Many were victims of sectarian murder. Others were IRA Volunteers who were shot dead when they could have been arrested.

Margaret McCorry walked into the path of a guy spraying a machine gun at the Army who hadn't a clue what he was doing. Apparently, as he ran away down

Kerrera Street from an Army stop and search patrol the next day he was shot down like a dog. The man who protested most about his shooting was Billy McCorry, the father of Margaret. Poor Billy! Tragic. Pointless.

My parents had a pretty rough time in terms of what went on later in the Troubles. Our house was rendered uninhabitable by a bomb attack that was an attempt to kill Paddy Cassidy in his shop next door. They then went to live in an apartment off the Antrim Road.

This whole experience had an immense impact on their nerves. My mother was held up at gunpoint in Kennedy's bakery shop, where she worked. My father was proxy-bombed by the IRA in 1974, and he had a particularly harrowing time in the aftermath. He came under automatic suspicion because of the fact that both he and his brother, Manus, had been interned during the war. The day after it happened, he woke up in the morning to find the British Army standing at the foot of his bed. He was arrested and taken off for interrogation.

It was a pretty trying time for him. He was very conflicted. He probably wanted to shoot the guy who proxy-bombed him but, on the other hand, he would not give the RUC any satisfaction in helping to identify him or say what exactly happened. It was a very difficult time. He was threatened by the hijackers that if he didn't do as he was told, they would make his family pay. Subsequently, I was approached by a messenger with an apology for what happened. My response isn't printable.

I have a short news clip of the van exploding where he had jumped out of it near Bairds Car Sales. It was supposed to be at the BBC. Mam and Dad spent the next four years working hard and renovating the house in Donegal in the midst of the ongoing turmoil. They eventually moved there in 1978 and settled into a different way of life.

Leaving Ardoyne

I had changed jobs and was doing well with the record label Pickwick – I got my car expenses, etc. The situation was deteriorating with random sectarian murders taking place almost daily. Our local newsagent, Mr Kelly, was shot dead in his shop just two hundred yards away, and we were feeling unsafe in the house.

In mid-1974, we were thinking about leaving and where we would go. We couldn't contemplate raising the kids in the atmosphere that existed. As fate would have it, I had a call from George Priestley wondering if I fancied going to Dublin to expand the business as trade barriers were being dismantled as part of the EEC membership. It was a no-brainer for us.

Mary and I moved to Dublin permanently in March 1975 and rented a house. I set about travelling around Dublin. I just had a map of Dublin with the names and addresses of offices. I kept banging doors until we got the business established.

There was a lot of guilt during the first couple of years in Dublin. Guilt about who was left behind in Ardoyne, and what was going on there. It was difficult. I had some friends who had also made the decision to move away.

We had the good fortune to be given a mortgage in 1976 and bought our home in Malahide, where we have lived for 44 years.

Looking Back

There were times when I suffered from the guilt of moving away, but when I was out of Ardoyne for a while I started reminiscing. I began to see things that I had already known but that I hadn't wanted to admit to myself. I know it was the right thing to do and that I am in the right place. Two of our kids are in Dublin, and one is in Clare. Now, we have six beautiful grandchildren who have been spared the trauma of what was still happening when they were growing up.

The community in Ardoyne has suffered untold hardship as a result of the Troubles, both at the hands of the Army and police as well as the people who professed to be their protectors. I have very fond memories of the people I knew as friends and neighbours and the strong sense of community in the district. The regeneration has transformed it into a different place from the one we left in the seventies, but my memory will always be of what it was in the sixties.

6

Sharon O'Connor

Ardoyne Connections

I currently work as a non-executive director holding a senior role in education; previously I was Chief Executive of Derry City Council, so I lived up in Derry for a while. It was funny then that when I started coming back to Belfast for work people would say to me, 'Did you drive down this morning?' They have forgotten that I am a Belfast person, but I am now back in Belfast and enjoying getting to know the place again.

My family comes from what is known as 'Old Ardoyne' and we have very extensive connections with the Ardoyne community, especially sporting connections. My grandfather was a founding member of the local Gaelic club, Ardoyne Kickhams. My dad and his brothers all played for the Kickhams at one time or another and at county level.

Ardoyne Kickhams also played a role in my early life. I have to admit to a few romantic entanglements over the years and at that time there were a number of families who were connected via school and club, certainly the McCallans. Their father was a very close personal friend of my daddy's. One of my most treasured possessions is a photograph of the Ardoyne Kickhams team. Two boys are sitting in the front row: one is Frank McCallan and the other is my daddy, and Frank has his hand holding my daddy's boot.

There were obviously other people, many whose names I am going to struggle to remember, but people like the Murphys, the Maguires, the Byrnes, the Clarkes and the Wassons were part and parcel of that whole scene when I was growing up in Ardoyne. It's a very close-knit place; Pat Murphy even told me that he saw me take my first steps – that's how close we lived to each other. By the time of the outbreak of the Troubles in 1969, however, my family had moved out of the immediate Ardoyne district and were living on the Upper Crumlin Road.

Family Background

The O'Connors were all grammar school boys. They did well in education but, despite Granny O'Connor's best efforts, there wasn't the money around for a university education for any of them. However, they all prospered in various professions such as accounting and engineering. My daddy was in engineering. He was a very hard worker, and had spent some time in the United States and managed to get himself a very good job. He really learned his trade in broadcasting in the United States while working for RCA and going to night school while he worked. Radio and television were much more advanced over there at that time. I suppose these days he would be called a 'migrant worker'.

Fortunately for me he came back here, as otherwise I would not have been born. He had come back home for a break and was thinking about returning to the United States when a job happened to come up with a new television station called UTV. It was the beginning of Ulster Television. Mummy encouraged him to apply, and he got the job. In local terms I suppose our family were reasonably prosperous, because my dad had a well-paid job. We had moved home, first up to Springvale in Ligoniel, and then in 1968 my dad bought a bungalow on the Upper Crumlin Road. I'm sure he felt that we had arrived with this beautiful bungalow on an acre-and-a-half of garden.

Everything was on the up for us in 1968/1969. I was in school in Chief Street in the old Holy Cross Girls' School, preparing for the 11+ examination; I was one of the first P7s to move to the new school later that year. I have strong memories of that year as an exciting time. My dad was a great consumer of newspapers and current affairs programmes, and I was also a very precocious child, which probably explains why I was very conscious of world events such as the civil rights movement in the United States and of the Civil Rights campaign locally. So while I may not have been very advanced in terms of a full understanding of what was going on around me, I did have some inclination of what was going on and why.

The 'Twelfth'

12 July in particular was something I was always conscious of. I remember one funny incident at our house over 12 July 1968. We got up on the morning of the Twelfth and had planned to go on holiday that day. When we looked out our window there was a Union Jack in our garden. My dad nearly went insane. He was quite a hot-tempered character and went outside, ranting and raving. When he eventually calmed down after about half an hour and examined the pole the Union Jack was on, he noticed that it was stapled the whole way along. At that point he realised that people don't have industrial staplers lying about the house, and that the flag had been put up by some boys from his workplace who were playing a prank on him! Thinking about the late 1960s, with parental permission (they were not sectarian in their outlook), I went to 'the Field' on the Twelfth with a friend's family and participated in the celebrations for the Orange parade with our neighbours. That innocence, though, was about to be shattered.

Growing Menace

I vividly remember the television pictures during the summer of 1969 of the Civil Rights marches and the trouble in Derry at the Apprentice Boys' parade. I was aware of the Civil Rights march at Burntollet, and have a vivid recollection of a front page photograph, I think in the *Irish Independent*, of a young woman in a miniskirt with her stockings ripped and her legs bleeding from where she had been attacked by a Loyalist with a cudgel that had some kind of nails in it.

We were on holiday on 12 July 1969 because my dad, like a lot of people from North Belfast, would have taken us somewhere peaceful for the couple of weeks over the Twelfth in order to get away from the tension. We were all bundled up in the Zephyr. I can't remember how many of us there were in 1969, but it was a big family, and we were all bundled up in the car. He usually took us as far away as he could get, places like Sneem, in County Kerry. In the background though was an awareness that something was brewing over that July period. However, the biggest adventure I was looking forward to that summer was getting ready to go to secondary school, getting my uniform and all that kind of stuff. These were the big issues going on for me.

Although we lived on the Upper Crumlin Road at that point, our lives still revolved around Ardoyne. I went to school in the district, Irish dancing and choir in Ardoyne, and would go to my granny's for lunch. We stayed in the district most of the day, and would be picked up by Mammy or Daddy later in the evening. They would pick us up by car and bring us up to what my granda called 'the Ponderosa', the bungalow up on the hill.

It was an interesting summer and I was certainly very conscious of the conversations that were taking place in the house about everything that was unfolding, particularly in Derry. This is why it was so satisfying for me to see Derry in 2013 when it was chosen as City of Culture. A glorious year, when frankly I had to pinch myself to believe that we could be a society at peace with itself, walking on the walls and over the Peace Bridge and hearing The Undertones playing 'Teenage Kicks' in Ebrington Square – truly days like this!

Innocence Shattered

I don't know why my memories of 1969 are so vivid as I was only a kid, but I remember people talking about what was happening around us. My great-aunt May had a little sweetie shop in the district, and we would call in after school to get free sweeties. I would have been wandering around the streets prior to getting picked up in the afternoon, picking up a lot of the local news and gossip. I have a vague recollection of lots of talk among adults about 'taking the pressure off Derry.' There were student protests and Civil Rights protests going on in different places.

I think on the day that Hooker Street was burned Mammy and I were down the Crumlin Road shopping. It must have been around the middle of August. There were lots of small shops on the Crumlin Road at that time, some facing Hooker Street and down the road beyond the Wheatfield Bar. I had urgently needed an item of clothing of a sensitive nature. I might as well say it – it was my first bra! We had parked the car and walked down the road to get this little item of clothing, which I was very excited about. This was a big occasion for me. Maybe that's the reason the events of that day are so vivid in my memory. The previous night there had been some trouble along the front of the road. There was a strong smell of burning in the air, for some reason that is a very vivid memory. However, apart from the smell and a few people standing about the road I didn't feel anxious and Mammy and I did our bit of shopping down the road, went back to the car and drove on home.

That night though, in our house on the Upper Crumlin Road with its large windows overlooking Belfast, we sat and watched fires break out in the city below us and the sound of what was happening in Ardoyne carried up the hill to us. The next night, relatives from Ardoyne came to our house for safety. I thought that this was all very exciting. Looking back it was such a dramatic interruption to normal life but I didn't fully comprehend the serious nature of it. I certainly had no sense at that time that these things were really spinning out of control in the way that they were. I was one of those children 'who missed nothing' and I listened to all the adult conversations and the news; I remember hearing my dad on the phone speaking to Vivian Simpson, who was then the Labour MP for the area. His voice was raised and he was saying, 'Something needs to be done. Something needs to be done.'

I overheard a number of similar conversations around that same theme. As the summer progressed, my mum and I would regularly come down to check on family, and I would have been with my cousins wandering about on the pretext of going to the shop to nosy what was happening around us. I remember being totally bewildered at the once tidy streets covered in wreckage and the barricades at every street corner.

Violence Erupts

Chronologically, some of the memories of that summer are confused, but I vividly remember the burnt-out houses, bits of prams lying around, people's possessions in the street, glass and all kinds of debris. Children were engaged in excited conversations and I just couldn't get over the scale of the damage. Then there was the smell of smoke in the air. People were nearly retching with the smell of smoke. That smell of smoke was all pervasive; indeed looking back it seemed to be ever-present in the place from that period on. Everything that was happening was shocking!

Buses, vans and all sorts of vehicles were parked across the streets. Paving stones were pulled up and thrown all over the place. Street lights were broken. These were the street lamps we swung from with our ropes, but none of the lights were working. People just seemed to be milling about on the streets. My dad probably wouldn't have known that I was down in the district; in those days children ran free and I wouldn't have wanted to miss anything!

Things seemed to settle a little bit once the Army arrived. Then there was an occasion when Mammy and I were in town shopping and trouble was breaking out at Unity Flats. We had parked our car down there and I remember running to the car to get away from trouble. There were mobs running about throwing stones, police turning up and all sorts of commotion. I was bundled into the car and brought home, and the rest of the summer just seemed to be more of the same!

'Long-Haired Louts!'

I remember there was a fashion that summer of 1969 for washed-out, almost white jeans, which is very aspirational in a community that didn't have great laundry facilities. The teenage boys were wearing these washed-out jeans and 'winklepicker' pointy boots. I remember one night when we were driving into the district and the headlights of the car caught some of the young lads, my mammy said, 'In the name of good God, would you look at them with their white jeans on, it's like an advert for Daz!'

Teenagers were dismissed then as they are now. Long hair was quite a thing then. My father made everyone get the standard short back and sides and strongly disapproved of jeans; he was extremely uncomplimentary of anyone with long hair, as they were judged to be undesirable. This give rise to one of my standout memories, which is my granny saying, 'It was those long-haired louts they talk about. They are the ones who were out trying to help.' Suddenly, in her eyes and in reality, these 'useless' teenagers were the defenders and heroes of the hour! So it was funny to hear my granny suddenly appreciate these young people.

Back to School

I started secondary school that September, and I was told by a teacher that I was precocious because I was telling the teachers what was happening on the streets. All I was really doing was repeating stuff I had heard. I did read the newspapers and listened to conversations, and the news seemed to be on all the time. Every time the television was on there seemed to be news or current affairs about what had now been named 'the Troubles'. So I had a strong sense that there is something really big happening here.

In the immediate aftermath of the trouble starting, it just seemed like normal life had been suspended. The whole of the district was like a battle zone. All the neat little streets were constantly covered in all manner of wreckage and debris. When I think about it, it was absolutely crazy. It interrupted normal life, things like our Irish dancing. Our classes were suspended because of what was going on in the streets around us. All sorts of things that were part of the norms of our social lives were disrupted in the aftermath.

I remember my father got very angry and the tension in our house rocketed. He had just bought a big house at a huge risk at the worst possible time, and whilst he was politically very interested and animated about everything that was going on, he was also very anxious about his work and his professional life. It would not have done to express a political view in his work at that time. I think that's one of the things that is very sad, and I am not sure it is much better today. It is still risky to express a personal view, but surely the mark of a normal society is to be able to hold a view without it making you a subject of attack or suspicion. That will be the mark for me of when we actually get to a better place. Freedom for people to be themselves and to disagree without personal risk. I caught a snapshot of it in

2013 in Derry during the City of Culture celebrations, where I really felt that there was a fantastic outpouring of peoples' ability to talk freely, and to be free in their language and talk about difficult subjects. In my career in local government I tried in my own small way to create safe, shared spaces. The Derry/Londonderry 2013 experience was one of mutual respect and people working as one community. It was a beautiful sight; sadly I think we have lost that ability again.

Making Sense of It All

As I grew up around Ardoyne I was aware of a growing consciousness of people being identified by their difference, of being Protestant/Catholic/Unionist/Nationalist. I had previously no idea of those things. I did have an pretty good understanding of what was going on in the Civil Rights Movement, and would have been very tuned in to what I was hearing at home, my parents' reactions to what was on the news, and what was actually happening in this community. I was certainly aware that the tension had rocketed off the scale during that period.

Much of my growing understanding of the events around me was influenced by my granny. I remember her talking about the 'pogroms' that took place in Belfast in the 1930s. It was like she was trying to make sense of the violence she was witnessing and so she was telling her memories. Her family were from the Short Strand, and I think they were burned out of their original home. She was talking a lot about these Troubles and about bombs that had been thrown in the streets at the time. She was saying, 'This is just the same thing happening all over again.' How right she was! It's not until you reflect back and see the totality of the conflict that you can identify the cycles of violence.

One of the things, though, that struck me when I was in Derry, talking to people and sharing our recollections of the Troubles here, is how different the experience was for the people of Derry from that of Belfast. Derry did not have the civil difficulty in terms of inter-community conflict and riots. They obviously had conflict dissatisfaction and disadvantage, but they didn't have the level of close-up sectarian violence that was part and parcel of everyday life here in Belfast.

I remember even before the Troubles began we had riots regularly taking place involving St Gabriel's and Somerdale schools and the pitched battles with knives and all kinds of things used. The reality is that there had been long-standing diffi-culty between the communities. You now hear people talking about 'the good old days', but the more you look back the more you realise it was literally just a lid resting ever so lightly on what was bubbling up underneath. When I went to secondary school in 1969, it became the only thing that was real. People were instantly identifiable from the uniforms they wore on the buses on the Crumlin

Road (including my sister Carol having her teeth broken by a boy from Somerdale); there was always stuff being said and done on the journey to and from school. Getting to school started to become a really, really difficult journey as we navigated that road.

I think it's only now, looking back on it all, that I am able to get some understanding of the personal impact. I think a lot of us who lived through the period never really took full cognisance of what happened to us. I watch television programmes about the Troubles, like *Pop Goes Northern Ireland*, that other, younger people probably look at it and find interesting and maybe even enjoyable. However, I watch that programme with a tension in my chest because, for me, my body is reacting to the fear and anxiety of the time.

The thing I was most conscious of about that summer, that I could not have put a name on for years, or even have identified, is the fact that children always pick up on the tension and the fear of the battles that adults fight. For the first time in my life I noticed that the adults were afraid – a real fear they were trying to hide, but such fear is a virulent thing. I was very affected by the tension. When I look back the facts are jumbled but the feelings and emotions return with perfect clarity. I often think of where my father found himself at that stage. Up to that point he lost everything he had worked for, everything in life, and what happened on the Crumlin Road had a massive effect on all of our lives. He actually thought about moving abroad. He investigated going to work in South Africa. We were inundated with lovely glossy brochures about the great education system in South Africa and so on. He gave us the choice of whether we went or not and being aware of apartheid I wasn't keen and we finally decided to stay.

Driven Out

One of the things I remain very aware of was the pace of escalation of the conflict. With the increasing violence it soon became apparent that we wouldn't last very long in our lovely bungalow overlooking Belfast. My dad tried his best to hang on to it because everything he had in the world was invested in it. I clearly remember the events of 1971 for all sorts of reasons, but the main reason being that we lost our home. When we called the police they didn't come until a crowd (one with a visible gun) had gathered and when they finally arrived they seemed to have a little chat with the mob and then they left us to fend for ourselves.

Although my family are from the district, we had the trappings of fairly middle-class life; we had a lovely home and we had this lovely shiny Zephyr, which I remember as an American-style car with fins on the back of it, and then we got a big new Zephyr in burgundy. One lesson I learned then, and feel powerfully now, is although we had the trappings of a secure, middle-class life, the reality is – and this personal experience makes me sympathetic to refugees – the veneer of respectability can disappear in an instant. When we turned up across the border in August 1971, I was grubby in my ripped dress. I was mortified. I also didn't know how my dad was (he remained to try to defend our home), or even whether he was alive or dead.

I identify very powerfully with refugees when I see them on television because we also lost our home. We fled our home with quite literally the clothes on our backs. When the attack came I was wearing a dress that my mother had made for me, and a little matching handbag. My brother Ciarán was six weeks old. We had to literally run for our lives. It was an awful wet night. I was carrying Ciarán and I ripped my dress as I went over country fences behind our house. A gunman had appeared at the front of our house and we watched him for what seemed like a long time. He was soon joined by others. We called the police, but they never came. My dad then phoned his brother, who came to an estate that was not immediately behind our house, but that was reasonably close. We literally ran out the back of the house and through the fields to be picked up and brought down to Mountainview to my uncle's house.

The next day we were in Gormanstown Army Camp. I don't remember leaving Belfast or who took us to the border; from there we were taken away on a bus to camps on the other side of the border. Daddy had stayed in the city to work as he was afraid of losing his job. Much of what happened then is a blur, but I vividly remember standing in Gormanstown Camp watching the television coverage of Ardoyne in flames. I was thinking that my granny and everybody I knew was dead. I remember that very, very vividly. It's quite extraordinary actually when I think about it.

It is hard to believe too that when we came back from Gormanstown we went back to our house and repaired the damage to live in the same house. It was difficult though; we ran the gauntlet going to and from school and there were further attacks. At one stage we actually had soldiers from the Parachute regiment living with us. A major had moved into Ardoyne and he had come to visit us. Of course, like many at that time, Mammy made him tea and sandwiches. He relaxed into the place, and I heard him telling my dad, 'Don't worry. I will protect you. You will be able to stay in your home.' We had soldiers from the Para regiment staying overnight in our house. I remember one, a Scottish guy, who called his gun 'the widow-maker'. I found that very chilling. We also had a Gaeilgeoir, a fluent Irish speaker from Letterkenny. He told us funny stories about being in a shop at the Pad in Ardoyne and the woman started speaking in Irish. 'Imagine her surprise', he said, 'when a Para answered her back in Irish.' As soon as the Para regiment left though, our position up there became pretty much untenable as the tension rose. People had been shot dead in a house not too far away from us on the Upper Crumlin Road. I believe they were brothers, shot dead in one of the small cottages up at the turn of the road.

The night after interment was introduced we listened to the gun battles all night. We watched the One O'Clock News and heard the plummy accent of the Prime Minister and it looked and sounded like a war. Later that year there would be a change in the Army regiment based in Ardoyne, and the next regiment told us that they couldn't afford us any protection.

Back to School

When I went back to school after that summer of 1971 we were given the usual September essay in English class, 'What I did during the summer holidays.' My teacher was from leafy South Belfast, and I wrote my essay about what had happened to us that summer. I have never forgotten her comment at the end. She wrote, 'Sharon, you must learn to be less dramatic.'

It was mad. As if I had dreamed it. Probably my language was a bit dramatic but what had happened to us was very real. I feel it even now. I realised very quickly that people who were not there, who hadn't experienced what we had, just couldn't understand. They had no understanding whatsoever.

At Our Lady of Mercy School we were about to get a very close-up and intimate understanding of the consequences of the conflict. In addition to students being attacked going to and from school, the school itself became a target and the school was attacked on numerous occasions right through my school years. There is a great photograph I came across quite recently taken by an international photographer. It records a riot where Loyalists are trying to get into the school. Those are the sort of things that were happening up there all the time. The Army would be outside the school and literally we would walk on the road and the Army land rover would drive alongside us. All of that would be unusual in terms of anybody's school experience but for us it was normality.

Personal Impact

I think there have been long-standing consequences for me given what we experienced as individuals and as a community in Ardoyne. I am only now beginning to realise that although my generation had these experiences, we never really processed them. If these same things were to happen now, statutory agencies and voluntary groups would be deploying response teams to support people to cope with these experiences. Then there was absolutely nothing. If anything, our experience was just passed off as 'normal'. There were no charities intervening, or people running to help. Even in school, and I am sure it is true of most of the schools, there was no quarter given. It was just an attitude of 'get on with it'. I remember going in to sit my English Language 'O' Level, and the school had been attacked the night before. The school was strewn with glass from one end to the other and, again, there it was the smell of burning all over. No remarks were made about it, nor did we get any discretion for any upset. I think we became resilient, but that doesn't mean to say that we were unscarred. Being resilient and being unscarred are two different things.

I got an insight into that recently when the Primark building went on fire (28 August 2018). There had been a wee bit of anxiety about potential bombs from dissident groups around the same time as that fire occurred. I was going into Belfast to get a painting reframed and was taking it to the art shop in Queen Street. I arrived into Belfast city centre and parked at the bottom of North Street. As I parked my car I could see the smoke and the flames. Mentally I said, 'Well, I have come to do this errand, and I am not letting this get in my way.' I came round the back of the Primark building again. There were explosions going off, obviously gas canisters or aerosol cans. I remember thinking, 'Why did I go ahead with this?' Then I realised that I went ahead to get my picture framed because that's what you did during the Troubles – you just got on with it!

I remember at one time getting my mother to drive me to a work 'do'. I was working at the *Belfast Telegraph*, which incidentally was blown up while I worked there. I remember getting her to drive through a riot while we were all glammed up, and we thought nothing of that. She could have had the car taken off her but you just went ahead and got on with it. We all have the scars as a consequence. I have no doubt that they are there.

Shot at the Disco

My daughters think this hilarious, but I was shot on the Antrim Road in 1972. When the Troubles started, our personal freedom was shut down overnight. My father was already a Victorian father, even without the Troubles, which of course had the effect of our lives being completely contracted and closed in. We weren't allowed out to go to Irish dancing for example, because I had to walk down the Crumlin Road to get to it.

So here was I at Our Lady of Mercy School, and all the other girls were going to the Barney disco. This was a disco that was held in a local secondary school, and it was the place to go as a teenager in North Belfast. The girls had been talking about it for weeks. I had been thinking, 'I would love to get to the Barney disco.' One night I told my parents an elaborate narrative about my plans for the night. I told them that I was going to be staying overnight with my aunt. That bit was true, but I didn't tell them that I was going to the disco in Newington first, and then going to her house afterwards. Two people had been shot dead on the road the week before, and I certainly wasn't going to raise this issue with them!

The disco was fantastic. On the way home, I walked down to the top of the New Lodge Road to get a taxi up to my aunt's house in Ardoyne. There must have been at least 40 people in front of me in the taxi line. People were all around me, and yet the bullet still managed to find me and my lovely new coat. It was my first grown-up maxi length coat too – out of Robb's in High Street, Belfast – not cheap! I was shot in the arm, but I only heard the shot after I was hit. A really weird thing. My face was cut because the bullets hit the wall, and I was hit by masonry as well as the bullet. I am now scarred round my chin, but the bullet was actually in my arm. I was afraid to move my arm because, although the bullet had gone through me, I was afraid it was still in me.

I ended up in hospital and then gradually began to realise that I still had to face the wrath of my father. I don't know which was worse. Actually, I think facing him was definitely worse! I was asking the nurses to keep me in the hospital as I didn't want to go home to face the music. To make it worse, my parents almost had a very serious accident on their way to me in hospital. All they had been told was that I had been shot. I was told by a policeman, the next day, that I had been shot from a passing car. I didn't know anything about it though. I was just standing there, got shot, and that was it; it was great fun growing up then!

Trauma Remains

The impact of getting shot remains with me. It still gets to me. My kids laugh at me because if I am in the cinema and there is a loud bang, I go on a vertical take-off. I can't cope with large explosions, noises, crashes. I am very alert to noise all the time, and that's a consequence of all that we went through. It is not just that one incident. I was in the offices of the *Belfast Telegraph* when it was blown up. So I had a whole series of events that would have shown in that physical reaction. My body reacts and my unconscious mind reacts, but it is only now that I consciously know I am reacting to those things that happened years before. That anxiety never really leaves.

I think I also have antennae for trouble due to my experience. I go to some places and get a very strong feeling of danger. I saw that strongly when I visited Nairobi. We got off the plane and got a taxi that brought us through these shanty towns. I immediately said, 'I really don't like it here.' We arrived at the hotel, which had been blown up as often as the Europa in Belfast! They were searching under the taxi and everything. I couldn't wait to get out of Nairobi. That was in 2007, and a few months later the place was engaged in violent community conflict.

I often get a strong awareness of my bearings, of where I am, and of being safe. I had a funny incident with a senior PSNI officer when I was in Derry. He invited me for lunch one day and we both arrived at the restaurant at the same time. We both dived for the corner chair – for the same reason. We both wanted to see the door and who was coming through it. It was really funny because we both went for the chair facing the door. It is just that idea of wanting to know where your exit route is and being able to see a way to get out in case something goes wrong.

Regrets

When I lived on Upper Crumlin Road I had a friend, Liz, who was from a Protestant family on the Silverstream Road. It was probably around 1968 and we were out playing in the street. I remember a flatbed milk lorry with this guy on the back of it shouting, ranting, raving. It was a famous political preacher, along with his acolytes. I remember Liz's mammy, who was obviously concerned, coming and getting us into the house, but I registered this loud booming voice shouting about papists, as that sort of thing kind of sticks with you down the years.

All of that was going on, and look where we are now as a consequence of it. Dreadful, but I get more appreciation of my parents when I look back and recognise that they went through hell and back, and never lost faith. My poor old dad is now dead and buried. He should still be pottering around on the golf course. His brothers all lived longer lives than him. My dad died when he was 56. He is a victim of the Troubles. I have no doubt about that. He is dead because of all the pressure and tension, losing everything. That is what killed him, without a shadow of a doubt.

Many of my generation just wanted to get out of here and many did. Most of the O'Connors went to the United States; we all wanted to get out of here. I stayed and I am grateful for the decent education I received and the opportunities I have had. It was only when I went to work in Derry that I realised how different Ardoyne and Belfast was. In Derry in the 1970s they also had division and separation but they did not experience the sectarian community conflict to the same extent. They didn't have the experience of being afraid of being attacked on the journey to school. It was extraordinary to talk to people of my generation from Derry, because their teenage experiences seem completely different. For people of my generation growing up there, while obviously having the ongoing conflict to contend with, that idea of walking home at night watching for passing cars was not something they were familiar with to the same degree. The fear of being kidnapped or shot was very real for many young people from Belfast as they tried to forge a life in the middle of all the craziness. My dad would often say to us, 'Run for your life. You are better getting shot in the back as getting taken away.'

When my family lived on the Crumlin Road, one of our neighbour's fathers was a surgeon at the Mater Hospital. The Shankill Butchers got him coming out of Queen's University one night, and he was savagely murdered. Our lives got even smaller after that, because my dad was so freaked out by that. Yes, I often wonder what it would have been like had we left earlier than we did...

A Place Apart

I take great pride in Ardoyne. Several recently published award-winning books have been written by people from this place and I also think of the aspiration of the people from Ardoyne. I am so proud of the achievements of all the people I meet who are from the place. It is really remarkable when you think that it is such a little space for the remarkable achievements and the talent of people who came out of it.

I was educated in redundant Second World War Nissen huts at the bottom of Butler Street where there was standing water and the occasional dead dog, outside toilets, broken windows. It was like a Third World country in terms of where we got our education, but what an education we received! The quality of love for language and all that I acquired here was just so important. When you think of the people who have emerged from within this place, very talented and resilient people, and when I see them I think, 'That's an Ardoyne person! Amazing!'

Ardoyne people have these incredible achievements. I get such pride from that. One of the special things about Ardoyne is that it is like an island. My partner comes from a remote Scottish island and to me it's sort of the same thing. I am rarely in Ardoyne now apart from funerals at the church and weddings (weddings less so with increasing age), but when I am here, even infrequently, this is like an island in that the family networks are extensive. I can be away 30 years, yet people instantly recognise me. Although they might not know me personally, they know my connections and my clan. They will say to me, 'which one of the O'Connors are you?'

The people here know you, and they just have to find out 'which one' you are. I have seen that with other families. I was talking about the McCallans. I was getting served one day in TK Maxx and I said to the young man serving me, 'Are you one of the McCallans?' He was maybe in his early twenties. He turned out to be one of Michael's ones. I recognised him, and knew who he was just from the physical appearance of him. So that's the clan thing, a sense of connection and recognition.

It may be different now. I am no longer inside that world and the last of my family have long since scattered to the four winds, so I don't know if that glue still holds, but certainly that network and layers of family we witnessed was very much like life on an island. That reality became increasingly more evident during the Troubles, because there was a period of time when it wasn't safe for people to go outside the district, to leave the island. At that time I used to beg my cousins, 'Can we go into town and go to the cinema or something?' Anything to just to get away from it.

There was a claustrophobia about living in Ardoyne. When you are young it feels big, but Ardoyne is actually very small; the houses and the gardens are very small, the streets are narrow. There is something positive to that, a close-knit feel to it, but the other dimension is that it can be claustrophobic. Everybody knows you, and knows everything about you. In and out of each other's houses. I have very fond and affectionate memories of all that. We were lucky in that. Although we had really very little by way of resources in terms of education, we were really rich in terms of the quality of the people who educated us.

7

Davy Wasson

Early Days

I was born in Ardoyne in 1953 and went to Holy Cross Boys' School. When I started primary school we were using the old Nissen huts still present in the Butler Street playgound, but I was only there a couple of months when we moved into the 'big school'. At that time, mothers might have brought their children to school on their first day, but after that kids made their own way to school! Ardoyne, though, was the kind of place where your parents felt safe to let children walk to school on their own. We walked to school from when we were no age, and we never worried about trouble or anybody doing anything. It was just that close-knit kind of community and I loved growing up in Ardoyne. After school we would play football on 'the Bone Heights', on the streets, or up in Ballysillan Playing Fields.

I became an altar boy in 1961 at seven years of age, and that had a great impact upon me. There were so many altar boys and so many priests in Holy Cross that there was a great sense of community. It was also a social outlet, as that's where we got to know people. There were people like Harry Patterson, Stuarty Baxter, John McCloskey, Brendan McFarlane, his brother Gerard, so many people. Paddy McCabe, the sacristan, was a great man who gelled it all together. He organised and refereed Gaelic matches on a Thursday night and even got a social club built out the back of the monastery for us to use. So many families were involved, the

Currans, the Shannons, the McKees. There were so many events happening around the church at the time.

I remember 'the Big Snow' of 1963. I was serving the 6.30 a.m. Mass and the snow was really deep. My father took me up on his shoulders, and as we came walking around the corner we met Raymond Mooney on his father's shoulders. People did things like that to make sure you got to serve Mass because the chapel was the mainstay of the district at that time. Everything revolved around the church.

The other great thing that happened to me was joining Ardoyne Kickhams Gaelic club at thirteen years of age. Antrim had brought in an under-14 district hurling league to promote hurling in Belfast in particular. So I started playing under-14 hurling and never looked back from there. We had a little club house up by Frank the barber's in Butler Street, and then we moved down to the old Working Men's Club, beside Toby's Hall. My days were filled with matches and as I got older my summers were spent in Ballysillan Playing Fields.

Ardoyne Kickhams

In 1968, the Ardoyne under-16 football team reached the semi-finals of the South Antrim Championship. We drew with local rivals Pearses but lost the replay in extra time. However, the 1968 team was very young and we knew that it was going to come through the following year as well. So come 1969 we were being looked upon as the team to win the championship. I was captain of the team that year, and from the beginning of 1969 everything was focused on winning this championship.

We trained throughout the winter up in St Gabriel's School, as we were totally committed to winning the championship. Brian McCargo was one of our trainers. I remember him because he was always running the roads. He was very fit, and when the bright nights of the summer came in we were training in Ballysillan Playing Fields just about every night. Brian McCargo had us pounding up and down the Ballysillan Playing Fields. We were super-fit and really gelled together as a team.

Brian was a tough guy who you would want to be on your side in an argument. There was one match where an incident took place somewhere up in the country and following a fight Brian McCargo ended up against the hedge. The opposition were coming at him, but he stood there like Muhammad Ali, just punching all round him. He just kept going. He was as tough as nails, and he looked after you. I was playing midfield against St Malachy's in Casement Park one day, and I was getting lumps kicked out of me by Liam Boyle, who was a county player at the time. For the kick-outs, Ted McQuaid (our goalkeeper) used to play the ball out the wing to me. I was playing half-forward, and would then move up to half-back to collect the kick-out. Brian McCargo pulled me aside and said to me, 'You just keep doing the same thing. Don't you worry about a thing.' Next kick-out I rose for the ball and collected it, and there was nobody near me. I looked round and Liam Boyle was lying in a heap, and Brian McCargo said to me, 'Away you go.' Brian was a tough man, no doubt about that.

Political Awareness

The first real awakening of Nationalist feelings that I was aware of was in 1966, with the 50th anniversary of the Easter Rising. The streets of Ardoyne were decorated with tricolours and the kerbstones were painted. All kinds of bunting and banners were put up to celebrate the Rising. I was amazed at this because I had always associated this kind of celebration with the Orange marches, when the Loyalists had their flags and banners up.

I was also aware of what had happened in Divis Street, with Paisley coming to the fore and the tricolour getting removed from the shop window. I watched the Civil Rights Movement starting out, and the famous incident when the protestors were attacked at Burntollet during the Long March to Derry. In 1969, particularly coming up to July time, there were various small riots in Hooker Street around the parades, but nothing major had happened so far. While I was beginning to become aware that tensions were rising, the main thing for me was being totally focused on winning that under-16 championship, so wider politics didn't impact on me too much at that stage. To me, the most important thing was that we were due to play in the championship final on 23 August. I didn't want anything to interfere with that and I never thought anything would until, as August progressed, things just seemed to get worse. Those early riots were probably what today would be referred to as 'recreational rioting'. Then 14–16 August came along, and everything changed.

All Changed

Over those three days of 14–16 August the trouble really sparked off, and it just seemed to spiral out of control. It started off with rioting between Loyalists and local residents across the main Crumlin Road, but then the police invaded the district. While I was living in Stratford Gardens and out of the direct line of trouble, my granny was living right in the middle of it in Brookfield Street, and we had to get her out to safety. Her sister lived at the top of Brookfield Street, near the Crumlin Road end, but she refused to move out to go anywhere, and unfortunately she was burnt out on the night of 14–15 August. The rioting was so bad that she couldn't even get out her own back door as it was blocked in. As a 68-year-old woman, she had to climb over her yard wall to escape the mobs who were coming down the street.

I saw the aftermath the next morning and became aware that people had been shot and injured. I remember Paul Coleman and myself coming out of Mass on 15 August, the Feast of the Assumption, and walking round the old district. We were shocked at seeing the devastation in Hooker Street: everything ripped up to be used as missiles and the burnt-out homes. It was like a battlefield. I just couldn't believe that this was happening. Bad as it was though, people were saying that it was just going to get worse later that night because of what was happening over in the Falls and in Derry.

Later on that day I was on the Berwick Road and saw buses coming from all directions. The people had gone up and taken the buses out of the bus depot. Anyone who could drive was encouraged to drive the buses, as well as some who obviously could not drive! I was standing at the corner as they were driving them into Northwick Drive, and they were hitting the lamp posts and anything else in their way as they went down the street. People who were driving the buses had no idea of what they could be walking into. They could have been arrested, shot or lost their jobs, but that's the kind of spirit that was alive in Ardoyne at the time, just that complete willingness to help out. People realised that we were under attack and were doing what they could to help. All these buses being used as barricades, and I was wondering, 'just what is going on here? What is going to happen tonight?' The night of 15 August again saw serious rioting and shooting, but for me Saturday 16 August brought the biggest fear to the district, because by then we thought, 'this is not going to be good tonight.' People were now being evacuated. My sisters were sent over to Andersonstown, and there was only my father and myself left in our street.

I always remember the Shoreland tanks sitting at the top of the Oldpark Road, all pointing down into Ardoyne. There was a very real, palpable fear among people about what was going to happen that night. At that stage I heard people saying that the Army had been sent into Belfast, but there was no sign of them in Ardoyne. Early on 16 August my father, who was a member of the trade union UCAT, had got in touch with a lot of union officials and got them up to Ardoyne and showed them around the district to let them see what was happening. They went through the Brompton Gap into Herbert Street and there was shooting coming from the other side of the Crumlin Road. Loyalists were firing shots at anyone who was moving, so you had to be careful as you moved around the district, but the big fear was of what was going to happen that night with the big Shorelands coming in. At sixteen years of age, that's when I really felt the fear. Only my father and myself were left at home. Everyone else had been evacuated and I had no idea what was going to happen that night. It really hit home then. This could be life or death. The people who did come out and fight were very brave. They were fighting bullets with bricks, but still put their personal safety and lives on the line to defend the district.

I remember Roy Kerrigan and myself getting involved in helping to move people out of their homes after they had been intimidated. Guys in lorries got us to go along with them to help families in Chief Street, Bray Street, Ohio Street, and other streets on the Protestant side of the road. Loyalist crowds would have gathered during the day as we were moving the families out. They didn't do anything at that stage, just look on at what we were doing. It was very menacing, but Roy Kerrigan managed to get his picture in the *Irish News* the next day as we helped the families to move out.

The Army Arrives

Around 6 p.m. on the Saturday evening, word came that the Army had come in from the Crumlin Road into Ardoyne. I was on the Berwick Road at the time and cut through the gap into Herbert Street to see what was going on. As I walked along I saw Martin Meehan walking along with a shotgun, coming through the gap. I remember someone shouting, 'Martin, what do you think? The Army is in.' I had been thinking, 'Thank God. At least we are safe now.' But Martin's response was, 'I don't like it, but what can we do?' I went up to the top of the road and saw the Army with their barbed wire and barricades. To be honest, I just felt relief.

Just seven days later, Saturday 23 August, we played St Gall's in the final of the Under-16 football championship in Casement Park. Normality in the midst of the craziness. It was played in glorious sunshine and we won the championship. It was a brilliant day, and such a different feeling from just a week before. We hadn't lost a match in the league either but for some reason that year, the county board decided to have a top four play-off to see who would win the league. We ended up playing St Teresa's in the final and lost by a point, so we just missed out on doing 'the double'.

27 June 1970

The next significant day that I remember in Ardoyne was 27 June 1970. Roy Kerrigan, Pat Murphy and a few others of us were in Ardoyne Kickhams' clubrooms beside Toby's Hall getting things ready for a club reunion that was due to take place that night. Next thing, we heard pandemonium break out. We went out of the club to go to the top of Brookfield Street only to see hordes of Loyalists coming down Brookfield Street from across Disraeli Street, Leopold Street and Palmer Street. They were running down Brookfield Street attacking houses as they went.

People came from everywhere in the district in response. My aunt Kathleen lived in Brookfield Street at the time, and as I passed her house she gave me an old sauce bottle to throw! Anything was used in what was practically hand-to-hand fighting. Then the shooting started. We ran into Hooker Street, and as I looked across the road I could see someone lying underneath a Young's lemonade lorry firing down the street. Next thing I saw was Jimmy Fennell's wife, Agnes, getting shot and going down.

People at this stage were standing at their doors looking up the street at the fighting going down in front of them. A guy who was with me said, 'You take this side of the street and I will take the other side. Get everybody inside their houses!' So we ran down getting people off the street, and as I came to the end of Hooker Street I saw this car pulling up on Butler Street. The car doors opened and two guys jumped out. They pressed the button on the boot and the boot opened. I was just amazed at what I saw next. It was stacked up with rifles. People were running and just grabbing rifles out of the boot. Next thing, the shooting really started. I think there were four or five people killed that day. I remember there were five people arrested and charged with the shootings and ended up on trial down in the Crum (Crumlin Road Court House), but they all got off. Of course, there was great celebration in the district because they had been released, and a lot of rioting from the Loyalists, also because they had been released!

Lookouts

The Army came into the district in force following the shooting and everything eventually quietened down, but there was still a lot of rioting going on in St Matthew's parish in the east of the city, so people were still nervous about what might yet happen in Ardoyne. Pat Murphy, Cathal Goan and myself were sent up by Cathal's father to the chapel, specifically to get up on the walls and to keep a check down the Woodvale Road, and to give the alarm if we saw Loyalists coming up the road. There was a fear that because St Matthew's was being attacked, Holy Cross Church would also come under attack. So the three of us were doing lookout and had positioned ourselves on the wall. Pat Murphy, of course, decided that wasn't good enough for him, so he decided that he would climb up one of the trees to get a better look. Next thing, Pat fell and broke his arm. Cathal's father wasn't a bit impressed, and we spent the night in the Mater Hospital with Pat. So we were the poorest lookouts ever!

The events of that day marked a turning point in Ardoyne. It was the day when people were adamant that what had happened in 1969 'will never happen again', and I don't think the Loyalists ever attempted to get back into Ardoyne from that day forward.

Personal Impact

Like many people in the district I had witnessed some extraordinary events, but despite what they had experienced the people had an attitude of just getting on with their lives. I continued playing Gaelic football as before. I played on the Antrim vocational schools' team in 1970 and then on the Antrim minor football team the next year. However, I was really influenced by a couple of the guys from the district – Tommy Ferguson, Jimmy Mailey, Pat Brown and Fidelus Ewing – who were all going to Australia. A dance was organised for them in St Gabriel's School, and they were brought up onto the stage and given a send-off. I thought that I would like to try that. I began to feel restless, and things in Ardoyne were changing with more shootings, more trouble, more bombs, constant riots. I was only eighteen and started to think about the possibility of going to Australia. In normal circumstances my parents would have said, 'you are not going anywhere at your age!' But people of my age were being arrested in Ardoyne. Barney Watt had been shot dead. Different things were going on and recruitment to the IRA was very high because of what had happened. I think my parents believed that I would be better off getting out of the way of what was happening around us.

Joe Smith was another guy who influenced me when he talked to me down in the GAA club. Joe was from Etna Drive and worked on the boats. He used to talk to me about travelling the world, and so in the end I decided to give it a go. Two other friends had agreed to go with me, Brendan McKeown and my cousin, Danny Wasson. Our interview date for processing the emigration was arranged for 9 August 1971, which turned out to be internment day. There was no way that Brendan McKeown and myself, coming from Ardoyne, were ever going to make it down to Castle Street in the city centre for our interview, although Danny was able to make it down from Andersonstown. The day after internment I was round helping shift Denis McMullan and some other people in Glenbryn after they were intimidated out of their homes. Danny ended up going to Australia a couple of months before Brendan and myself, but we all eventually ended up in Sydney.

New Life in Australia

Saying goodbye and going to the other side of the world was difficult. My father came down to the boat with some of my brothers and sisters. My mother didn't go down as she thought she just couldn't say goodbye at the boat, so we said our farewells in the house.

Australia though was marvellous. I really enjoyed it, but it was also daunting as I suddenly realised that I was in the place I had always wanted to go to. I was quickly brought back to reality when I went to the hostel where I was staying. It was very regimented and it was as if I had joined the Army rather than gone to a brave new world. I got a job as a ticket clerk on the railway system, a bit similar to the Underground in London. I thought I was getting on well until one morning someone came up and asked for a return ticket to Burwood. I told him the price was, 'Eighty-eight.' He stood back in amazement and didn't say a word. We just stood back and looked at each other, and an official behind me took me to one side and said, 'What did you say to that person?' `

I said, 'Eighty-eight.'

He said, 'Oh, he thinks you have called him an idiot!' Of course I meant eighty-eight cents, but my Belfast accent was causing me language difficulties!

One day someone came to the door asking for me, and it turned out that he was Tom McCallan, who was a relative of the McCallans from Ardoyne. Someone had told him that I was out in Sydney, and he called round to see if I would like to play for the Young Ireland Gaelic team. Through getting involved in Gaelic games I met lots of other Irish guys and that helped me get settled in Sydney. We had a league in Sydney, but a New York team was coming across that had a lot of very well-known Gaelic footballers playing for them, so a New South Wales team was selected to play against them. Everybody wanted to play in these matches, and I was lucky enough to get picked for them. We were playing against Mick O'Connell, a great Kerry legend, and Christy Ring, the legendary Cork hurler who was actually playing football on this tour. It is amazing just to be able to say that I was on the same pitch as these legends. This was 1973, and Christy Ring was probably the most famous name in all of Gaelic games, and I ended up marking him. I was playing top of the right and Christy was left-fullback. I got the ball and – remember I was just twenty and Christy was easily in his fifties – I just sailed around him. Next thing, a rugby tackle and Christy brought me down. We got a penalty, and Mick O'Connell went into goals. A Kerry man was our designated penalty taker. Needless to say, when this Kerry man faced his legend in goal, he blasted it over the bar! Coming from Ardoyne and being on the same field as these legends. Amazing.

I stayed in Australia for about two and-a-half years, but about a quarter of that Ardoyne under-16 team went away and never came back. I wanted to come back, but I know others felt safer where they were and decided to make a go of it, and they never came back.

A Team Torn Apart

The Ardoyne under-16 football team of 1969 had the potential to go on to achieve great things, but it was team that was to be decimated directly because of the Troubles. Raymond Mooney was on that team. Raymond was shot dead up in the grounds of Holy Cross Church. Ciarán Murphy was kidnapped by the Shankill Butchers on the Cliftonville Road and assassinated. Others left Ardoyne never to come back. Roy Kerrigan went to England and never came back. I had gone to Australia. My cousin Danny went to Australia and never came back. Other members of that team had their own struggles to deal with. John McMahon emigrated. Pierce Moss emigrated. Liam Millar stayed in Belfast. Raymond McClurg emigrated. Tommy Ferguson emigrated and came home again. Pat Murphy stayed in Belfast but his brother Ciarán was assassinated. Roy Kerrigan emigrated to England and never came back. Jim Murray stayed in Belfast. Leonard Cooke emigrated. Danny Wasson emigrated. Michael McKervey stayed in Ardoyne. Ronnie Harrison stayed in Belfast. Martin Mallon emigrated. Gerard Rosatto's father was assassinated. He emigrated and later returned. Paul Coleman stayed in Belfast. Brian Carville stayed in Ardoyne but his brother was assassinated. Frank and Michael McCallan's brother was assassinated. Liam Corr emigrated and his father was assassinated. Kevin McAleer stayed in Belfast. Frank Mulgrave left Belfast. Emmanuel Millar stayed in Belfast. Other guys on that team just never played again.

The Ardoyne Kickhams team suffered deeply because of the Troubles. There is no club that suffered to the extent of the Kickhams. Tommy McAuley was playing senior football for the club at that time, a brilliant midfielder. Tommy got shot and never played again. Despite the escalating conflict and our playing resources becoming more limited, Ardoyne always managed to get teams out on to the pitch. We lost Ballysillan Playing Fields when Loyalists intimidated the club out of the grounds, and that caused major difficulties in arranging both training sessions and games. Up to then our summer nights just revolved around Ballysillan, and there were days when I played up to three games in one day. Having such an interest in the GAA and growing up as an altar boy gave me discipline, and instilled a sense of needing to be careful about the choices I made in life. There were times when the Army stopped you, beat you, dragged you down an entry, put you up against a wall when you were coming home at night. I could easily have made different decisions about my life, but I had that discipline of knowing that there was always another way of doing things and that stood by me.

Ardoyne Kickhams was very important within this community. Not only in terms of keeping a lot of the young people away from trouble and giving them possible opportunities for development, but it was a driving force in helping young people keep their discipline. It gave you something to live for, a reason to look forward to playing matches or to have some involvement in the club. Members of the Gaelic club also played a major role in the defence of the district or in rehousing families who had been evicted from their homes.

In the middle of all the mayhem, the Gaelic club stayed loyal to the principles of the GAA and managed to maintain a unity in the face of the wide range of political affiliations that were then present in Ardoyne. I was on the club committee at one stage and there was pressure on the club to get involved with the Hunger Strike campaign. Other committee members who were personally very sympathetic to the campaign made a decision that we could not get involved as we were members of the wider GAA and that we had to stay faithful to the principles of that organisation, which said that we were non-political. That was a very hard decision for those members, but it demonstrated their integrity.

The Gaelic club lost a lot of members through violence. Members ended up in prison. The club never had its own ground, and every match was an away match. We lost out on so many potential successes. We really could have been a great team but the Troubles decimated us and kept us down. In many ways, the Gaelic club was a microcosm of the wider community. Some were killed, others ended up in gaol, some emigrated, some just got their heads down and got on with their lives. The story of the Ardoyne Gaelic Club is the story of the Ardoyne community.

Final Thoughts

Ardoyne is a Catholic enclave, surrounded on all sides by Protestant areas, but growing up I never thought that things were going to get as bad as they did. I remember when the Army came in thinking that things were never going to be the same again, but I never realised just how different they would become. I never thought that it would get to the stage that it did. Never for a moment did I think that we would witness so many shootings and bombings. I thought that after the initial trouble there would be a stand-off and people would keep their distance from each other, but the kickback from those three days in August 1969 was immense. The IRA grew in strength. People couldn't go outside their own area for fear of attack and the whole social scene changed with the growth of so many social clubs in the area. To leave the area you left yourself open to the possibility of assassination. That was a very real fear, and a very real possibility.

People from Ardoyne, though, never lost that sense of pride in the community we come from. From growing up in Ardoyne you get caught up in that community spirit. Like Mrs Quinn from my own street, she was the 'rapper upper'. She went round in the morning rapping people's doors to waken them up for work. People looked after each other in Ardoyne. Even as a kid, those we knew as 'the big lads' looked after us, and they wouldn't let anything happen to you.

Yes, Ardoyne is very insular, but I always felt that I was part of a community that would look after itself as the people looked after each other. The focal point was the chapel on the hill. The chapel was the major influence in the life of this community. Every part of the community had its own priest and as altar boys we were serving Mass from 6.30 in the morning. There is maybe lots that can be said about Ardoyne people, but no matter where we go we will always be Ardoyne people. No matter about the bad press that it has got, when people ask where I am from I tell them, 'I am from Ardoyne, and I am proud of it.' I was born in Ardoyne. I was reared in Ardoyne. I played for Ardoyne. I was privileged to serve Mass in Ardoyne. I love Ardoyne. It's a great community!

8

Jackie Donnelly

Family Background

The Donnelly family would be described in modern-day terms as 'Castle Catholics'. My grandfather had joined the British Army just prior to the First World War. This was maybe a good thing for him, as he got properly trained up as a soldier, whereas had he been conscripted he would not have got the same level of training. As with many who served with him, my grandfather was wounded on the battlefield and later became a prisoner of war.

He was still in the British Army when he married my grandmother, Jane Alexander. She had been born and reared in Middle Chatham Street, Ardoyne, and after their marriage they moved to a house in Flax Street. My grandfather was still in the Army in 1939 when an RUC man, a drinking friend of my grandfather and based in Leopold Street, called up to their home in Flax Street and asked to see my father, Frank. My grandmother Jane asked him, 'Why? Has he done something wrong?'

'No, we only want to see him down in the Barracks for an hour.' My father went down to Leopold Street Barracks and found himself interned for the duration of the Second World War because of his suspected sympathies with the Republican movement. So as the war was raging, my grandfather was in the British Army, while his son, my father, was interned.

Alongside the obvious contradiction, there were also the hidden painful family consequences. My father was obviously the black sheep of a large family of four brothers and four sisters. While he was interned in Crumlin Road Gaol for six years, my grandfather was still attached to the British Army, and because of this my father never sent him 'a visit' out (a pass to visit him in prison). He sent visits to my grandmother, to his brothers and sisters, but he would never send a visit to his father.

Ironically, during the period my father was in gaol the family home in Flax Street got blown up during the Blitz. For anyone who remembers Flax Street, as you walked down old Flax Street there were about four houses then a gap where four houses, including my family home, used to be. My father certainly found that very ironic. He married my mother shortly after he got out of gaol at the end of the war and they settled in what was known as Glenard.

Republican Influence

My father was very proud of his Republican beliefs. He was the only one of the Donnelly side of my family who would have claimed to be a Republican, and this was passed on to me. It wasn't that he browbeat anything into me. It was just the atmosphere and the stories he told me that drew me into Republicanism.

Another intriguing influence on my Republicanism came from my mother's connection to a woman we called 'Mum Fay', who was a regular visitor to our house. She was my grandmother's sister or cousin, a lovely lady. It turned out that 'Mum Fay' was related to Tom Williams, an IRA Volunteer hanged in Crumlin Road Gaol in 1942. In fact, she was the last visitor to see Tom Williams before he was hanged. So that was always an important memory in our home. My mother remembered Tom Williams, and anytime she heard the song about Tom Williams she would always end up in tears. That was the kind of atmosphere I grew up in.

Childhood Memories

There were three children in the family: my younger brother, Frankie, and my older sister, Betty, with me in the middle. Only five years separated the three of us. We lived with my grandfather, Johnny Doherty. The Dohertys were originally from the Docks area, and during the Second World War they came up to Glenard and squatted. They eventually got the house in which they had been squatting.

My immediate family lived in Highbury Gardens. It was a great boxing street. We had Jimmy McAreavey living facing us. He was the legendary Freddie Gilroy's manager. Freddie was an Ardoyne man who boxed in the Melbourne Olympics in 1956 and was the first Irishman to win the Lonsdale Belt. John Duffy lived two doors above us. He was Freddie Gilroy's assistant trainer. Ernie Regan lived two doors beneath us. He was the first boxing promoter in Belfast and was probably one of the first people in Ardoyne to own a telephone. They were all referred to as our 'aunts and uncles'. This had nothing to do with family connections, but more a reflection of the kind of close-knit street in which we lived. Jimmy and Big John also ran the John Bosco Boxing Club, so naturally enough we all joined the boxing club. Great memories.

Sonny Liston became World Heavyweight Boxing Champion in 1962 when he knocked out Floyd Patterson in the first round. The following year he visited Belfast, and we were totally amazed when he arrived into the John Bosco Club on the Friday night, along with a photographer from *The Newsletter*. For some reason he took a shine to me, and there were photographs published in the *Belfast Telegraph* and *The Newsletter* of me sitting on his knee. I was ten years of age at the time. There was another one of him holding a punchbag for me. That was the type of loving and happy childhood that I enjoyed.

Along with boxing, we also had a great soccer following in Highbury Gardens. We had our own street team. A guy called Jim Rocks lived in Holmdene Gardens. He was our player manager. Although we were young, we all had jobs. I actually had two jobs, one as the milkman's helper in the morning and the other a paper round at nighttime. I got paid the equivalent of £1.50, about 30 shillings, from the milkman, but to earn that I was up for work at 5 a.m. through to 9 a.m. seven days a week, but the 30 shillings made it worthwhile. I actually gave that to my mother. I told her that I would keep the paper round money, which was one pound. My mother was so proud of me, but what she didn't know was that I also had my own wee private paper rounds. I was getting £1 off the paper man on the Ballygomartin Road, but I was also probably getting £2 from my own private round. My mother was getting short-changed!

I went camping with friends every year, but it was the football that we were really into and we wanted to own a set of jerseys for the team. Jim Rocks was the treasurer, and he decided that we would all put together a shilling every week towards the football rig. We thought that was a great idea and the collection went on for months. There were only two sports shops in Belfast at that time, the Athletic Stores in Queen Street and McGlade's in Gresham Street. One day Jim made an announcement, 'Listen, McGlade has got us a football rig. Now all I need to know from you is that it is alright to get it.'

We were delighted. 'Sure, go ahead and get it. Bang away.' We arrived in the Ballysillan Playing Fields for our next game, anxious to see our new rig. Up comes Jim with the big bag with the rig in it. He opened it and put the jerseys out onto the grass. Pure orange! It was that bright an orange that even an Orangeman wouldn't have worn it! He said, 'But I got it cheap!'

'Maybe' we replied, 'but who would wear it?' It ended up that we did eventually wear it! Those were great times.

School Life

I got on well at school. I actually passed the 11+, but I didn't go to grammar school as would have been expected. I had my own reasons for that. It may sound stupid now, but I was very much aware of the cost to my parents for me to go to St Mary's Grammar or to St Malachy's College. On top of that, the main factor was that all my friends were going to St Gabriel's, and that's where I eventually went.

I was in the 'A' class up until Third Year. Although I was small, I was a fairly good footballer for my age and my height didn't really matter. We got into the semi-finals of the Schools Cup and the prefects, rather through jealousy or whatever, decided that they would give us a run out in preparation for the big game. The semi-final was to be played on the Saturday morning, and the warm-up was arranged for the Wednesday after school.

One of the teachers took it upon himself to referee it, and the prefects were giving us a hard time, myself in particular. I remember thinking, 'If this keeps up, I am going to get hurt and miss the match on Saturday.' After a particularly hard foul, I decided that I had enough and left the pitch. I had a row with the teacher refereeing about leaving the pitch, but I told him that as it was after school I was going into the dressing rooms, whether he liked it or not. He grabbed me by the ear. I was wearing a pair of Tommy Doherty football safety boots with big toe taps on them and I hit him such a kick on the shin. It was just a reaction and I then ran on into the changing room.

Another fight developed ten minutes after I had left, and the rest of the team came into the dressing rooms. Of course, the word got around the teaching staff that I had 'assaulted' the teacher doing referee. I tried to explain to the other teachers what happened, but some of them decided to get their retribution through the strap, and some of it was pretty vicious. Some of the prefects intervened on my behalf, but it was not a pleasant experience.

The school chaplain also heard about the incident, and he decided to give me a thumping as well! I ran out of school and eventually got around to telling my mother what had happened. She of course then told my father. My father was well respected in Ardoyne. He wasn't big in height, but he was built like the side of a house. He was even-tempered most of the time and, in all honesty, he never once lifted his hands to us in the house. I told him what happened and all he said was, 'Fair enough.' That was as much as he said.

Next morning as I left for school, I noticed that my father was still in the house. This was not like him as he never took a day off work. I went on to school and into school assembly. As I came out of the assembly, I noticed my father with his arms round the chaplain's shoulders and he said, 'Listen, I have heard my son's version of what happened. It might be right. It might be wrong, but if he needs chastising, I will chastise him.' He then walked out, leaving the staff wondering what had happened.

Early Exit from School

At that time, if your fifteenth birthday was before the start of the summer holidays in June, you left school in June. If your birthday was after June, you left at Christmas. One day after the incident on the football pitch I was sitting in geography class, Class 3A1, and the teacher said to me, 'Young Donnelly, I need to see you.' When I walked up, he handed me a leaving kit, essentially papers you got when leaving school. I was due to take my Intermediate exams, so I told him that I was not due to leave until December.

My father had told me, 'You are going to get your examinations. If you don't manage that then you will get an apprenticeship, but you will get one of the two.'

I said to the teacher, 'You have me down to leave in June, but my birthday is not until August.'

He said, 'You better go and see the headmaster.' So up I go and rap the office door. The secretary told me to wait. I must have waited about ten minutes, but I hadn't a care in the world. It was a genuine mistake as far as I was concerned.

I went in and said, 'Is there a mistake here sir? I got a leaving kit here, but I'm not due to leave until January.'

He said to me, 'You are leaving son. You are either leaving or you are getting expelled. You assaulted a master.' That was it. No arguments. I was sent home.

There was no way I could tell my father that I had been thrown out of school, and I realised that I had from then until the end of December to find a job before he would find out what had happened. I hunted continuously, and eventually got a job as a plumber's mate with a firm called Central Merchants up in Musgrave Orthopaedic Hospital.

By this stage it was then safe to tell my father that I had got my apprenticeship. This was the beginning of 1967, and Feldon House had opened up their apprentice-ship centre. As an incentive they had promised employers £400 if they sent them an apprentice. So John Dowling, owner of Central Merchants, sent me there. Seven months into my apprenticeship at Feldon House, Central Merchants folded, but Feldon were obligated to get me a firm to complete my apprenticeship. I ended up with an apprenticeship with Rotary Mechanic, who had moved over from England. So, it all worked out fine for me.

Political Education

My father made no bones about being a Republican, but he didn't force his beliefs upon us. In 1968 I was seventeen, and I was aware of issues such as civil rights, the Vietnam War and the Israeli Six-Day War. This was all part of my growing up during the 1966 hippy phase. I got my apprenticeship with Rotary and was working in the Halls of Residence in Queen's University. I saw this group of students standing outside Queen's University protesting. I knew one of them, Frankie Murphy. He explained to me that the protest was about civil rights. This intrigued me. The people I was running about with were fairly intelligent. I got interested in what they were doing and went to a few protests and it rubbed off on me.

I remember vividly January 1969, the Long March to Derry: Belfast to Derry. The marchers were attacked at Burntollet. There had been rioting with the cops before that, but it didn't amount to much. Watching the attack on television, though, I realised that this just wasn't right. The protestors eventually reached Derry after being attacked at Burntollet Bridge by Loyalists and 'B' Specials, and then attacked again at Irish Street, leading to the Battle of the Bogside. I don't know how word got down, but after two days there was word that the people in Derry needed help. Riots then began in Belfast 'to take the heat off Derry'.

There was always tension around 12 July. It wasn't anything new in Ardoyne. The opening of the new boys' school at Somerdale for Protestants around 1965 was marked by a riot on the Crumlin Road between St Gabriel's and the new Somerdale School. It went on into the evening and eventually spilled over into the Savoy Cinema further down the Crumlin Road that night and a young Somerdale boy was stabbed.

Tension was also a constant reality in working-class areas such as Ardoyne because of issues such as gerrymandering or 'one man, one vote'. This tension was magnified by the high level of unemployment in Catholic/Nationalist areas, largely due to pure discrimination against Catholics. When Catholics applied for a job, the question asked after giving your name and address was the one about which school you went to. This of course defined you as a Catholic or a Protestant, and you were guaranteed not to get that job. That played a big part in people realising the depth of sectarianism and discrimination. Discrimination also played a major part in the distribution of housing. It was always there. Society needed that spark, and the Civil Rights Movement provided it.

Ardoyne Riots

I remember the word went around that we need to help the people in Derry. They were being besieged and we needed to start rioting. To be honest, that was brilliant news to us. I think it would be fair to say that most people who were rioting probably didn't have a political bone in their body at that stage. This was their way of getting their pound of flesh back. The rioting went on from January 1969 right through to the summer period. They would call it 'recreational rioting' these days. They were bad. They were really bad. I was also terrified of getting caught, as there was a mandatory six-month prison sentence. Nobody wanted that, but I also really worried about getting caught because of the physical beatings I would get from the cops, and there were people who got those bad beatings.

There had been a riot near enough every night. The whole idea was to get the RUC and the 'B' Specials into the area and attack them. To be honest, it didn't take much to get them to come into the area. They played on it as much as we did. Some people probably had political motivations and could see a bigger picture than we could, but, to be honest, we just enjoyed the rioting. This was our way of getting our own back and we were doing it in our own territory.

I remember the night of 14 August when Neil Summers lost his leg. I didn't actually see it, but I was quite close to the place where it happened. The whippet (armoured car) came up Butler Street and I was at the junction of Fairfield Street and Butler Street. During a riot you lifted anything you could get for ammunition. One of the things available for lifting was the cast iron gratings. These were often broken or even missing altogether. I think what happened to Neil was that when he was running up the street he didn't notice the grating cover missing. He went down through the grating and rolled over and his leg was badly injured. The whippet, along with the 'B' Specials and the RUC, made a beeline to him. Nobody knew at the time that it had happened. The crowds were scattered around different parts of the district but eventually the news about Neil spread. At the time somebody said his leg was severed clean off, but I didn't get close enough to see that. Regardless, as a result of what happened he did lose his leg.

Anyone who lived on the Crumlin Road or the top end of Hooker Street/Brookfield Street/Herbert Street lived in a war zone. There didn't have to be riots for them to get attacked. They were getting attacked and windows broken on a nightly basis at this stage. The word 'sectarian' wasn't in our vocabulary then. It was 'them

Orange bastards attacking us again!' That was it. I hadn't even heard the word 'sectarian'.

There were three bars on the main Crumlin Road: Kilpatrick's, Logue's and, further down, the Wheatfield. They closed at 10 p.m. on a Saturday night. You could set your watch to it. As soon as they closed there would be fights. Guys coming out of one of the pubs would congregate and this would be followed by the police coming down the Crumlin Road. The police would be attacked and next thing the Loyalists from the other side of the road would get involved. It was all stone-throwing in the early stages. There were also some bad fights in which people got injured, some badly injured through being stabbed for example, or darts being thrown, but that was an ongoing occurrence. It would be fair to say that even on the night of 14 August nobody expected shots to be fired. It was just an ordinary night of rioting that had been going on for six or seven months. This was going to be no different – until the shooting started.

In hindsight, I had been given a forewarning about what was about to take place. I was serving my apprenticeship, and every Wednesday night I was given a list of fittings to bring up to the job on the Thursday. I had to go down to the workshop in Howard Street, which runs between the Shankill and the Falls. This was also the place from where we collected our wages. I went in on the Wednesday night (13 August) and handed the list over to the guy behind the counter. To this day I don't know his full name, but he was a big Protestant man called Big Sammy, from East Belfast. I handed him the list of fittings and said, 'Sammy, I will get them in the morning after I get the boys' wages.'

He said, 'Don't you be coming down here in the morning.' I looked at him but paid no heed. I got down the next morning, Thursday 14 August, at about 8.20 a.m. I rang the bell to get the gate opened and Big Sammy came out.

He just grabbed me and turned me round, saying, 'I told you not to come here this morning', and he pushed me away. I didn't know what to do, and I rang the bell again. He came out and said, 'I told you to fuck off. Now I mean that!'

I have often thought about that incident. Big Sammy had obviously known beforehand about the sectarian violence and intimidation that was about to erupt, and he was trying to protect me.

The Night of 14 August

That night I finished work and as we had just gotten paid, I had ten shillings in my pocket. That was a fortune then! I was almost seventeen and didn't drink, but I loved the atmosphere in the clubs in Ardoyne. I went up towards the League but didn't manage to reach it. I got as far as the Hibs club in Herbert Street, and the fighting had already started. A bunch of guys were round the back of the Hibs, so I went to join them. You could walk from there up the back of Butler Street to Elmfield Street. So I went up there with a few guys to see what was happening up at the League.

It was still early evening, I think around 8.30 p.m., when the rioting started to get really bad. At about 9.30 p.m. we were standing at the corner of Butler Street and Elmfield Street, what we called 'the League Corner'. We were making petrol bombs when we heard the shooting, although at first we didn't realise that it was shooting, 'What's that?' someone shouted. It was a really loud bang. Somebody else said, 'That's shooting.' Then there came a long prolonged burst of gunfire and it was really loud. It amazed us. Everybody ran down towards Herbert Street. As we were running down, there were people running up Butler Street and shouting, 'What's happened? What's happened?' Others were answering, 'The 'B' Men have opened up!'

At first it was a bit of excitement. We were making plans as to where we would attack them. Would we go up to the Crumlin Road? Would we go down to Chatham Street/Herbert Street? Then news came through that a man had been shot dead. I couldn't believe it. People were calling each other liars to be honest: 'You shouldn't be saying that! Don't be saying things like that!' But it was true. Sammy McLarnon had been shot dead.

What I also remember about that night was the number of people on the streets. You could hear them before you could see them – this mass of people heading along the Berwick Road. They appeared to be coming out of every street in the district and coming towards Berwick Road. I remember thinking, 'This is great. More people coming to help us.'

A rumour had also been started that the monastery had been attacked, and people with no previous interest in getting involved in the rioting were now out on the streets on hearing that the monastery had been attacked. Whoever started that rumour, deliberately or not, it worked as a great strategy because next day it wasn't just the young people out rioting. Everybody was out. Along with this, Michael Lynch had also been shot. People you would never have expected were out on the streets as the whole community came together. The growing fear and tension had gelled us together.

I was one of what later came to be known as 'the so-called long-haired ones'. We were all around sixteen to eighteen years of age. All of us had long hair, and most of us wore sky-blue denims that sometimes appeared to be white. The older generation, people maybe in their twenties or thirties, resented the fact that we had long hair. We were seen as sort of 'layabouts'. 'Look at the state of that. Long hair like girls!' We had our beetle boots, our kaftans, our polo necks. I remember my father saying, 'Look at the state of you'.

'I am trying to grow a beard!' I would reply, to which he answered,

'Watch it doesn't trip your soup!' It would have taken me ten years at that rate to grow a beard!

We might have been the butt of jokes for jags, but in those early fearsome days of August 1969, it was 'the so-called long-haired ones', as described by Bobby Rogers in his song about the violent attacks of those days (called 'The Long-Haired Ones'), who 'stood steady and true.'

I particularly remember the hijacking of the buses, mainly because of my father's reaction. The word had come that the buses had been hijacked from the bus depot and the next thing I knew about it were the buses coming down Estoril Park. My father would have been about 47 or 48, a fairly young man, and he couldn't get to work that morning. It was one of the few days that he didn't get to work. He was just floating about. I remember him watching the buses and the windows being smashed. He went mad at that, 'What are you doing? That could stop a bullet and you are breaking them'. Every street was covered by the buses. It was amazing. That wasn't done by the IRA. This was the community pulling together.

Role of the IRA

The IRA was not behind the rioting. It was a spontaneous reaction by the people themselves. It was an act of preservation. People were being forced to answer questions very quickly. What can we do to defend ourselves? What do we need to do? What is possible to do? Making use of the buses was one of the suggestions. We have ready-made barricades here.

To be honest, I remember the frustration of my father at the time that the IRA was not to be seen. There were individuals there like my father, whom everyone considered a Republican, but there was no organised Republican structure in the district. The fact that there was no structured IRA was difficult for Republicans to live with.

Friday 15 August

I remember Friday 15 August, around 7 p.m. It was total daylight. My father heard that some people had been trapped in Brompton entry beside the Millie Dam. He went along with a neighbour to find out what was happening. He stopped when they got to Brompton Park/Etna Drive and looked up the street. A bullet struck a wall some 15 feet above them. The shot had come from a part of the nearby mill in Flax Street that had railings round it and protruded up from the rest of the building. It was either a 'B' Special or UVF man carrying out the shooting.

I also remember the next day when the Brits came in. Everybody was out on the streets. My father just walked round to the house. I said, 'It's great that at least the Brits are in!'

He replied, 'That's not a good thing son. Once they are here, it will be hard to get rid of them.'

We then had the 'honeymoon period' when the local community reached out to the Army to welcome them. I don't blame the people at all. Then came the time of the split within the IRA. My father, a lifelong Republican, washed his hands of everything. He was remembering what had happened during the Civil War and refused to take sides, although at the end of the day he became a staunch supporter of Adams and the Provisional IRA. I can understand why the split came about. The Republicans within this area got abuse and they took the abuse. Veteran Republicans like Billy McKee, Prionsias MacAirt and people of that ilk knew that the structures then existing in the IRA were not good enough and that we needed a new IRA.

I am told that there were about 40 Volunteers in Ardoyne around the time of the split in January 1970. Ardoyne predominantly went with the new Provisional movement. There was also a sort of an autonomous group alongside the district structures of the IRA who went about getting weapons for Ardoyne along with the Citizens' Defence Committee.

Citizens' Defence Committee

The CDC played a pivotal role in the defence of the district. They were brilliant. You expected Republicans to behave like Republicans and to take proactive measures, and to take roads that Republicans could go down. The CDC were guys who were not outwardly Republican or who you would not put down as Republicans, and they had only one thing in mind – defend the district. 'This is not going to happen again, and this is what we are going to do to make sure it doesn't.'

The CDC consisted largely of GAA members. When Ardoyne Defence was mentioned, GAA came into our heads right away, and I still have that thought today. If people wanted to get into the Citizens' Defence, they went to the GAA. If they wanted into the IRA, they went to an IRA source. The CDC people played their part when attacks on the district happened on a regular basis.

The CDC were a different kettle of fish. The IRA had not really gone on the offensive against the Brits at this time. So far, most actions had been in defence of the area when it came under attack. There were guys involved with the CDC whom you would never have associated with the IRA.

Journey into the IRA

I am a firm believer that Republicanism is in your genes. 1969 hadn't so much an effect on me. I was still serving my apprenticeship, sitting back and reflecting upon what was happening around me. I remember the words of my father, and I could slowly see the circumstances changing. One thing he said to me was, 'Do you notice where their guns are pointing, son? They are lining up on the Crumlin Road and their guns are pointing down towards us!'

Saturday 27 June 1970 marked a major change in the dynamics of Ardoyne. There had been a prior warning that, due to events like the Orange parade in West Belfast, there was a possibility that trouble would spread over to Ardoyne. The IRA on that day was ready for the attack, and when the attack happened it was able to defend the area. Three Loyalists were shot dead and the attack was repelled.

I watched events unfold in August 1969 and could see people treating the Army well. I thought that was fair enough, but then I saw events turning after 27 June 1970, when those same soldiers began to wreck houses in the search for weapons. I could see that they were taking a completely different attitude and being obstructive. The ordinary squaddies were doing what they had been ordered to do, but there was a realisation that they were out to take our only source of defence.

This was what we had to do to defend ourselves, and the Army was taking weapons off us and leaving us open to what had happened only a few weeks earlier. Rioting then started against the Brits, who in turn started firing CS gas. The honeymoon period soon ceased, and the Republican movement was now being overwhelmed with recruits, including myself.

I was subsequently charged with planting a bomb in British Oxygen, up at the top of the Castlereagh Road. In those days, when the police arrested you for an incident you were interrogated in the nearest barracks to where that incident occurred. As it happened, I was taken to Castlereagh. This was before it became famous for being an interrogation centre. They gave me a bad time, but I refused point blank to make a statement. This was something my father had drilled into me so as not to incriminate myself. I was charged, and was on remand for about 11 months or so before eventually the charge was dropped.

I was then interned in 1973. I remained interned until the end, when I was the second last internee to be released. I got married on 17 December 1976. When I came back from my honeymoon, my aunt Betty said, 'The RUC were round looking you.'

'That's par for the course,' I replied, and it didn't really bother me. I didn't really stay out of the house or anything, but on 4 January 1977 I was arrested and taken in for questioning. At this time, the sectarian assassinations were going haywire, and a group of detectives focused solely on sectarian killings were based in Tennant Street.

The jeep opened after a short time and I knew that I wasn't in Castlereagh Barracks as I had expected. I then realised it was Tennant Street station. I had an idea the charge was something fairly serious. They held me for five days and they weren't very nice, to say the least, but I still didn't make a statement. They charged me anyway. The way I was looking at it, at that particular time, was that this was internment by demand.

This is when I met Bobby Sands. I didn't even know he existed before that. I had been through the internment period; I had been arrested in 1971 or 1972; I was remanded to the Crumlin Road gaol and I thought, 'same old, same old!' But it wasn't. The screws' attitude was distinctly different. It was 'Call me sir!' Well that wasn't happening as far as I was concerned. I remember the particular screw – who eventually turned out to be fairly friendly with me, but on that particular occasion he grabbed me like a wet rag: 'When I shout "shite" you stand on the shovel!' Those were his exact words.

I saw the governor and he gave me all the old spiel, and then he said, 'You are going to "A" Wing.' As soon as I went through the circle in 'A' Wing, there were two gates with a screw in between the gates. I went in and just looked to my right and saw this guy with long hair and a leather jacket and pair of jeans. I thought nothing of it. The screw was signing me into his book, and he says, 'You are in Cell 15. Take your gear up there.'

As I walked up this guy came over to me and asked, 'Jackie Donnelly?'

I said, 'Aye'.

He said, 'The boys in "C" Wing were talking about you. Sam Faulkner told me that you might be coming to "A" Wing. I am Bobby Sands. I am OC of the wing.'

He talked to me for less than an hour, and he was explaining to me about the criminalisation policy that the screws were trying to implement and that if I got sentenced I would be going to the H-Blocks. He had such an air about him. It is easy to say now, but he gave me confidence, and I had never met the guy in my life before: 'You are not on your own here. We are in this together and we will all pull together.'

Bobby was very inspirational. I was in for about six months when that second charge was also dropped. I was in for a total of eight or nine years, and I had no convictions. When I heard that Bobby was going on hunger strike, I had no doubt in my mind that if it came to the point that this guy would go the whole way.

I was never a 'blanketman', because I got charges dropped in January 1977. Kieran 'Header' Nugent was sentenced in March and he became the first 'blanketman'. I was out of gaol by then, but I was arrested again under the 'paid perjurer system' due to allegations by the paid informer Christopher Black. I was one of the lucky ones. I didn't know Black. I hadn't a clue who he was. I remember about two or three months before when I was in Castlereagh and one of the Branch men turned around and said, 'See the next time you come in Jackie, you are not going out. We will verbal you if we have to.' (To say that I had admitted committing an offence.)

I remember being arrested that morning and going into Castlereagh. These two Branch men came in and didn't even introduce themselves. They sat there, and they actually had holiday brochures in their hands. They were talking as if I wasn't there. I thought, 'This suits me'. After about five or six hours, a rap came to the door of the interview room and one of them walked out. When he came back in, he went over and whispered to the other guy. The two of them stood up and went to either side of the door. One of them opened the door, and this guy, uniformed and with all the braids, walked in. He stood to one side and then this face appeared. It was grey. I am not talking about his hair. His face was a grey colour. The penny hadn't dropped for me yet, but the guy with the braid said, 'Do you recognise anyone in this room?'

And a shaky face said, 'Yes.'

'Who do you recognise?'

'I recognise John Jackie Donnelly.'

'Do you know John Jackie Donnelly?'

'Yes.'

'How do you know John Jackie Donnelly?'

'He is a member of the IRA.'

'Out!'

This all took place in fifteen to twenty seconds. I was sitting there thinking, 'What was all that about?'

Christopher Black's name never even came up.

'Jackie, you are not going home son,' said the Branch man. 'That is one of your comrades who has decided that he is going to tell everything he knows about everybody.'

I was sitting thinking, 'Well, if I don't know him, then he doesn't know me.' They threw me down into the holding cell, and never came back near me for five-and-a-half days. They held me for another three days and then said, 'We are going to charge you. We are going to read you these rights and then you are being charged and brought down to Townhall Street. You are being charged with being a member of the Provisional IRA.'

I thought, 'Is that it? That's not too bad like!'

The logic behind that was getting informers like Christopher Black to only tell things that they could corroborate. If he had said that there was a shooting incident at Flax Street, they would make sure that it was down in the books that there was a shooting incident at Flax Street. Christopher Black's problem, as far as I was concerned, was that he didn't know me, so he couldn't prove anything against me. Despite this he said that I was a member of the IRA. That was the only charge against me.

On Trial

My trial lasted eight months, but they were the longest eight months of my life. I tried to sleep through most of it in court, but we were found guilty anyway. Donald Deeny was my defence barrister, and he went on to become the high sheriff of Belfast afterwards. He called down to my cell after we had been found guilty and were about to brought up to be sentenced. He said, 'Jackie, I need a few details.'

I asked, 'Like what?'

He said, 'Things like your age; how many children you have.'

I said, 'You already have this information. What do you need that for?'

He replied, 'This is for your mitigation.'

I asked, 'Mitigation for what?'

He replied, 'Mitigation for you.'

I said, 'Donald, hold on a second. We have spent the past eighteen months saying that he was telling lies. You are telling me now that because Basil Kelly [the trial judge] has found us guilty, that we are going to say, "Alright, we have been saying the past eight months that he is telling lies, but now that you have found us guilty will you go easy on us?" That's not happening. I don't want you to put mitigation.'

There were over thirty of us waiting to be sentenced. I was the last in the line. Then the magistrate, Basil Kelly, got up and asked, 'Representing John Donnelly?'

Donald Deeny got up with his folder, and I was just uneasy with his manner. I then got up and said, 'I told you that I do not want mitigation.' I sat down. He just dropped his glasses.

Basil Kelly looked after me and said, 'Six years for membership.'

Donald Deeny said to me, 'If you hadn't opened your mouth, he probably would have given you a suspended sentence.' But sure, that was the way it went.

Family Tragedy

On a personal basis I have no problem with that. I was fully aware that there was a price to be paid. I was one of the fortunate ones. So many guys got arrested, but so many also got killed. That's the long and the short of it. I was one of the lucky ones who got arrested. My brother wasn't so lucky. I personally paid a terrible price that way with my brother being killed. It still has an effect on me to this day. Dinny Brown and Jim Mulvenna and I were very close friends. We actually drank together, and I was with them an hour before that tragic incident. It is the price that other people have paid that has an effect on me. I am personally at peace with what happened to me.

Dinny and Jim, along with Jackie Mailey and my younger brother, Frankie, knew the possible consequences of what they were involved in. The same as any Volunteer in this district. Unfortunately, there were times when the worst possible consequences did happen. They should not have happened regarding Dinny, Jackie and Jim, and possibly it should not have happened with Frankie either, but that is neither here nor there. It happened. It's their families who I feel for. When I look at their families then I see who really paid the price. They paid a terrible price. Jackie's wife, Rosemary, was six months pregnant when he got killed. My brother's daughter, Frances, never saw Frankie, her daddy. If you look at Frances Donnelly, you are looking at our Frankie. Sometimes that makes me stand back. That's the price I paid, standing watching the price that they paid, and continue to pay to this day.

The way I got the news about Frankie's death was bad and, strange as it might sound, it was bad probably for all the right reasons. I was living in Etna Drive when the shooting happened. I had heard that there was an IRA operation going to happen early in the morning. When I got up that morning, though, it had gone out of my head. Then I heard an explosion, not a massive one, but something like a dull thud. Then I heard people running in Etna Drive. I took my time and got dressed. I said to my wife, Kathleen, 'I am going up to see what happened.'

As I headed to my cousin Eddie's house further up in Etna Drive, I saw the Brits across the bottom of Northwick Drive. I saw two particular Brits, who would normally have gone out of their way to give me a lot of abuse, standing at the bottom of Northwick. I noticed them looking at me and then turning away. I thought nothing of it at the time. I looked up Northwick and saw what seemed like a wall of people. I couldn't see past them, but I did see the light of the ambulance. I went on up and into Eddie's house. There were at least three, maybe four, people there. I asked them, 'What happened?'

They said, 'We are not sure.'

I asked. 'Is it Loyalists or what?'

'We are not sure.' I honestly thought nothing about it because the subject was then changed.

I then remembered that I had a set of keys that I had to give to a bloke. I said, 'Listen, I am going to head on down.' I walked out, and by this time all the crowd was away. I had stayed about half an hour in Eddie's, and as I walked down Etna Drive I saw Jim Duric, and I think it was Frankie Kane who was with him. Jim stopped when he saw that it was me approaching. 'Alright Jim?' I said.

He replied, 'You don't know, sure you don't?'

'Know what?' I said.

'That was your Frankie and Lawrence Montgomery who were killed this morning,' he said.

That's how I found out that my brother had been killed. I was totally shattered. What annoyed me, although they did it for good reasons, was that nobody had told me when I was in the house. To be honest, although Eddie and I are very close, I have never asked him why he never told me. What happened after that wrecked me.

At about eleven o'clock that morning, I thought I better go up to see my aunts Betty and Margaret to see how they were after getting the news. My mother had died when I very young, about thirteen or fourteen, and they had reared us. I went up Highbury Gardens. An RUC jeep came speeding around the corner and literally pulled up in front of me.

'Jackie Donnelly?' he said. 'You have to come with us.'

'What do you mean I have to come with you?' I replied. 'Are you arresting me?'

'No,' they said.

'Well then I am not coming with you,' I said.

'You have to come,' he said. 'We need you to identify the body.'

'I am not identifying the body', I told him.

'If you don't identify the body, then we will arrest you', he said.

'Well you may arrest me, because I am not going with you to identify his body.'

Then a cousin and an uncle came out, Jackie and Fra Doherty. There was a big argument with the police and then my uncle Fra said, 'It has to be a next of kin, any next of kin to identify him. I will go and identify him.' They went off then to identify Frankie's body.

The reason I did that was because I had been talking to Aldo Brown and Pat Mailey a while before our Frankie had been killed. They had told me that when they went up to identify the bodies of Jackie Mailey and Dinny Brown, the police had messed them about. First, they showed Pat the body of Dinny Brown, then Jim Mulvenna and then Jackie Mailey. They then showed Aldo the body of Jackie, then Jim and then Dinny. There was no way I was going to allow them to treat my family like that.

I am at peace in my mind about making the decision not to identify Frankie's body. I had seen our Frankie the night before, and that how I will always remember him, but that hurt me. It still hurts.

No Regrets

I can honestly say that I have no regrets. What I do hope, and I sincerely believe that it will come about, is that because of what happened, what people died for, a united Ireland will come. If not in my lifetime, certainly in the lifetime of my daughter or granddaughter, and I am under no illusion that if the IRA had not have mounted their campaign this would not be the case.

I remember back in 1973/74, a Belfast man called Tommy Taylor, who was OC of the internees, got us all together and said:

> 'Listen lads, we are sending these hankies out saying "Freedom '73" or "Freedom '74", but we have to be real about this. You have to get this into your head. Internment is not going to last forever, but you are not going to drive the Brits into the sea. We have to put ourselves in a position where the Brits will say: "Enough is enough. Let's talk about this."'

And that's what happened. The IRA did not enter talks through weakness. After two years of getting nowhere through talks, the IRA put a bomb in Canary Wharf and showed what they were capable of. The IRA was in a very strong position but it also realised and stated in 1977 that this was going to be a long war. What had to be taken into consideration was that our people were burned out by conflict. We needed popular support, but people were growing tired.

I often reflect upon my life and see it in all its different stages, but my reflection tells me that each stage was meant to be. It started with me rioting on the street, for whatever reason. It wasn't a political reason initially. It went in stages from there to how the district was nearly burnt out, people were getting killed, and there was no way of defending ourselves, until we found a way to defend ourselves. Through that way of defending ourselves it became a way of getting involved to get rid of whatever had caused this injustice in the first place. I think the sixteen- or seventeen-year-old Jackie Donnelly would have been at peace with that.

We were normal people who were forced into an abnormal situation. The vast majority coped well with it. Different people went in different directions, but I would say that about 95 per cent of the Republican population who went through gaol would never have seen the inside of a police barracks, never mind a gaol, only for the conflict. Ordinary people in an extraordinary situation, and part of that extraordinary situation led some of them to gaol, and some of them to death.

The Need to Remember

I am renowned for and very proud of my role in the building of the Volunteers' Wall in Herbert Street for those who died in action. The Republican prisoners took that on as a project. We did the fundraising and we got plaques made. I compiled and read out all the orations and I have made the point of mentioning both the men and the women of the district. People like Essie McDade, Ellen Doherty, Mary McLaughlin, Minnie Black. Without people like that we could not have survived. When the conflict was going hot and heavy, people were giving their beds up to let you sleep. People took care of you within this community and there is a plaque that states that we need to appreciate the help of the people who are no longer with us.

How will people remember me? All I know is that nobody will remember me for a bad thing. That's all that concerns me. Nobody will be able to turn round and say, 'Jackie Donnelly. He was a bastard!' Other than that, I am not worried. My family loves me. I am happy. I don't make enemies easy. Having said that, I can often say things as soon as they come into my head, but I don't mind apologising if I am wrong.

All in all, I am just one of those 'long-haired ones', an ordinary guy caught up in an extraordinary situation. As long as nobody has anything bad to say about me, I am very happy. It is extraordinary. You need to be an Ardoyne man to appreciate it. I have been all over Belfast, Derry, Tyrone, but Ardoyne people are a different breed altogether. If anybody's in trouble, then Ardoyne is in trouble. It's their trouble. If anybody needs help, as we have seen so often, the people pull together. I am not saying it doesn't happen in other communities, but it definitely happens in Ardoyne. I think it is a privilege to be able to turn round and to say, 'I am from Ardoyne.'

My daughter is 41 now, and is a teacher in Motherwell. She has been there for more than 22 years. Ardoyne is in Francine's heart to this day. One thing that Francine is certain about is that she doesn't come from Belfast. She comes from Ardoyne, and if people don't like that, then that's their problem.

The British Army at the top of Brompton Park initially welcomed with cups of tea by the community (above) (© Hugh McKeown)

Soldiers erecting a barbed wire barrier at the corner of Brookfield Street in an attempt to prevent further attacks (below) (© Jim Moreland)

An Ardoyne resident uses the seat of a hijacked bus to rest and read about 'Strife Torn Belfast' in the *Irish News* (© Jim Moreland)

Brian McCargo introduced Gaelic football and hurling into the RUC (Brian McCargo, Image bh012233, Bobbie Hanvey Photographic Archives (MS2001-039), John J. Burns Library, Boston College)

The Ardoyne under-16 football team that won the South Antrim Championship (Davy Wasson: back row, fifth from left; Pat Murphy: back row seventh from left; and his brother Ciarán: front row first on left) (© Ardoyne Kickhams)

A card issued to members of the Citizens' Defence Committee (CDC) (anonymous) (below left)

Brendan McFarlane beside the grave of Bobby Sands in Milltown Cemetery (courtesy of Peadar Whelan, *An Phoblacht*) (below right)

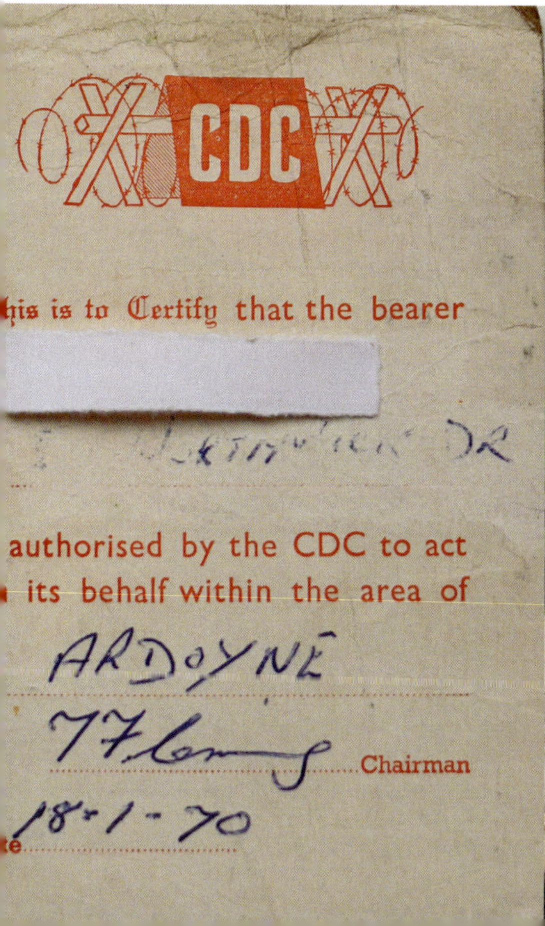

Edenderry Inn (known locally as Kils) (above) boarded up following stone-throwing attacks from Loyalists (© Hugh McKeown) and (below) burned out following petrol bomb attacks from Loyalists (© Jim Moreland)

Mothers make their way through the rubble of a night's rioting with Holy Cross Primary School in the background (© Jim Moreland)

Cars, buses and rubble form a makeshift barricade at the top of Herbert Street facing onto Crumlin Road (© Jim Moreland)

Burned out home at corner of Chatham Street and Hooker Street (© Jim Moreland)

The Wheatfield Bar the morning after being burned out (© Jim Moreland)

Mary McAleese and her husband, Martin, on a visit to her home parish of Holy Cross, Ardoyne (© Thomas McMullan, *North Belfast News*)

Loyalists gathering at Burntollet Bridge to attack the People's Democracy March to Derry (© Pacemaker Press)

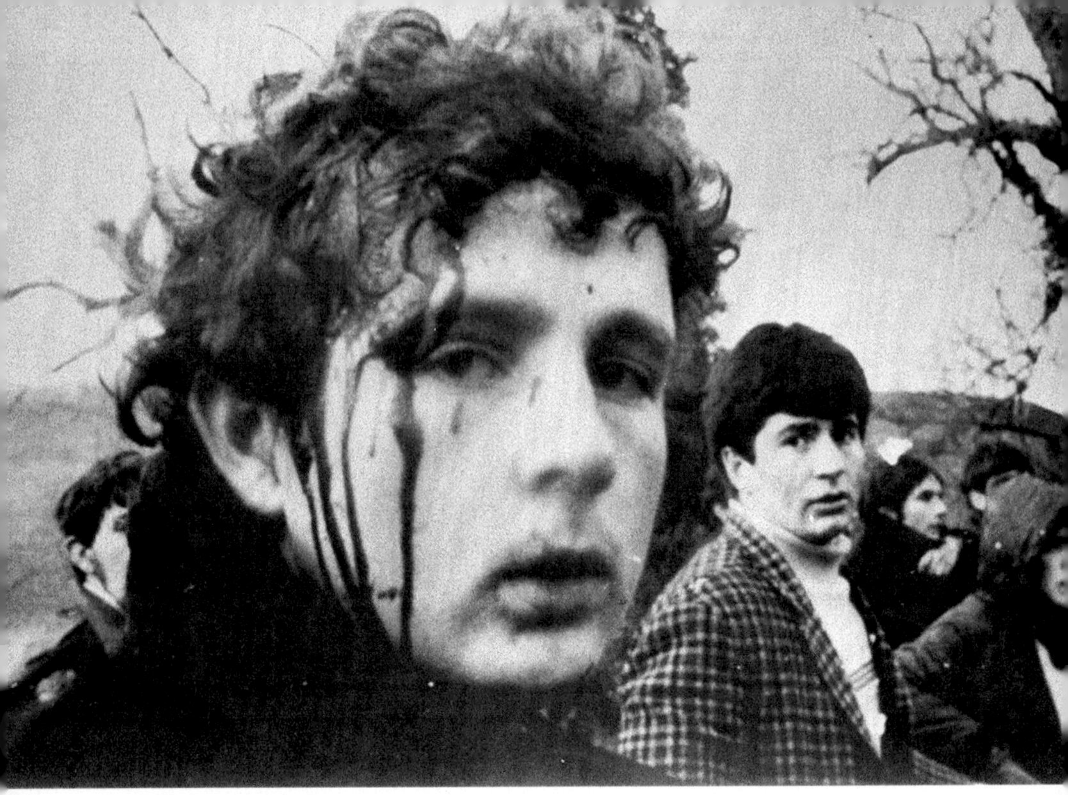

People's Democracy marchers attacked by Loyalists at Burntollet Bridge (© Pacemaker Press)

Pat Murphy on the right with his brother Ciarán on the left. Ciarán was murdered by Loyalists in 1973, at the age of seventeen (courtesy of the Murphy family)

9

Eugene McEldowney

Childhood Memories

I was born in Belfast in 1943 and grew up in Brompton Park in the north of the city, in what was then known as Glenard to differentiate it from the older area of Ardoyne. This was a new estate with gardens and bathrooms, and many of the people who lived there had been driven from their homes in other parts of Belfast in the sectarian rioting of 1935.

At the time I was born, the Second World War was raging and my parents often spoke of the Blitz – the Luftwaffe bombing raids which had devastated Belfast during the conflict. One such raid, at Easter 1941, had killed 900 people and injured a further 1,500. The effects of the war lingered into my early childhood. Outside our house, there was an air-raid shelter where people were meant to gather for safety during a bombing raid, although many people apparently preferred the sanctuary of the open fields around Ballysillan.

Another relic of the wartime period – rationing – continued into the 1950s. I remember my mother taking her ration book with her whenever she went shopping. Even children, like me, had to produce a ration stamp to buy sweets in the little shops that abounded in the area.

At the age of four, I was sent to Holy Cross Boys' Primary School in Butler Street, which I could see from my bedroom window. Beside it was an abandoned mill dam where we could catch sticklebacks, or 'spricks' as we called them. There was also a story that a young boy had drowned in the dam one winter while skating on the ice.

The other early impression I have is of the mills which dominated the skyline with their enormous chimneys. There were at least five mills in the Flax Street area and they provided employment for hundreds of girls and women from the Ardoyne district. This was welcome because many of the men in the area were unemployed. I remember the noise of the mill horns calling the girls to work. They made a loud wailing sound which could be heard all over the district. I can still picture the bands of mill workers marching down the street with arms linked and milk bottles filled with tea as they proceeded to work.

School was the first major challenge I faced. My mother had told me I was going to enjoy it. I was a big boy now and I would learn to read and write and count. So I was looking forward to the experience as she walked me down to Butler Street and handed me into the care of my first teacher – Nell Farrell, who lived in Chief Street.

The scene that met me should have put me off school for life. About a third of the boys were crying for their mothers. Another third were trying to escape out the door while Nell Farrell valiantly tried to restrain them. The rest of the class were sitting bewildered at their desks. I soon settled in and made friends: Joe Higgins, Kevin Shields and Frank McQuillan who lived further up Brompton Park, Gerard McMullen who lived in Holmdene Gardens, and Sammy McLarnon of Herbert Street who was shot dead in his home in August 1969.

I liked school and particularly enjoyed reading. By this time I was in possession of a library card and used to haunt the Oldpark Road library, devouring three or four books a week. Television hadn't arrived yet and I found reading books and comics a great way to pass the time.

The Christian Brothers

When I was eight, my mother decided to take me out of Holy Cross and enrol me in St Patrick's Christian Brothers' primary school in Donegall Street near the centre of town, which meant getting a tram to school. Later, my brothers, Gerard and Seán, would join me there. This was a much different environment to the one I had been used to. For a start, the brothers were mostly from the South – the Free State, as Northern Nationalists called it. They were firm disciplinarians and most of them carried a leather strap in the folds of their soutanes. But they had a reputation for being excellent teachers, which was why my mother moved us there.

They were also fervent Nationalists, very strong on the GAA and all things Irish. It was from the Christian Brothers that I got my first introduction to Irish history and the wrongs that the British had inflicted on Ireland down the centuries. And it was there that I learned the patriotic songs like 'The Croppy Boy' and 'Boolavogue', which I still sing to this day.

In due course I passed the 11+ exam, the 'qualifying' as it was called then, along with thirty of my classmates, which saw me transfer to St Mary's CBS Grammar School in Barrack Street. Here I met boys from all over the city but mainly from West Belfast, including some who would later become well-known, such as Gerry Adams and the businessman Paschal Taggart.

Off to London

In 1960, I passed my Senior Cert exams. By now I was totally bored with school and desperate to start earning money, which would enable me to buy smart clothes and go out with girls. So I headed for London, along with many thousands of young Irish teenagers, and got a job as a clerical officer in the British civil service. I was to remain there for the next four years.

I can still remember arriving at Euston Station on a warm summer evening with my suitcase in hand after a lengthy trip by boat and train. I was seventeen and had never been away from home before. I didn't know a single person in London. I was hungry and exhausted. I had a letter in my pocket from my new employers advising that accommodation had been arranged for me in Clapham. For those who don't know London, I should point out that Clapham is in the south of the city. Euston, where I had arrived, is in the north. The two places are miles apart. I asked a porter for directions and he answered me in a broad Cockney accent. I couldn't understand a word he said. So, I set off into the milling crowds, dragging my suitcase behind me. I was determined not to use the Tube underground train for fear that it might take me out into the countryside and I would be totally lost.

To this day, I don't understand how I managed to arrive at my destination. I can remember asking various passers-by and getting on and off a number of buses. But I did get there in the end and was warmly welcomed when I arrived. I was given a meal and a bed and fell asleep tired but happy, as they used to say in the best boys' adventure novels. 1960 was a good time to be in London. The British economy was growing strongly after the austerity of the post-war years. This was the era of Carnaby Street, Mods and Rockers, Mary Quant and the Beatles. There was a sense of optimism abroad that things would get even better.

Some time later I was living in a bedsit in Fulham in south London when one evening I happened to pass the offices of the local branch of the British Labour Party. There was poster in the window inviting members to join the Young Socialists, which was the junior wing of the party. My parents had always voted Labour;

indeed, two years earlier, in 1958, they had helped to elect Vivian Simpson, who held the Oldpark seat in the Stormont Parliament till 1973 for the Northern Ireland Labour Party. So I joined the Young Socialists. Although I didn't know it at the time, it was to change the direction of my life.

Two of the issues which were dominating British politics at this time were apartheid in South Africa and nuclear disarmament. The Second World War had ended only fifteen years before and many people were worried that another war might break out, which this time would involve nuclear weapons. I got involved in marches and demonstrations and was elected as a delegate to the annual conference of the Young Socialists. I also managed to get motions adopted for the annual conference calling for reform of the political system in Northern Ireland and the abolition of discrimination against the Catholic minority.

Membership of the Young Socialists wasn't all about politics. There was a lively social context and barely a weekend went past when someone wasn't having a house party or a barbecue. Invitations increased when people learned that I could sing. And they particularly enjoyed hearing Irish rebel songs, of which I knew quite a few by this time. One memory I have is of singing 'Kevin Barry' for the Lord Mayor of Fulham, who was a Labour Party nominee, in the local town hall.

Many of my friends in the Young Socialists held down well-paid jobs in the private sector, insurance companies and business institutions. They were earning far more than me. Slowly, the realisation began to dawn that one of the main reasons for this was that they were better educated. They had been to university and held degrees in various disciplines. I began to consider the possibility that I too might make it to university.

Getting to University

I had left school at seventeen with several O-level and one A-level subject. I made enquiries and discovered that to be sure of getting a place at university I would have to get further A-level qualifications. I investigated further and learnt that I could enrol in the East London College of Further Education for evening classes and sit another two A-level subjects. I chose English Literature and History. It would be a hard grind for the next nine months but it was possible.

So that was what I did. I cut back my involvement in the Young Socialists and buckled down to a rigorous regime of study after finishing work each day. I quickly began to enjoy my new regime, although there were some nights when I didn't crawl into bed till two or three o'clock in the morning.

It paid off. The following August, the results dropped through my letter box. I nervously opened the envelope and discovered, to my joy, that I had secured good grades in both subjects. I had already applied to Queen's University for a place in the Arts faculty. I forwarded the A-level results and began another period of waiting. But this time, I was more confident. In due course, the letter I was expecting arrived from QUB. I had been accepted for the course, starting in October.

I was about to embark on one of the most exciting periods of my life. I was back living with my parents in Ardoyne so I didn't have any rent to pay. I was also in receipt of a student grant from London County Council. And I had saved some money from my job in London. I wasn't wealthy but I wasn't poverty-stricken either.

Queen's University, when I arrived in October 1964, was a very lively place. There were numerous societies a student could join – debating clubs, drama groups, sports clubs, writing groups, political groups and the Queen's Folk Song Society, which I joined on my first day and where I was to make many friends over the next four years. I became a regular attendee at debates hosted by the New Ireland and the Literific societies, where I first came in contact with inspiring speakers like Eamon McCann, John McGuffin, Cyril Toman, Bernadette Devlin and Michael Farrell – figures who would feature prominently in the years ahead.

I also joined the student newspaper, *Gown*, as a reporter and later news editor. This was to shape the future direction of my career, although I didn't realise it at the time. I thoroughly enjoyed my spell on *Gown*. And there was an additional benefit. I became the paper's film critic, which entitled me to attend cinemas free of charge.

Of course, it wasn't all fun and games. The principal reason I was at the university was to further my education. In my first year, I studied English, History and Scholastic Philosophy, where one of my teachers was Cathal Daly, who later became a cardinal.

In my second year, I concentrated on English. I made some lifelong friends and came under the guidance of some wonderful teachers, including the poets Seamus Heaney and Philip Hobsbaum, both now sadly passed on.

Political Life Changing

But while Queen's was a vibrant environment for a young person to study, it wasn't divorced from the realities of life outside – particularly the political life of Northern Ireland. 1966 marked the 50th anniversary of the Easter Rising in Dublin and there were demonstrations and marches in many towns and cities in Northern Ireland, including Belfast, where a large parade took place in West Belfast.

In that same year of 1966, an important election took place in the West Belfast constituency for the Westminster parliament. An emerging politician called Gerry Fitt decided to contest the seat. It looked like he didn't have a hope but, nevertheless, I volunteered to work for him. He sent me into Hurst Street School in the heart of Loyalist Sandy Row as a personation agent. My job was to challenge anyone who I suspected was using another person's vote. This had always been a problem in Northern Ireland elections and gave rise to the slogan 'vote early and vote often'. In the end, I didn't have to challenge anyone for word had obviously gone out that Fitt had a personation agent in the station.

However, I was witness to one interesting episode. An elderly man came in and couldn't remember who he wished to vote for. Myself and the Unionist party agent were called together and the elderly man was asked to declare his vote.

He kept saying, 'The Labour man.'

'You have to give his name', the returning officer insisted.

The old man struggled for a few minutes and then said, 'Fitt. I want to vote for Gerry Fitt.'

I had the pleasure of placing his mark against Fitt's name. Later I wrote a song called 'They're voting for Fittsie, down Sandy Road Way'. I took it to the late Billy McBurney, who owned the Premier Record Shop in Smithfield and he recorded the song, which went on to dominate the record charts for several weeks.

The following year another significant event took place. The Northern Ireland Civil Rights Association was formed to campaign for reforms to the electoral system and the removal of discrimination against Catholics. It began a protest campaign of marches and demonstrations to draw attention to its cause and got the support of politicians like John Hume, Austin Currie and Gerry Fitt. Many of these demonstrations were blocked by supporters of the Rev Ian Paisley. The RUC was drawn in, with rioting often ensuing.

The Long March to Derry

The civil rights agitation found supporters in the university. A protest march was organised by students but the demonstrators were stopped at Shaftesbury Square by a counter-demonstration of Paisleyites from Sandy Row. The students sat down in the street and blocked the road. Eventually, they returned to the university and held a large meeting where they decided to form their own organisation – they called it People's Democracy.

On 1 January 1969 People's Democracy set off from Belfast City Hall to march to Derry. This event became known as the Long March. The students were harried by Paisleyites along the route and the march was disrupted at several points. I had missed the start of the march but was having a drink with a friend in the Spanish Rooms on Divis Street – a pub owned by a genial man called Jimmy Coyle, who lived on the Crumlin Road near St Gabriel's School and was later murdered by

Loyalists. I regretted missing the march but then had a brainwave. I rang Gerry Fitt MP and asked him if he could help me get there. He promised to send a car and a driver and two hours later myself and my friend were dropped off outside the town of Claudy in Co. Derry. We quickly joined the rest of the marchers and that night we were billeted in the hall attached to Claudy Catholic Church. Most of us slept well that night, little knowing what awaited us the following day.

We set out early the next morning for the final leg of the march into Derry city. We were in jubilant mood. Despite setbacks and disruptions along the way, we were now in reach of our goal. As we neared a place called Burntollet Bridge, the march was halted by the RUC and we were warned that there was a counter-demonstration ahead. The marchers decided to press on. In a few hours we would have entered Derry and achieved our goal.

Suddenly, I saw a hail of missiles, large stones and bricks descending on us. The people in the front rows of the demonstration were attacked by men wearing masks and armed with cudgels who were running down from the adjoining hillside. The crush meant that many marchers, myself included, were pushed off the road and over a ditch into a field.

When I picked myself up, several men armed with scythes and bill hooks were running into the top of the field. It was the most terrifying ordeal I have ever experienced. I was convinced I was about to be murdered. There was nothing for it but to try to escape across the river. Myself and others, including several young women, were compelled to wade waist-deep across the Faughan river in the icy water of early January. But our ordeal wasn't over. We straggled out onto a road and after half an hour several motorists stopped and gave us a lift into Derry city.

The scene that awaited us was one of devastation: the road was littered with more missiles, including smouldering petrol bombs. When I finally reached the sanctuary of the City Hotel, I was exhausted. I managed to get a lift to Dublin from a couple of RTE reporters and the following morning I hitchhiked back to Belfast.

Outbreak of Violence

Throughout 1969, the political situation continued to deteriorate. A major event occurred later that year that was to shape the future direction of Northern Ireland and leave its mark on Ardoyne in particular. On the night of 15 August disturbances broke out on the Crumlin Road at the bottom of Hooker Street. Loyalists invaded the district and burned dozens of homes. Several people were killed, including my schoolfriend Sammy McLarnon.

I was on holiday in Portstewart with my girlfriend and learned the terrible news next morning on the radio. I returned to Belfast and went at once to Ardoyne.

Thankfully, my mother's home in Brompton Park had not been damaged but in Old Ardoyne I met a scene of desolation. Houses were still smouldering and in Butler Street School families who had lost their homes were being billeted. A sense of shock hung over the district. But a grim determination seemed to have overtaken the people. I sensed that a seismic change was taking place and that things would never be the same again.

Later that year, I graduated from Queen's University and got a job in St Malachy's College teaching English. Several of my students were from Ardoyne. In 1970, I got married and my wife and I moved to live in Deerpark Road near the corner of Alliance Avenue. It was a mixed community with Catholics and Protestants living peacefully together. But the political situation was continuing to deteriorate and it exploded again on 9 August 1971 when the British Government introduced internment without trial. Of the 350 people arrested only one was from a Protestant background and that was my old friend from Queen's, John McGuffin, who was an anarchist and a strong civil rights supporter.

Internment

I can remember going around to Ardoyne later that day to find the place deserted and the burnt-out remnants of cars blocking the streets. People I knew were no longer living at home and had gone on the run. From then on my wife and I would lie in bed at night listening to the gun battles going on in the district. They became so frequent that we got to know the sound of the weapons being used – SLRs, machine guns, even shotguns. There was a sense that events were sliding out of control and that something very serious was taking place. Little did we know it would continue for another 36 years.

Moving to Dublin

I enjoyed working in St Malachy's College. I liked my students and my teaching colleagues. But my heart was in journalism. I had continued to write articles and get them published in the *Belfast Telegraph* and *Fortnight* magazine and the *Irish Times* in Dublin. In January 1972 I was offered a permanent job on the *Irish Times*. I got a small bedsit and went down to Dublin on Monday morning and returned on Friday night. In the meantime, I looked for somewhere to live in the city that was to be our new home.

In July 1972 we sold our house and moved permanently to Dubli,n but we continued to visit Belfast and particularly Ardoyne.

Innocent Children Become the Victims

Although I had moved to Dublin, I also kept an interested eye on events that happened in Ardoyne and I was particularly struck by the events that led to what became known as the Holy Cross Blockade. On 19 June 2001 a young Loyalist putting up flags on the Ardoyne Road in North Belfast claimed to have been attacked by Nationalist parents coming from the nearby Holy Cross Girls' School.

No one ever succeeded in getting to the bottom of the incident but it sparked off one of the most disgraceful episodes in the 30-year history of community conflict in Northern Ireland – the 12-week blockade of the school by Loyalist protesters.

In that protest, children as young as five years old and their parents were subjected to indignities and abuse that plumbed new depths of hatred and were to shock millions of television viewers across the world. The children and their parents were spat at, taunted, hit with bottles, stones, sticks and bags of urine, and, on one dreadful occasion, a blast bomb was thrown. Passionist priests from Holy Cross Church, who courageously accompanied them each day on their journey to school, were confronted with placards accusing them of sexual crimes and were cursed and vilified. The parents were physically attacked and beaten. The protest revealed, for all to see, the vicious sectarian cancer that could on occasion be at the heart of Loyalism.

For the parents, the issue was clear-cut from the outset. Their children had a right to education and they had taken this route to school for more than 30 years. To give in to the protest and take the longer alternative route through another school and across a football pitch to the back door was to accept that they were second-class citizens in their own land. Worse, it was to tell their children that this was so.

But what about the protesters? How could apparently rational adults behave like this towards innocent children? The Loyalist residents of Glenbryn, where the school is situated, did have grievances: they feared the decline of their own district in the face of the expansion of the adjoining Ardoyne area, and they were frightened by the growing confidence and assertiveness of their Catholic neighbours. There also seems little doubt that they suffered from stone-throwing attacks by Nationalist youths across the peace line between the two communities, although Catholic residents on the Ardoyne side also experienced attacks from Loyalists.

The initial protest seems to have been spontaneous and there is some evidence that the Glenbryn residents initially believed the police would prevent the parents bringing their children to school along the direct route. In some vague way they believed talks would result and their demands for a new wall to separate the communities would be conceded.

But the police took the decision that the children must be allowed to get to school and so the stand-off deteriorated into a test of wills between the parents and the protesters that was to last for three months.

What the protest also revealed was the absence of sophisticated political leadership on the Loyalist side, which must bode ill for the future. Some of the more perceptive among the protesters saw from the beginning that this was a battle they could not win. To pit Loyalist thugs against small children was unlikely to gather them much support. Yet the few moderate voices went unheeded. Like lemmings going over a cliff, the protesters persisted with the madness.

There is an uncomfortable gulf separating the two communities in Belfast and massive work that has to be done if Northern Ireland is ever to resemble a normal society. We can attempt to give a balanced account of the awful events that took place in this community, but there are occasions when balance is impossible because the behaviour is so vile that there can be no mitigation – and the siege of Holy Cross School is one such case.

Gone But Not Forgotten

I left Ardoyne in 1972 just as the Troubles were really kicking off. But I maintained a close interest in the district and its inhabitants and this was reinforced by regular visits to my family in Brompton Park.

To watch what was unfolding was heart-breaking for me. I knew the residents of Ardoyne to be hard-working people who wanted nothing more than to have a decent life for themselves and their children, and I defended them whenever required.

I went back to Ardoyne recently and it was a joy to see the transformation that has occurred in recent years – neat, terraced houses, well-kept gardens and the atmosphere of normality that surrounds the place. Of course, the air-raid shelters and mill chimneys that I remembered as a child have long gone. But the neighbourliness and the sense of community and basic human decency still flourish. Long may it continue.

10

Anne Tanney

Early Influences

I was born and brought up in Stratford Gardens, in the heart of Ardoyne. My mother had been reared near the city centre and had gone to school with the Mercy nuns. She also had an aunt who was a nun, so when it was time for me to go to school I was sent to Mercy Primary School, which was further down the Crumlin Road at that time. I then moved on to St Dominic's School on the Falls Road. My mother had been in the Legion of Mary, and so I also joined along with my sisters when I was ten years of age. We did our work for the Legion within Holy Cross parish, so we got to know Ardoyne well. The Legion put on carol services every year, and it was at one such service that I met my future husband, Pat. My sisters and I were part of the harmonising group in the choir, and one evening Pat came over and said to us, 'Excuse me, but you are putting us all wrong!'

My sisters were indignant and said, 'Who does he think he is?' Not a great start!

I was also working for Fr Myles at the time. He was then a young priest who had come to the parish to work with the youth. It was 1961, and I was sixteen years of age. My sisters and I all joined the Fianna Páiste (parish youth group) and helped him to organise a weekly dance in St Gabriel's School. It was what we would call 'a decent dance', as we had the Confraternity prayer at the very beginning, at the middle and at the end! I eventually qualified from the teacher's college at St Mary's Training College, and Pat and I got married and moved into Chief Street.

Awareness of Difference

Pat's maternal family, which included nine children, had come to live in Chief Street in 1917. They had moved into the city from the country when their business had failed. Chief Street was a street on the 'Protestant side' of the Crumlin Road, but half the street was mainly Catholic, so there was always that awareness of the Catholic/Protestant issue. There were street parties held at the end of the Second World War and again for the coronation of the new queen in the more Loyalist areas, but many Catholics in the area didn't really participate. We did not experience what could be described as a real animosity, just an awareness of the need to be cautious. Catholics played openly in the Woodvale Park and in Chief Street, staunchly Protestant areas, but it was always different when it came to 12 July, the Twelfth. We developed what could be described as a shell around us, an awareness of the need to be careful when we were living or moving in Protestant areas.

We were always conscious as Catholics of being 'up against it' when it came to applying for jobs. There was an election in 1959 and Pat went down to the nearest polling station in Tennant Street, which was in the middle of a Loyalist area. At that time you just went into the polling station and gave your name and address. The polling officer said, 'Oh, I am sorry, your vote has already been taken. We can get you a pink slip and you can use that as a vote, but that will only count if it is a dead heat in the election.' Pat remembers that as the time when he knew that things had to change.

Married Life Begins

Pat and I got married on 8 August 1968, and were unaware of any trouble at that time. We moved into the house in Chief Street that Pat's mother had been in since 1941. When Pat lived there, along with three other children, the house still had the outside toilet and one cold water tap. We decided that we could buy the house as a sitting tenant and we had plans to renovate, extend it and then maybe eventually sell it. The Civil Rights Movement was really just getting going, but we were so busy just getting ourselves sorted out. I had just got a job teaching in Holy Cross Girl's School in Chief Street in September 1968. It was one of three sites for the girl's school: Chief Street, the huts in Butler Street and the parish hall on the Crumlin Road. So we were living in Chief Street, where there was a row of Catholic houses facing the school. Pat was digging foundations, pouring concrete, putting in a new kitchen, putting in a new bathroom and we didn't have much time to be aware of much else happening around us.

Tension had been growing though since the beginning of 1969, starting with the attack on the Civil Rights March at Burntollet in January, and continuing with other attacks on Civil Rights marches in various other places. A momentum was growing through the summer period until Tuesday 12 August, when an Apprentice Boys' parade was stoned in Derry and the RUC attacked the Bogside. The trouble was not confined to Derry though. There were increasing episodes of stone- throwing at the police on the Crumlin Road and as a result we had started parking our van in the church grounds as it became so difficult to drive into Chief Street. During the week of the Battle of the Bogside, we were walking towards Chief Street and asked one of the young Catholic stone-throwers what was happening. He replied, 'We are taking the heat off Derry.'

Violence Hits Our Street

On Thursday 14 August we were preparing to go to Stoke-on-Trent in England for the wedding of my sister Nora, which was to take place on 16 August. In the early evening, a group of men wearing white armbands coming from the Shankill Road direction ran up Chief Street and tried to set fire to the Catholic school, which was across the road from our house. I had taught in the school until May, when it had moved to its current site on the Ardoyne Road. We heard breaking glass and shouting and went into the front bedroom upstairs and looked out. We saw the police talking to the men and heard one say, 'Go you on home. You're not really helping us.' The mob then moved on with the police towards the Crumlin Road. This was a determined attempt by Loyalist gangs to wipe out the Catholic population. We realised that Catholic houses were being attacked on the front of the main road, so we began to fill any containers which we could find from the renovations we had been carrying out on the house with sand and water. We put them in the front room as we were afraid that the mob would turn on Catholics who were living on 'their side of the road'.

Pat and I didn't really didn't know what to do. I went and sat on the floor of the bathroom and started to read a book of short stories! I used the bathroom as it had the smallest window should the house came under attack. Pat was busy putting more sand at the front bedroom window and at other places in the house. It became dark, but we didn't dare to put on lights at the front of the house and we were afraid to go to bed. At one point we heard gunfire and looked at each other in horror. We couldn't believe it. We prayed that nobody would be killed that night.

As the night got darker I thought that I would make a cup of tea, so I went out to the kitchen at the back of the house. The houses in Chief Street had no back doors into the entry behind. There was only a wall and a big drop to the entry and because we were extending the kitchen, we had taken the roof off the old kitchen and had a piece of polythene covering the kitchen instead of a roof. About two o'clock in the morning I was standing at the cooker under the polythene, with the tea pot in my hand, when I looked up and saw a man sitting on the yard wall. I thought that the Loyalists were coming in from the back. I kept my voice calm and said, 'Would you like a cup of tea?' While he was getting down from the wall, I hurried into the living room to get Pat but he was upstairs. I shouted up, 'Pat, there is a man here and I'm giving him a cup of tea.' Pat came tumbling down the stairs. He had been straining out the attic window trying to see what was happening on the Crumlin Road. I was surprised to see that Pat was wearing a helmet and was brandishing a stick with a spike on it. (He later told me that he had found the helmet and tent pole in the attic.) He rushed past me and then stopped and said to the man, 'Oh hello, do you want to get out the front door?' I was shocked.

Pat had recognised the young man as a Catholic who had bought a house further down Chief Street towards the Shankill Road. He had been crawling along the yard walls to try to get to a place of safety when he eventually reached our house. The young man refused tea, and as there seemed to be a lull outside he slipped out into the dark to try to make his way to the other side of the road. We hoped that he would get to the Catholic area safely.

The trouble seemed to quieten down, so we lay on top of the bed and Pat got up for work as normal early the next day. I had to get packed for the wedding as we had arranged to collect my family later to go to the boat. Pat came home from work early and went over to Butler Street to try to buy some hardboard from Marian Kane's father, Mr Toal, whose shop was inundated with people wanting hardboard to protect their windows. While Pat was boarding up the front windows, a van came screeching into Chief Street from the Crumlin Road with the windscreen smashed. The man driving it stopped near our house. He put his head down on the steering wheel and seemed to be sobbing, so we approached him and offered him a cup of tea but he said that he needed to get to safety, so we gave him a drink of water and he drove off towards the Shankill Road. Not long afterwards a young woman who was very distressed came along pushing a scooter. She did not seem to know where she was. She said that her husband was a policeman and she had thought that she would bring him a fish supper but the road was blocked and she was caught up in stone-throwing. We pushed her scooter into our passageway and brought her in for a cup of tea. When she had calmed down, Pat walked with her towards the Shankill Road and gave her directions to get into town.

We eventually managed to get ready for the boat to get to the wedding. We walked up to the church to get to our van and drove to my mother's house in Stratford Gardens, where my brother-in-law Bobby was waiting to bring us to the Liverpool boat. Bobby drove our van and we all piled into it. My mother sat in the front with Bobby while my father, Pat and I, and my two sisters sat on cushions in the back. There was no chance to get a taxi. We just managed to get out of Ardoyne through the barrier at Etna Drive. Bobby left us off at the boat and we went on board.

Army on the Streets

After the wedding breakfast on 16 August we were watching the television in the hotel in Stoke when we heard that the British Army were on the streets of Belfast. To be honest we were delighted, as we were sure that Ardoyne and other Catholic areas could not survive the concerted attacks of Loyalists and the police. We left to return to Belfast that night but sat up all night on the boat – that was three nights without sleep. We arrived home exhausted on 17 August and Bobby collected us at the docks. Things were much worse than we had thought. We could not drive into Ardoyne as there were buses across the top of the streets, so Bobby left Mammy, Daddy and my youngest sister at the top of Estoril Park and they climbed through a bus to get into the street to walk to Stratford Gardens.

We went with my sister Maire and Bobby to their home in Bray Hill, then drove our van back to try to get into our house. We couldn't get down the Crumlin Road so we drove down Woodvale, parked the van on Woodvale Road and walked down a flight of steps at the Woodvale/Shankill Road end of Chief Street. We were confronted by a large Army Saracen across the road and we couldn't get past. We spoke to the soldiers and explained that we actually lived in the street behind the vehicle, so they allowed us to climb through the Saracen from the back to the front and alight in Chief Street.

The place was a sorry sight. The Army was everywhere and soldiers were billeted in the school facing our house, which, of course, had all the windows boarded up. When we opened our front door, we found that the lights had been left on all weekend!

Fear of a Child

The next day, a little girl called Bernadette came to see me. Bernadette, one of my pupils, was about eight years old and was looking very tearful. She told me that, although she didn't want to, she would have to move to another school as her house on the front of the Crumlin Road had been burned. She described how 'guards' (the police), and other men were screaming outside her house and she and her family were terrified. Her mother had told the children not to be afraid and started to bless the rooms with holy water. Then the men began to break their windows and petrol bombs came into the room and the curtains caught fire. They all ran out of the house and her granny lost her slippers and got glass in her feet. They ran across the Crumlin Road and a kind Protestant woman took them into her house and sent for an ambulance. Then her daddy could not find her brother and thought that he was in the burning house and ran back into the burning house to look for him, but luckily the little boy had got out.

I listened to little Bernadette and did my best to comfort her. When she finally left, I sat down and cried and thought, 'My God. What kind of a society are we living in, when children have to go through this?' I wrote a letter to the *Belfast Telegraph* about Bernadette and her family but it was not published. I suppose there were so many other terrible tragedies at that time. I have never forgotten Bernadette Brady and I really hope that she and the other poor children who had to endure such trauma in Ardoyne and in other places during the Troubles were able to go on to have happy, peaceful and successful lives.

Defence of the District

There is no doubt that the young men who defended Ardoyne in August 1969 prevented more families being burned out, and more children like Bernadette losing their homes and loved ones. They deserve to be remembered. I know that the priests also did their very best to help their people, who were facing annihilation. Father Marcellus was instrumental in moving the buses from the depot to barricade the streets and other priests were also out in the streets with the people. It was the Catholic bishops who appealed for the Army to come to help the beleaguered Catholic community.

A few weeks ago we attended a Mass in Holy Cross Church to celebrate the lives of Samuel McLarnon and Michael Lynch, who were killed by the RUC on that awful night of 14 August 1969. Little did we realise when we had heard shooting that night that those two poor men had been shot dead. After the Mass we stood in the new car park at the side of the church and looked down to where our house had been in Chief Street and remembered what had happened.

For the people who lived on the front of the Crumlin Road and the streets running off the Crumlin Road opposite Chief Street the nights and days of 14 and 15 August were a nightmare. They suffered much more than we did. Fortunately for us, the attackers did not realise that there was a row of Catholic families living in Chief Street, on their side of the main road (the Protestant side), and because of that we were not attacked and our houses were not burned.

We were witnesses to what had happened though. It was a determined attempt by Loyalist gangs to wipe out the Catholic population, and we gave a statement to a representative of the Scarman Tribunal. The man who came to take our statement, though, told us that our testimony might not be used as we were still living in Chief Street, and it would have been too dangerous for us if they were to use it. It was as if we were living a different world, and the whole place just seemed to be going crazy.

Back to School

As teachers we were dreading going back to school in September. I think we were all so shocked, both teachers and children, that very little was said about the events during August. We tried to keep things as calm as possible. We had moved into a brand new school just six months previously, but now everybody was on edge. There was a whole list of children who hadn't come back after being moved out of the district that summer due to the violence. As we went down the class list, the school record had stated beside their names: evacuated, evacuated, evacuated. We tried to keep things 'normal'. We smiled at the children whenever we could, but everything had changed. Riots, rubber bullets, children being taken out of school. Fear was erupting all around us and we just couldn't believe it was happening.

A New Reality

A lot of our neighbours were moving out of Chief Street at that stage, but we stayed. We had just bought the house and obviously still owed the mortgage. When the soldiers first came in, they barricaded us off from the Crumlin Road, as they presumed that we were all Protestants on that side of the road. When we pointed out that there was a whole row of Catholics living in the street, they put another barrier at the other end of the street as well, so we ended up living between two barriers!

On one occasion, Pat's mother had visited us from Andersonstown and we were driving her home. When we got to the end of the street we were stopped by Loyalists at a barricade who interrogated us as to where we were going. We were diplomatic in the answers we gave so that we wouldn't be identified as coming from the Catholic end of the street. They gave us a card and said, 'Show this card when you are coming back this way.' The card was from a very reputable building suppliers firm in Agnes Street, and they had put a bit of red tape across it. They then asked us, 'What end of Chief Street do you come from?' We said, 'the middle!' Of course one end of Chief Street was mostly Catholic, so we decided that when we were coming home we would be like the Holy Family and take a different direction home.

The Violence Hits Home

Adults could rationalise what they saw happening around them. In Ardoyne particularly, people had experienced similar intimidation in the 1920s and 1930s, but for children at the time it was just beyond their comprehension. The Army arrived and things began to get back to what we thought was normality. We turned our attention back to the house renovations and we had a party in our house at Christmas 1969. Life was far from normal though. At various times we could hear a Protestant mob coming up Ohio Street, on the Protestant side of the road, to get into Herbert Street on the Catholic side of the road. We would go to bed, but heard the noise of the mob breaking stones, roaring and shouting.

In the summer of 1971 Pat had left his job and been successful in getting into St Joseph's Training College. We decided that we would travel around France, sleeping in our Morris Minor camper can. We had already done that successfully around Ireland, and decided to go to France to do the same. We were down near Bordeaux and I was speaking to a man in French. I said something about coming from Belfast. He said, 'There is terrible trouble in Belfast.' I thought that he was speaking about 1969, but we got a French newspaper, and on the front was a picture of Farringdon Gardens burning down. We then proceeded on across France to Lourdes. The pilgrims were praying for peace in Ireland and, of course, Pat and I were thinking that when we got home it would be all over. Out of the blue we met a group from Ardoyne who were on pilgrimage. Some of them had their homes burned down in Farringdon, but as they had already paid their money for the pilgrimage they had come on over to Lourdes. They didn't know though what had happened to the homes in Chief Street. We stayed in Lourdes for a few days and then went up to see the French Alps. When we eventually got back as far as London we phoned Pat's mother, who said, 'It's a pity they didn't leave your front door.'

I said, 'They didn't leave our front door?'

We then met my sister, who told us, 'Well it's like this. You have nothing left.'

We had left a house pretty well renovated and all intact. Following the introduction of internment though, Catholics were fleeing from homes in Protestant areas, and as a result of the subsequent violence Loyalists had looted our home, taking everything. I think the Travellers (i.e. people from the Travelling community) had salvaged our piano and a pile of books, but when we got home we found hundreds of Edel Quinn (Legion of Mary) leaflets blowing up and down Chief Street! That was one way of spreading the good news!

Our home was severely damaged, but Pat made a new front door and put a few planks across it, thinking that if the house was locked up it might deter people from entering it, but there was really no point. Before we had gone on holiday in July, Pat had gone down to the police station and said, 'I am going on holiday and will be back towards the end of August. We live in No. 36 Chief Street.' The officer wrote it down. When we came back, we were so angry at what we saw that Pat went back down to the police station and said, 'We were on holiday. I told you that we were going on holiday and you assured me that you would look after the house.'

'Oh really,' was the response, 'what damage has been done? How many yards of copper pipe have been taken?'

'I have no idea', Pat replied. 'Our house is wrecked, and I just want you to put it down on record.' He then got a detective or plain clothes policeman to come out, who noted down the damage. We ended up getting £200 for the total damage that was done but, despite the obvious mass damage to homes in the street, they wanted us to prove that the damage had been caused during a riot that had so many people involved in it.

We went down to see Johnson Solicitors because we were refugees and we were offered a flat in Andersonstown, but we were staying with my mother and decided to just remain there. On one Sunday afternoon in December 1971, we went round to see if there any houses for sale and we came across the house we are still living in today. It was overgrown and obviously uncared for, but it was in a quiet area and we saw it as a real possibility. We went down and saw the estate agent and then enquired about a mortgage, but as we still owed £800 on our mortgage for the house in Chief Street, a lot of money in those days, that proved a to be a big problem. However, we eventually moved into the house on 14 February 1972 and it has been our home ever since.

Impact of Violence on the Parish

I think there are a lot of unresolved mental health issues in the parish, and a lot of that stems from people living through times of fear. Fear was prevalent in the community, but at the time we didn't realise the immensity of the impact of that fear on our community. No counselling was available at the time, and people really didn't know how much we needed to talk about we were going through. There was an immense impact upon children who were watching that fear in their parents. There is nothing worse for a child than to think that their parents cannot deal with a situation. Children rely so much upon their parents to deal with things. There is nothing worse for a child than to see their parents not coping with that fear, or to witness a parent being killed. A child needs to grow up in a world where they feel safe and secure. Children at that time were robbed of that security, and we are living with the consequences of that today, as that trauma is being passed on through the generations. That is the kind of legacy this community has been left to deal with.

When we heard of the outbreak of violence while we were in Lourdes, we reflected upon how best Pat and I might respond, and we knew it had to be through non-violent means. We joined the SDLP, which was just beginning. We also joined the ALJ (the Association for Legal Justice), and went around the country taking statements from people about what happened to them. People were regularly disappearing and being taken away by the Army and the police at this time. We were taking statements in the Ard Scoil, an Irish language centre in Divis Street on the Falls Road. I went into Long Kesh every week with other teachers, where we talked to people and brought materials in for subjects like Maths and Art. I still have a painting that was done in Long Kesh, with all the names of the men in Cage 4 on the back of it.

The People's Assembly

We got very involved with Fr Myles when he came into the parish. I was one of the chairpersons of the People's Assembly, an association set up within the parish by Fr Myles in the absence of any real help from the Government. Every street elected its own representatives, and the assembly was an attempt to help people improve conditions within the area. I was chairperson of a group called the Holiday Committee, needed because many different organisations had offered lots of holidays, particularly for the children of the area. I was also involved in the Education Committee and through that we contacted the local authority at Stormont, lobbying for things like a library, which we eventually managed to get. A community centre was set up, followed by providing meals for pensioners in Holyrood Hall in Butler Street, but we had to fight for that! I then started evening classes in St Gemma's School, and then in the boys' school in Butler Street. We went door to door and recruited over 200 people for the evening classes, which eventually ran for over four years.

We formed a choir from the four schools in the parish that eventually went to Rome in 1975, about 80 children in all. Fr Myles was always available to help people, and he was really the brainchild behind all this. At one stage he was lying in a garden in Etna Drive while shooting was going on around him. He told me that while lying there he thought, 'I am not going to lie in this garden again. I am going to do something about this.'

During this time, the Army turned all the street lights out in the parish and the whole district was in the dark once night fell. The People's Assembly had been set up by Fr Myles to stand up for the people of the parish, and after a meeting with the local Army commander to stress the need for street lighting to be restored had little success we ensured that a light was put up outside every house in the parish and they were all turned on together, ensuring that we had light.

When the Parachute regiment were stationed in Ardoyne, they shot people dead in this district just as they did in Derry and in Ballymurphy. We organised a march against their actions. We stood on the front of the Crumlin Road and the Paras came and stood and looked at us. I thought that they were going to charge into us as they had done to the people in Ballymurphy, but we stood our ground and told them that we were going to stay there. Along with Larry Toolan, we met their commander down at their barracks in the mill, and because we had been elected to represent the people from the streets it brought us some authority in standing up to them. The People's Assembly was an important means of empowering people to stand up for themselves at that time.

On one occasion I was walking down Butler Street and heard screaming coming from around the Fairfield Street area. A young man by the name of Larkin was lying on the ground, surrounded by four paratroopers. His wife and child were there with him. I confronted the Paras by saying, 'Excuse me, I am a member of the People's Assembly. Can you tell me what is happening?'

He said sneeringly, 'We are identifying this man.'

I said, 'But sure that is his house, and that is his wife and child beside him. What else do you need to know?'

He turned to me and said, 'We will do whatever we like.' I was standing beside the young man, and they reversed their vehicle back towards me and then they grabbed him, threw him into the vehicle and tried to hit his head off the edge of the metal seats. I put my hand in between his head and the seat. We both ended up in the vehicle, but I then fell out. The vehicle moved up Butler Street with my bag still inside it. My bag eventually fell out of the vehicle, followed by the young man. As the Army vehicle then passed by me they fired the rubber bullet gun into the crowd that had started to gather. I phoned Fr Myles from the advice centre that the People's Assembly had set up and told him, 'There is absolute mayhem here.' He then contacted the paratroopers' commander and they were withdrawn from the area. I was contacted by the police who asked if I would like to make a statement about what I had witnessed because the Paras had accused the young man of attacking them. I made my statement and the Paras subsequently withdrew their accusation. It was obvious from their attitude that the police didn't like the Paras either.

I believe that when people react violently, the first thing that happens is they destroy themselves as well as the people they are attempting to destroy. The People's Assembly was based on that premise, and were always conscious of it when we were taking statements from people who had been taken away by the Army. Some cases, though, stand out for their brutality. One young lad from Ardoyne had been walking to work when the Army lifted him near York Street. They threw him into a Saracen and burned him, urinated on him, and basically sexually assaulted him. He had the wits to go to the Mater Hospital and show them his burns and other injuries. I took a statement from him for the Association for Legal Justice, who took statements from people and represented them in court, and the Paras were eventually forced to admit what they had done and he got some compensation from them.

Given our experience on the streets at the time, it was clear that if the community of Ardoyne had not been organised with initiatives such as the People's Assembly, then we would have suffered the same fate as Ballymurphy at the hands of the Paras.

Internment

In the trouble following the introduction of internment, houses in Farringdon Gardens were burned down. Roy Bradford was the Minister for Development at the time and the Government wanted to knock down all the houses. Fr Myles thought differently, and he set up a Farringdon Gardens Committee, which included people like Larry Toolan and Seamus Goan who wanted to save Farringdon Gardens. Fundraising took place in England and the United States. The campaign was to reroof the houses before the winter set in and was called 'There Is No Place Like Home'. There was always some humour around though, even in the darkest times. Some government official arrived one morning and asked to talk to Fr Fernando, another Passionist involved in saving these homes. He was told, 'He is away back to the monastery with an art attack.'

The official went up to the monastery and said, 'I believe that Fr Fernando had a heart attack.'

'No,' came the reply, 'but he is with an architect!'

Holy Cross Blockade

The well-documented Loyalist blockade of Holy Cross Girls' School began in June 2001. After the summer break, it began again September and lasted until 23 November. During that awful time, the school children and their parents ran a gauntlet of abuse every day on their way to school. I was principal of the school at the time, and after the ending of the blockade we organised counselling for over one hundred children, but I was aware that the parents were often more upset than the children, and I tried to get support for them as well.

Everybody in this community has a story to tell. We live in a very divided society, but under the skin we are all the same. As Pat puts it, 'When two four-teen-year-old boys realise that they can take over a bus, terrorise people, steal the conductor's money and wreck the bus, is it any wonder that they lost interest in education?' Put that alongside the fact that many of their parents and relations had been traumatised or beaten up, that puts the task of getting them to value education into perspective.

Gratitude

Ardoyne is a very special place. There was always a sense of comradery and caring for people. If someone died, everybody rallied round. We had very good friends here. People like Phyllis McBrierty, who went out to tend to people when they were hurt or wounded in times of trouble. I am so grateful that nobody within the immediate family of Pat or myself were killed.

I think, for all our sakes, there are two great lessons which must be learned from 1969. The first is that peace is precious and that we must work for peace, based on justice and mutual respect; the second is that all our children have the right to grow up, free from fear, in a secure, loving environment.

11

Rab McCallum

Born in the Shadow of the Chapel

I was born and bred in Elmfield Street, very much in the shadow of Holy Cross Church. In fact, the chapel was always my compass point. I was in prison a couple of times, and I always remember that when I was released from prison and would walk up Butler Street, seeing the twin spires of the chapel always told me that I was home. Elmfield Street was in the part of the district called 'Old Ardoyne', as opposed to the newer part of the district, called Glenard.

I have great memories of growing up in Ardoyne. They were hard times though, and the fun we had as kids was that which we created for ourselves, building huts in back entries, football in the street, playing tig, being boisterous and probably annoying people as we rapped on doors and tied string to letterboxes, but it was never anything vindictive. Occasionally we would hear of someone breaking into a house and robbing the gas meters, but that was seen as really horrific and we would look down on people who did that. We also knew who they were because the community was so close-knit.

People were great neighbours to each other. I remember running up to get the midwife, or more often to the woman who had been designated by the local women as midwife to deliver babies, going down to the pawn shop or bringing a bag of washing down to the launderette for some woman across the street. They were not always things that I wanted to do, but my ma made sure that I did it if I was asked. Ardoyne always had a good community spirit. If I went down to the shop at the bottom of the street, it was often done on tic – that is the shopkeeper trusted that the bill would be paid later when people had the money. If I went down and asked for sausages, bread and meat, and then added on a bar of chocolate to the list (even with my ma's permission), I would be immediately sent back by the shopkeeper to get a note from my ma to make sure that I wasn't chancing my arm.

It was a community where people didn't have a lot but people helped each other out. Doors were open and we would often walk into each other's houses. I remember when colour television came in and people were walking into houses just to see this new thing. I don't remember having any real concerns as a child.

Although there was a great community spirit, there was also fierce local rivalry not only between streets, but also within streets in the district! Chatham Street for example, was very close to us and it was divided into three sections – top, middle and bottom – known locally as Heaven, Purgatory and Hell. The section of the street you lived on though often made a big difference. I lived in the top end of Elmfield Street, and we were fortunate to have baths in our house. The houses in the bottom end didn't have a bath. But while we had a bath we had no hot water, and our house still had an outside toilet. Having a bath in the winter wasn't so bad, as the fire in our house also heated the water. In the summer, with no fire lit, we had to heat water in the twin tub washing machine and then pump the water into the bath.

Football and snooker were my favourite hobbies. My back door was right beside the League, the local working men's club, so I could walk from my house straight into it. It very quickly became my favourite place to go to hang out and play snooker. First thing Saturday morning I would be in the League trying to be first on the snooker table, but there always seemed to be something to do in our spare time. During the school holidays we would be out the door at eight in the morning, with a bottle of lemonade and some biscuits, and away we went up over the mountain and not coming back exhausted until after ten at night. Kids would never be allowed to do that kind of thing these days!

Political Awareness in 1969

I was fourteen in 1969. I knew what the Easter Rising commemorations in 1966 were about. I can remember the riots on the Falls, but I knocked about with Protestant guys from Chief Street, and the launderette was in Disraeli Street, both on the 'Loyalist side' of the road. I never had any real concern walking over there. When

I went to the cinema further down the Crumlin Road with my mates we would make sure we got out before they started playing the British national anthem, 'The Queen' as we called it, at the end of the show, and we knew that there was a potential to get chased. So there was always that awareness of tension, but it wasn't a big issue that disrupted my life. Of course, we could all sing rebel songs like 'Kevin Barry', but we weren't embedded in Republicanism. We weren't even embedded in Catholicism at that stage! It was a chore to go to Mass, or to avoid going to Mass.

Changing Climate

I vividly remember the issues that were rising in Derry in 1969. I saw the Civil Rights marches and events like Burntollet on the television, but they still didn't have a big impact upon me. Then I got a wee job after school in the Wheatfield Bar on the corner of Leopold Street in the summer of 1969. I picked up the tensions there and the way people were talking. The first of the riots started and I remember Michael Lynch and Sammy McLarnon being shot, basically at the bottom of my street. Michael Lynch was brought into Basil McAfee's house when he was shot on the street. Basil was a very good friend of my da's. I remember seeing Michael Lynch lying there and they couldn't get an ambulance into the district. The first aid people were working on him, but there was no priest. Someone suggested getting a priest, but we couldn't get up into the chapel as the cops had the road blocked. We were trying to get him across into the Bone area, but the police whippets were all across the roads.

I remember the tension that night. People were rioting, and as fourteen-year-olds my mates and I were collecting bottles and making petrol bombs and getting involved in the rioting. There was pandemonium and a palpable fear of what was happening. I remember particularly 15 August. People were out on the streets with bottles, petrol, rags, vinegar (as a protection from the CS gas) and getting prepared for what they thought was going to happen following the previous night's violence. I was also trying to avoid my ma, who was out looking for me. I was only fourteen years of age and I was right in the middle of all that was happening. There was a definite understanding that we were facing a serious situation as we were defending our homes. We knew that if we were going to be out on the streets, then we had to be wholeheartedly involved in what was going on.

Whole families moved out of the area on 15 August. All my family except my da moved out and I was supposed to go with them. I refused to go and was aware of a real fear that the Loyalists were coming in that night to burn out the remainder of the homes in the district. There was a real doomsday sense of what was going on, but for me there was also a sense of being alongside the men of the district to defend my home. My ma went off to Andersonstown with the other kids and neighbours from the street. I watched them going, and on the afternoon of 16 August people were standing around the street corners. There was a sense that this was like high noon and we knew that something really ominous was about to happen.

Ardoyne Ignites

I remember the scene on the street that night: petrol bombs exploding, tracer bullets going through the air, wimpeys (armoured cars) sitting at the corners of the streets. A cameraman was standing at the Brompton Gap and he was using the camera to look at the two wimpeys on the Bone Hills. Conversations were going on about the IRA and people were asking, 'Where are the IRA?'

There were people in the IRA in the district, but they were not a major influence. I remember them coming into the League club with the *United Irishman* newspaper up their coats as it couldn't be sold openly. I knew bits about the IRA since the celebrations in 1966, but to be honest I heard more from my granda about the Mass Rock and how Catholics were persecuted than I did about the IRA. While we knew and sang the rebel song 'Kevin Barry', the hymn we sang at Mass, 'Faith of Our Fathers', was more like the national anthem. It was emphasised that we were Catholics before we were anything else, and I didn't really know much about politics. Those events leading up to the summer of 1969 were my first real political insight. I see myself as a '1969 baby' – from then on everything changed in my life.

Saturday 16 August

The morning of 16 August I was up and out of the house first thing to see what had happened the previous night. As I walked around the district it just seemed like a scene from the Blitz. I was in and out of houses and then breaking up pavements to help build the barricades up again that had been knocked down by the police vehicles the previous night. Women were running out with buckets of water and vinegar to combat the CS gas.

Things changed on Saturday 16 August and Ardoyne became like a ghost town. People were standing about waiting for something to happen. The night of the 14th was bad, the 15th got worse and then the buses came onto the streets. The riots were escalating and on that Saturday morning people were genuinely expecting to be killed in their own homes that night. They were confused as to how they could stop that as we only had petrol bombs, bricks and whatever else we could get our hands on. There were no guns. I remember standing with my da along with Basil

McAfee and four other guys. It was the first time I had stood among men and felt like I was treated and spoken to in an adult manner. I felt included in what was being said rather than being dismissed off to the side as a kid.

Sights and Smells

I remember the dirt and the smell. Some people had been in around their houses trying to get belongings out of them. Electric wires were hanging down and everything was black from the burnt soot, but we had to go into these houses to help people retrieve their belongings. That brings to mind one of the nights at the back of Kilpatrick's pub. People were bringing out kegs and bottles of beer that hadn't been burnt. I think Hooker Street entry had about thirty to forty basins and when the people burst open the kegs the beer flowed into them. That was all part of the scene of what was going on.

What stands out most in my mind is standing outside Reid's shop at the corner of the street on the Saturday afternoon, and the awareness of people waiting for what was to happen next. Tension was heightening and people just did not understand what was happening. News came on the Saturday afternoon that the Brits had come in, and a real and tremendous sense of relief could be felt right round the district when the Brits arrived.

People cheered when they realised that their worst fears were not going to realised. That was the first reaction and there was no other kind of political thought, just that the Brits were in to defend us against the Loyalists. My thoughts were, 'We are not going to be killed in our beds tonight. The British Army is here to defend us.' That initial sense of relief lasted for weeks. I remember Barney McKenna, a well-known local Republican, coming up to Reid's shop where the people were giving the Brits tea and saying, 'This is going to turn into tears. These people are not here to defend you. They have another motive.' I remember not understanding what this old Republican was referring to, but he was saying that things were going to change and that we needed to be aware of that.

It's hard to tell the difference between I have learned since and what I actually thought then, but to be honest, all I thought was that the Prods wanted to wipe us all out. They wanted to kill us. People were saying that the Loyalists were coming in to drive us all out, and that was the only sense I made of it. I didn't see anything political in it, just that they wanted to kill us. That was my sense at the time of what was happening. What we were trying to do was to defend the area from those coming in to kill us, and trying to make sure that didn't happen.

I didn't have any other great sense of why it was happening, although I was aware of the relief of Derry: people coming to the area and telling us that we needed to take the pressure off Derry. I recall someone on the back of a lorry talking about the people of Derry being killed and that we needed to show support.

Life Ambitions

All my mates had gone to St Gabriel's School, but I went to the Christian Brothers school. My only ambition at this age was to get out of the Christian Brothers and into St Gabriel's to be with my mates, which I eventually managed to do. My only thoughts about a job was that I would get one somewhere, but, other than that, none of my family had ever gone to university and I didn't have any aspirations then of doing so. Most guys like me thought that they would probably end up getting a trade of some description and would stay in that for good. I remember though at one stage wanting to go away on the boats. I always had an inclination to go to sea, which probably came from being in the League so often. A lot of men came into the club who worked on the boats, and they just happened to be the flashiest guys we saw in the club – lovely suits, polished shoes, fancy cigarettes after coming back from New York or Southampton, so it was no surprise that going away on the boats appealed to me. The start of the Troubles distorted all that kind of ambition though. School went out the window, and many of us never finished school. The main thought we had when we did go to school was of the daily riot that was going to happen when we got home again.

I left school in 1970 with no thoughts of exams. Everyday life was tempered by what was going on around me at that particular time. Making plans and having ambitions for life didn't really come into my thinking.

Tensions in the Background

There was always some kind of trouble going on around Ardoyne and the neighbouring areas. Even as kids when we would have gone across to friends who lived on the other side of the road in Chief Street, there would have been scuffles with some of the local Protestant guys. I also had a paper round along with four other guys from Ardoyne down in the Eagle Newsagency in the Loyalist Ballygomartin Road. Even after the events of 1969 I still had that paper round, delivering papers around the mostly Loyalist areas of Ballygomartin and Hesketh, until it eventually become too dangerous to do so. I would get stopped and asked where I was from, and fights were even starting among the paper boys ourselves. One of the guys from Ardoyne had trouble finishing his paper round up in the Loyalist Springmartin estate and had to dump his paper bag. He got the sack and I knew then it was time to stop.

27 June 1970

The most significant day that changed the course of my life was 27 June 1970. I remember that vividly. Due to having a paper round I had a few pounds in my pocket and had gone to McMurray's clothes shop in Lower North Street to get a corduroy Wrangler jacket and a pair of horsey boots. Danny Mullan, Paul Donnelly and myself had come back from town and I was upstairs getting my new boots and jacket on. Someone shouted up, 'Fuck, get down here quickly! The Loyalists are coming into Hooker Street.'

I rushed down the stairs and we went bolting down Chatham Street to be confronted with the rioting going on, with both sides throwing stones back and forward across the Crumlin Road. There were bits of barbed wired already up along the road and I remember getting my horsey boots ripped on it. I was raging at getting my new boots ripped! I had only bought them twenty minutes beforehand. I then saw a guy with a white shirt and an orange in his hand throwing stones across the road near Kilpatrick's pub, when suddenly red spots appeared on his shirt. Even when people knew that somebody was firing from the Loyalist side we just carried on. We ducked down behind a wall and then came out again to throw things. Next thing a car drew up and some guys got out. The boot opened and they moved to the corners of the street and shouted, 'Get the fuck off the street.' The shooting started and for me it was, 'Fuck! Crazy!'

A number of people were shot that day. I remember one guy falling off a lemonade lorry. He must have had a pistol as he had been positioned behind the crates on the lorry shooting into Ardoyne. People had been shouting, 'He's on the lorry. He is shooting from the lorry.'

For me this was a key moment. The car had pulled up, guns had been distributed, and the IRA had stopped the mobs coming into the area. From then on I was a Fianna boy, and then into the IRA, and that set the course for where my life went after that.

Member of the IRA

Joining the Fianna, and subsequently the IRA, felt to me that it was something I had to do. It was my duty. The Kevin Barry stuff was always there, the young guy who died for Ireland and all that kind of talk. It didn't come from having a lot of political ideals about what a united Ireland meant. It was purely and simply to defend the area. The Loyalists had come in to attack the area, and the IRA had defended it and showed us what needed to be done to make sure these things never happened again. I looked up to that.

When the Army came into the district that afternoon, they were firing CS gas and I remember running up Hooker Street with my eyes burning, tumbling and falling, trying to get away from the gas. As fifteen-year-old boys, the group I hung about with would stand at the corner of Fairfield Street and we were constantly harassed by the Army. At one stage there was an unofficial curfew, where if you were caught by the Army on the street after 10 p.m. you got a beating from soldiers. We never obeyed that curfew, but certainly tried to avoid running into the Army! I was always clear about the cops: they had come in with the 'B' Specials to burn us out in 1969. These were the people we had issues with, and once the Army came then they were seen as helping the others to attack us. That was the issue I was trying to deal with. I never saw it as an issue with the Protestant community. Of course I was aware of the UVF, but when I got involved in the Fianna we learned a bit about history. We did our drilling, but we were there to give assistance to the IRA. Then it got the stage where someone came round to me and said, 'Right, you are the right age now.' We had a talk and I was asked if I wanted to go into the IRA. I was told, 'If you go into the IRA these are the options – you could end up in gaol and you could die. Now go off and think about it.'

To be honest I never really thought about it for a second, because I never thought either of the two of them would ever happen to me. I was then sixteen and by the time I was seventeen I was in gaol. It was a short initial career. I got caught for robbing a bank in Crossgar, but getting caught was almost inevitable as there was something happening almost every day at that stage. I was seventeen when I went to court and the other guy was thirty-five. He was presented as the 'godfather' and I was the young guy who was getting manipulated, but we all ended up getting a sentence of eight years. I suppose that was also the way that my mother would have looked at it – being manipulated – but for me, I went into it with my eyes wide open. I was always aware of what was happening, and I was never press-ganged or pressured to do anything that I did not choose to do or felt needed to be done. Out of my teenage group of twelve guys who used to hang about the corner of Elmfield Street, only one of us did not join the IRA and end up either dead or in prison.

Life in Gaol

I was in Armagh Gaol first and then taken down to the Crum (Crumlin Road Gaol). They then opened up the Cages and we were moved up to the Kesh. I had an eight-year sentence, but it was with political status, so we were in our compounds with our own command structures, although sentenced prisoners and internees were kept separate.

Two memories of my time in prison stand out for me. I vividly remember my ma coming up to visit and being distraught. She was shedding tears and asking me, 'What have you done to yourself?' I also remember the whole interrogation experience. It was frightening, but regarding going into gaol I had no real expectations. I didn't really know what it meant when I was told I was going to prison, so I wasn't really scared. Then when I walked in, I was kind of in awe. I think the television series *Porridge* had just started and everyone had this picture of a Victorian prison. When confronted with the reality I was wondering just what was going on, and then just getting used to the routine, especially as a kid. I got into the routine very quickly though and knew what the expectations were. In Armagh, for example, there was somebody singing every night. There was a Loyalist estate right beside us and the UDA would come out and parade out the back on the waste ground and we could see them out the window of the prison. There was an article in the *Sunday World* about the local people complaining that their kids knew the words of the 'Broad Black Brimmer' better than they knew their Sunday hymns because they were being sung so often in the prison beside them.

I ended up doing twelve years of a sentence altogether. My first spell was from 1972 to 1976, but four months after I was released I was caught again, and back in prison from 1976 to 1984. I had gone in at seventeen years old, and when I was in I became more politicised and had a better understanding of what was going on. My own family background was mixed, as my granny was a Protestant from Disraeli Street, and I would stay with my granny and I knew people who were Protestants. When it came to the week of the Twelfth though, we were always shipped back to Ardoyne and not allowed anywhere near the area. Sectarianism was never a feature in my upbringing, and given my family background I have always been aware that had I been born in Disraeli Street I would probably have been in the UVF. I am conscious that I am who I am because of where I am from. I understood where people from the Loyalist community got their particular perspective on things, and for me in the early days the whole focus in the conflict was to engage with the British Army and the cops. I had no time for sectarianism.

Facing Change upon Release

When I came out of gaol in 1976 there was a whole different scenario. I was now more politicised, but I was walking into a situation where people were almost engrossed in a sectarian campaign. That shook me for a while. Ardoyne especially had a reputation that if you wanted Prods killed you went to Ardoyne and they would do it. I knew some people who if they had a choice of planting a bomb or shooting a Loyalist, they would have chosen to shoot a Loyalist. That was due to the whole growth of sectarianism both against and within this area.

When I came out of gaol I believed that the IRA was being drawn into a campaign that was not where I thought we should be going. We were spending more time looking at Loyalists rather than the Brits and the cops. When I went back into gaol though and had time to reflect, I thought that this was being deliberately manipulated so that the Brits and the cops would not become the targets, and they were being presented as the neutral sheriffs between these two warring groups. It later transpired that was what was being deliberately done and the Loyalists were being fed information by the police, and the Loyalists had decided to attack the supporters of the IRA if they could not get directly at the IRA.

Up to 1974 the whole focus of the IRA campaign was to target the Brits. Then the sectarian element came in, and that didn't happen by accident. If we can't terrorise the IRA, then we will target the Nationalist community, and hopefully they will make the IRA stop. There was also the strategy from the Brits that they wanted to be seen as the neutral players in the conflict, trying to keep these two sides apart. So it was then portrayed as a sectarian conflict rather than as a struggle against the Brits.

Second Gaol Term

The second time I was in the Kesh was during the blanket protest, the no wash protest, then the hunger strikes and right up to the escape. I was on the blanket protest for the whole of my four years when I was back in the Kesh. I was on the blanket from the time I was sentenced right through until the protest ended. When people hear about the blanket protest and the hunger strikes they say, 'That must have been rough!' But when I think about it, I had a much harder time in the Cages than I had on the blanket.

I was only eighteen to twenty years of age when I was in the Cages, and the simple routine of what went on every day just drove me nuts. It was just the same thing that happened every day. I got up in the morning and went out and did parade. You came in and you washed up. Then you might have had a bit of football. It was just sheer monotony every day and visits were the only thing that really broke up that monotony. Playing cards, having a bit of craic, but I knew what every day would bring in advance. The winter was especially hard as with the bad weather we were locked up more and not able to get out to the yard so often.

While there is no doubt that being on the blanket was hard, it was also a challenge to be faced every day, so one day was never going to be the same as the next. Each day had a purpose to it, and I was part of a larger organisation working together with a common purpose. Even with the food protests, when we were throwing food over the wire, there was the excitement of the internees smuggling in a parcel for you. Being on the blanket was rough but mentally I was more alert; it was more of a challenge with a definite purpose and I felt more alive when I was on it.

I was lucky because I had no close family connections, but some guys were not seeing their kids and loved ones. Of course my ma was there, and while your ma is your ma, she is not your wife and she is not your kids. It's not that I didn't care for her. My ma was a convert and like many converts she became very Catholic, and if I had been going into the darkest jungles as a missionary her attitude would have been, 'Good for you son.' So gaol was just a different life that I had to get used to.

Community Involvement

I was finally released from prison in 1984, but at that time the war was still on and I went back to doing what had to be done. It wasn't until later, when the cease-fires came, that this idea of getting involved in community issues – like internment commemorations, bonfires and parades – came about. Along with other former combatants I was involved in setting up the Fleadh in Ardoyne, but some of the statutory organisations would say, 'We can't talk to you. There is a housing associ-ation here.' The housing association was closely aligned with the Church, and there was always this tension between the Church and Sinn Féin in the area at the time. All the people making decisions in the district at the time seemed to be associated with the Church. So when we tried to organise events around the Fleadh, obstacles were put up against us. In response to that, we started setting up housing asso-ciations and committees for the local community, simply to get the opportunity to talk to people to tell them what we were planning to do. Subsequent wider community involvement from Republicans was rooted in that original concept.

Transition to Peace

The transition from being a man totally committed to the IRA, and who went to prison for that commitment, to a man totally committed to peace-building didn't suddenly come out of the blue. It came through an evolution, from a situation where people believed that in responding to their disempowerment there was no other option but violence, to a situation where Republicans were exploring other options than armed struggle.

My experience in gaol enabled me to engage in discussions on what the armed struggle meant and where it needed to go to. Conversations took place in gaol that could not have happened outside it, like the inevitability that at some stage the armed struggle would come to an end, and how we might then move the Republican ideal forward. Although people were aware that we would be in a prison for at least another few years, these conversations were going on and strangely there was more freedom in prison to have these conversations. Speculative conversations were encouraged and not seen as a threat to any factions on the outside of prison.

Engagement with Loyalism

My engagement with Loyalists in my role of working to remove the Peace Walls is essential for me. As a seventeen-year-old I may had this vision of 'driving' the Brits out, where the jeeps would retreat and the Brits would get on the boat as we waved them goodbye. We would walk down the Crumlin Road to City Hall and take down the Union Jack and put up the tricolour. That phase of this conflict is never going to happen. For me now, the big struggle is how to engage the people who live across the road from me and who have different political aspirations from me.

I am currently involved in a Peace Walls programme called Twaddell Ardoyne Shankill Communities in Transition (TASCIT). This explores people's attitudes towards living near the Peace Walls and interfaces and how we can create the confidence within communities to get to the situation where we make Peace Walls redundant. I carry out that work through a group called North Belfast Interface Network, a group that was brought into being to deal with interface conflict, primarily as a result of the inter-community rioting that broke out following the Good Friday Agreement. To work our way through that we built up relationships that saw a major reduction in interface violence, and therefore the next phase was to deal with the most striking manifestation of community division, and that is the Peace Walls themselves. We also engage people in a programme called 'Challenging Conversations', which recognises that the transition to peace is not just about getting people to engage on issues in which they have agreement, but also to face up to issues that we don't agree on.

Regrets

I was in gaol at seventeen and lost a lot of that teenage life experience. I spent all of my twenties in gaol. There are a few things that I regret, like never being away on a 'boys' holiday' with teenage friends. I didn't go on a foreign holiday until I was 32. I think it would have been great to have been able to live with no responsibilities, but if someone was to turn around and ask me, 'If you were able to change things, would you?', I would say, 'No.' There is not a single thing that I would change in the experience I had.

When I look back at some of the things that happened and some of the things I was involved in, I wish they hadn't happened, but even with that I can't say that I would apologise for them, because at the time I thought they were the right thing to do. I have regrets as in 'I wish that didn't have to happen', or regrets that some specific things happened, but I can't apologise for things that I believe were needed at the time. Am I remorseful? I am remorseful for what happened to some of the people who were involved, but I genuinely can't turn around and say 'I am sorry', because I believed at the time that these things needed to be done. It would be disingenuous for me to turn around now and say 'Sorry.'

Personal Convictions

Some people from Ardoyne joined the IRA and some people didn't. Some people did not see the armed struggle as the way to respond to the injustices. I did. I joined the IRA as a reaction when I was a kid, but I continued in the IRA because I had considered what I thought to be the best way forward, and I genuinely thought that being in the IRA was the best way to deal with the injustice. As the struggle moved on I knew that we were not going to put the Brits on the boats, but I believed that we could bring about a conclusion to the ongoing struggle. I always knew that the armed struggle would ultimately end up in a political struggle. We were never going to just drive the enemy out.

The evolution into the political arena legitimises the struggle. People of course have different opinions on the need for the ongoing armed struggle. Some believe that there was no need for the IRA as it had been solved in 1972, but I don't believe that. I believe that we have been brought to the way things are today by the way the struggle evolved.

Are there things that were done in the name of Republicanism that I am ashamed of? Yes. Things happened that should not have happened, but if you bring a group of young men together and you give them some scope, then sometimes they will do things that are not well thought out and are not good. That happened in Ardoyne, especially in terms of sectarian incidents. So yes, there were things that happened that I am not proud of, but I understand why they happened. I can understand the context in which they happened, but I don't think they should have happened. When I came out of prison in 1976, I was shocked by some of the things that happened. They were not what I saw as being necessary. It was like we were trapped in a sectarian conflict, and I was ashamed of some of the things that happened. They were not good. They should not have been allowed to happen, but I cannot just disown them. I can say that on occasions when some things were being discussed, I very clearly made the point that this was not what I joined the IRA to do. I knew clearly what I saw as a legitimate target and what was not. That, of course, was after I had spent four years in gaol and had come out into a situation where people who had not been in gaol had a very different perspective.

Ardoyne Through and Through

I married a girl from Andersonstown and initially went over to the Falls Road to live. Eventually a guy came to me and said that he had a house available in Ardoyne. I didn't give a toss what it was like. I took it and we came back over to Ardoyne to live for the next fifteen years. Our kids were brought up here. Ardoyne is my home and every time I come back, like the times I came home from prison, the chapel spires let me know that I am home, and home will never be anywhere else. My friends are all there. The League club that I first went into as a teenager is still like an extended family to me.

I now live back in the Falls as we bought my wife's family home. It was a difficult transition for me. I work in Ardoyne. I socialise in Ardoyne. Some people say that it isn't the Ardoyne that it used to be and that it is a very different place these days. I remember a group of the older guys in their seventies in the League, and my da was one of them, arguing about some club that used to be near the boys' school. One of them contradicted what another had said, and the response was, 'What to fuck do you know? You are not even from here.' This was despite the fact that he had been living in Ardoyne for 70-odd years! That's the way it is in Ardoyne, and I know that I have this notion that 'Old Ardoyne' is the real Ardoyne, and Glenard is just Glenard, and the Bone is the Bone! There was a joke that in 1969 people in Glenard put the buses up as barricades to keep the people from Old Ardoyne out! Even though what I knew as Old Ardoyne no longer exists, it is where I am from. I guess other areas think the same. An area of a few streets will determine where you are from. Even my friends now make fun of me for being a 'Westie', but Ardoyne is where I am from. That will never change.

12

Pat Murphy

Mixed Background

I was born in 59 Strathroy Park, as were my younger brother and older sister. My mother was from the Lower Falls area, while my father was from Berry Street, Carrick Hill. My ma was a member of the Hannaway family, and trade unionism played a big part in the life of the Hannaways. My grandmother, Alice Mulholland, was the first to organise the garment workers in the mills around Rathfriland, in County Down. She was a personal friend of the leading socialists at that time, and they sent representatives to her funeral when she died of sepsis. This was in the 1920s. My grandfather was secretary of the Barman's Trade Union, so the whole family was coming from a trade union, Fenian, Young Irelander's background.

My paternal grandfather didn't share that background. They were professional British soldiers and along with his brothers my grandfather had fought in the First World War and the Boer War. My grandfather's experience of the British Army was a fairly chequered one. He had been pensioned out of the Army, and then ended up in the Belfast Brigade of the IRA. He was a Collins man. He supported the Treaty and went into the Free State Army. After Collins' death, when the Free State Army started executing the Republicans, my grandfather went over to the Irregulars (anti-Treaty), and took the contents of a magazine with him. As a result of his actions he was then afraid to put in for his pension. He reckoned that the regular army would be looking for the twenty rifles he had brought with him, and he gave up all his pension rights which had transferred over into the Free State Army.

My father, from the time he started to think, appears to have been a Republican, or a Republican socialist. He would have been a big fan of the Irish Republicans who formed the International Brigade to fight in the Spanish Civil War but was too young to join them. He pestered the guys leaving from Belfast to take him with them, but they wouldn't do it. He ended up being interned in the 1940s. He died very young, in his late forties, in 1967.

Early Political Awareness

I knew of Republican families such as the McGlades and Patsy Quinn on the Bone, and, of course, the McGuigans from Ardoyne. These were all well-known Republicans and contemporaries of my father and mother. The McGuigans were great friends of my family and members of our families had been interned together in the 1940s. I also knew about Phil McTaggart, who escaped out of Crumlin Road Gaol in 1939. When it came round to the council elections, the people sympathetic to the Republicanism stood as Republican Labour, but the bulk of the people were going with the Northern Ireland Labour Party, represented by Vivian Simpson and Gerry Fitt. The Republican supporters in the district at that time were in the minority. There were so few Republicans in Ardoyne at the time that I knew who they all were. It would have been quite easy at that stage to round them up. I remember one occasion, though, when the police caught Gerard McGuigan's mother and one of the Halls carrying out drilling practice over in Ardilea Street.

The first time I saw a real gun was in Strathroy Park, and it was an RUC man who had it. We were playing football, and at that stage you would get a fine for playing ball in the street, either handball or football. It was a fine of half a crown or 7/6 or something. Not too many families had a car at the time, but there was a family called Campbell who lived at the bottom of the street. I think he worked for the Customs, but the ball got kicked and it stuck under the exhaust pipe of the car. I got down and crawled in under the car to get the ball. I pulled the ball out and as I was reversing back out from under the car I could see a big pair of boots to the left of me and a pair of boots to the right of me. The boys had all taken off, thinking it was a great joke to play on me: 'We will not wire Murphy off that the cops are there!'

I was never getting away. I remember scrambling out and being confronted by the cop. He had a big .45 Smith & Wesson, but it looked like a yard of a gun on his hip! It looked like a cannon to me. I was only eight or nine at the time. I suddenly thought to myself, 'Jesus! That's a real gun!' He was the sergeant, and the guy at the other side to me was a constable, so he took the notepad out and started writing me a ticket. I was thinking, 'Fuck, my da will kill me!' Not for getting the fine, which would have been hard enough to pay, but for getting caught! You know what I mean, that would have been the big disappointment for my da. My ma would have gone nuts about the fine though!

The constable said to me, 'What is your name?'

I said, 'Murphy.'

He said, 'First name.'

I said, 'Pat Murphy.'

The cop said, 'Where do you live?'

I said, 'Up the street.'

The big sergeant said, 'Is your da Johnny Murphy?'

I said, 'Yes.'

He said, 'That's alright. Just tell your da that the sergeant let you off.'

My da was fucking raging, and simply said, 'The bastard.'

That was the first time I had encountered that kind of hostility, and I was asking myself, 'How does that policeman know my da?' My da though was a prominent Republican and I started picking up on political differences from that time on. I have to say that looking back on it though, when I was fourteen years of age Ardoyne was the most apolitical place you could ever come across.

RAF – No Recruits in Ardoyne!

The RAF visited St Gabriel's School in the mid-1960s. My father was still alive, so it was pre-1967. The RAF had come into the school on a recruitment drive and they put on a film show in the school assembly hall. It was the talk of the district. About four or five members of what would become known during the Troubles as an Active Service Unit came into the school with hurley sticks and beat the crap out of the projectionist. They smashed up his projector and wrecked his films. They came in shouting, 'Irish Republican Army.' I believe that Martin Meehan was one of the people involved in it.

It was the talk of the district that the 'Ra had gone up and fixed the RAF. Mind you, it was probably some old boy like me who was the projectionist! But all of a sudden I was thinking, 'So the IRA still exists!'

Interest in Politics

Politics was beginning to be a growing area of interest around 1965/66. People were aware of the Paris riots and were starting to become familiar with wider politics.

My da was a big hero of mine, and he would give me books or articles about people like James Connolly to read. I remember going to him when I was about twelve years old asking him to get me into Na Fianna Éireann, the junior wing of the IRA. He said to me, 'Not a chance! You come back to me when you are eighteen and tell me why you want to join the movement and, if I am convinced about your reasons, I will put you in touch with them. If they get you now, they will brainwash you. If they get you at twelve years of age they will turn you into a machine, but I will facilitate you when you are older and when you can tell me your own point of view.' This was coming from a lifelong Republican, but my da was always a socialist before he was a Republican.

Coming into fourth year in St Gabriel's I was reading about the Soledad brothers (three African-American inmates charged with the murder of a white prison guard at California's Soledad Prison on 16 January 1970), and the economic conscripts. I was dabbling in *Marx for Idiots*, the writings of Connolly and that type of thing. St Gabriel's at this time was a great school and producing great results. We were hitting the highest percentages for 'O' Levels and 'A' Levels in the country. There were some very intelligent guys there, and the bulk of them were left-wingers! A lot of them, like Brian Quinn, God rest him, were in the Official IRA when the Troubles got going. The Black Panthers, the revolutionary political organisation founded by Huey Newton and Bobby Seale in California, came on the scene. Then we had the Springboks coming over to Ireland, with large protests organised in Dublin when the guards beat the shit out of us. The natural progression for me was into People's Democracy.

People's Democracy

I joined the PD and went on marches but I remember Battler Boyd, my Maths teacher, warning us that he better not see us at any of those PD marches because we were doing 'O' Levels. I was thinking, 'What a load of horse shit! I am more worried about the Special Branch spotting me at one the marches than you, no harm to you!'

I went along to the first PD march up Royal Avenue and the sit-down at City Hall, but the level of my political engagement depended upon what my ma was prepared to let me go to at fifteen years of age! I also walked up the Antrim Road as part of the Burntollet March. Major Ronald Bunting had organised a protest against this march, and the Loyalists had walked up the Antrim Road before the PD march. (Bunting's first involvement with politics was as election agent to the then Republican Labour MP Gerry Fitt, but he later became a close confidante of Rev Ian Paisley, playing a leading role in Paisley's campaigns against the Civil Rights

Association.) They stopped at Bellevue Zoo to await the PD march. Well, that drew a lot of comments, like, 'Are you going home Ronnie?'

Imagine stopping outside the zoo. You would have thought he would have waited until he at least got to Glengormley! Eamonn McCann, one of the organisers of the march, and all the older guys gave him dog's abuse about being outside the zoo. But I turned back myself at that stage, as my ma would have killed me had I gone any further.

Trouble in Ardoyne

I already mentioned that Ardoyne was a totally apolitical place, but now we had trouble in Derry. Paisley was causing trouble with his counter-marches attacking the protestors, but Ardoyne had been largely quiet at that stage. As far as I can remember there had been a row in Kilpatrick's Bar on the front of the Crumlin Road. In the process of this row, it had spilled out onto the street and a guy had a heart attack in the middle of it. People had sent for an ambulance and as it came up the road with lights flashing a crowd of Prods had gathered on the other side of the road. So the two groups were facing each other on opposite sides. The cops arrived and did what the cops did in so-called Northern Ireland – they baton-charged the Catholics standing outside Kil's Bar, and that degenerated into the first riot in Ardoyne at Hooker Street.

It was the talk of the school next day of how the cops had baton-charged the crowd and of the hand-to-hand fighting. There was sporadic trouble stemming from that, but the real vicious stuff started following some people coming into Ardoyne in a big black motor. I remember them saying that there was trouble in Derry, and people needed to take the pressure off the people in Derry. That's when the so-called 'long-haired ones' of the song started a riot at the end of Hooker Street.

It all seemed so weird at that stage. I was just fifteen years of age, so I could defend the district all I wanted until it was time for me to go home to bed! I was out throwing petrol bombs at the peelers, the 'B' Specials and the Orange hoards who were attempting to burn down Ardoyne, and then it was, 'Right lads, I have to go home!' Maybe somebody got defending the district longer because their ma let them stay out later. I had to be in 11.30 or 12.00, and I remember on the way home thinking, 'Guevara never had to do this!' Then going home and shouting, 'Right Mammy, I'm in.' It was that mad, surreal sort of situation.

On that Friday night (15 August 1969), the Loyalists and peelers had taken over the mills and were banging heavy fire into the district. I went home and put on a Hitchcock movie, thinking, 'We will get some tension here, some edge-of-our-seat stuff here Ma!' I could hear the gunfire in the background as I sat and watched Hitchcock with my ma. The whole thing had gone mad. Watching Hitchcock to get some tension while the district was in flames with gunfire everywhere! Sammy McLarnon and Mickey Lynch were killed that night. Mickey's father and my father were great mates.

Street Fights

There was so much confusion at the time. It was also the first time I had seen anybody get shot. Brian Quinn was running down Kerrera Street with me after we had just fired off a load of bricks at the 'B' Specials and we had turned to run back down the street. I always remember a Special stepping out with a sten gun and he spread the street as we were running back, but there was this clown running about the district shouting, 'I was in the British Army for nine years. They are only firing blanks! They are just trying to scare us boys!' So we ran back, pissing ourselves laughing at them firing the blanks at us, when somebody said to Brian Quinn, 'Fuck Brian! You're bleeding from the back!'

Brian had been hit by a round that went in his side and came out of his back. Somebody then said to Mickey Rosatto, 'Fuck Mickey, you've been shot.' We all looked at each other, asking what do we do if somebody gets shot? 'I suppose you better lie down!' So Brian and Mickey lay down. We were all around sixteen at the time, although Brian Quinn was few years older, but we shouted to the CDC men for help: 'Hey, mister, these boys are shot!' I remember some of the older men giving out to us because they thought we were joking: 'You boys shouldn't be shouting things like that!' But they eventually realised that it was no joke, and that the boys had been shot.

This was when the old western movies came back to haunt us. In the westerns, when somebody was shot and the bullet came out the other end they presumed the guy who had been shot was okay, but if the bullet was still in them, then there was nothing that could be done for them. Well, Quinn had been shot and the bullet went clean through him, but the other guy who had been shot had the bullet still in him, so the presumption was that nothing could be done for him. So they carried the two guys into the house of one of the wee 'shawley' women (women who constantly wore a black shawl) who used to live in Ardoyne. She lived beside the green electric junction box that was at the gap in Butler Street. They put Mickey on the floor thinking he was dead as the bullet hadn't come out the other side. Then about seven Knights of Malta people tried to bandage Quinn up, because they presumed that he was okay as the bullet had come through him.

Mickey later said he was lying there, just looking over and not one person came near him, because they thought he was a goner! The old woman of the house then came over to Mickey, who was a raging atheist at this stage, and kept saying the rosary in his ear. He said all he could think was, 'Would you clear fuck off Mrs and give my head some peace!' It turned out though that he was alright and they took them both of them out to Whiteabbey Hospital.

There was no IRA or weapons to speak of in Ardoyne at the time. There were a couple of shotguns, but that was it. Somebody actually produced a .22 at one stage but it had maybe nine rounds in it at the most. The locals emptied the nine rounds into various gables and up into the air, but it wasn't fired in any particular direction. I remember the old *Beau Geste* bit, where the guys with a shotgun at the corner of the street would fire and then run down to the next street and fire off a round, and then on to the next street, and so it went on. That was about the height of the armaments that I saw.

One guy lay behind a masonry barricade with a big 'duck catty' (catapult). He had it full of marbles and he would sit up and fire a marble down the street and then lie down again. The return gunfire was hitting the barricade from the other side, and he would then sit up and fire off another marble down the street at them.

The Citizens' Defence Committee basically sprang up in those few days, along with CESA (Catholic Ex-Servicemen's Association). These were guys who had been serving members of the British Army. They played a leading role in organising the defence of Catholic areas against Loyalist attacks in the absence of a meaningful structure within the IRA. They were organising the first aid centres, letting people know where the incursions were happening, and sorting out temporary accommodation for those who had lost their homes. They eventually morphed into the Citizens' Defence Committees in the various areas.

Making Sense of the Mayhem

I found myself in the middle of a mad situation. We were throwing stones and petrol bombs at the peelers. It was great. Then there was the shock of the deaths of people I knew. People like Mickey Lynch. I knew Mickey well, although he was older, and I knew Sammy (McLarnon) to see and he was one of my brother-in-law's best mates. Mickey's family were wrecked by his death, and I think they moved to England after it. Seeing the two boys shot brought the realisation that this wasn't just a laugh. This was serious stuff. One of the speeches that impressed me at that period was the 'Ulster at the Crossroads' speech that was broadcast on the BBC by Terence O'Neill, the then Prime Minister in Stormont. It was a foreboding warning to Loyalists about the future should they not compromise.

As a Nationalist I got what he was saying. If you want to hold on this statelet, you have to accommodate others. Carson had spoken about having to cherish the minority. If Unionists had taken Carson's advice and cherished the minority, I don't think that there would ever have been a border campaign during the 1940s and 1950s by the IRA. Catholics just didn't have the stomach for it then.

At one stage during the conflict Ardoyne accounted for almost 30 per cent of security forces casualties. Such a situation was ironically created by the Unionist State. Unionists will not get that though, because they are immune to irony. To get into the DUP you have to prove that you are immune to irony! We had one DUP guy saying that they were not going to support 50/50 recruitment anymore, because 'that is just entrenching sectarianism.' He was totally straight-faced when he said that. I was thinking, 'If English comedians came off with that we would falling about laughing!'

The Impact of 14–16 August Upon My Family

While the rest of the district was being evacuated out to Gormanstown and Andersonstown, my ma went to Silverstream, a staunchly Loyalist area! My ma would never do anything simple. I had a brother living in Silverstream Parade and that's where she was on the Saturday night with my younger brother. She was also the first woman back into the district the following morning.

That Saturday was a beautiful morning as the Brits were getting ready to move in. The district was eerily quiet and you could have heard a pin drop. The kids were all gone, evacuated. Fifteen- and sixteen-year-old lads were the youngest still present in the district. It was basically like a ghost town. There were just lads standing about the corners doing vigilante. Then at about four o'clock, two RUC Shoreland tanks came on to the two tarmac pitches on the Bone Heights. They came in the gates and stopped beside the changing rooms that are still there to this day. They then trundled across the pitch. Brendan McKeown and I were walking along the Berwick Road and he said to me, 'Here, have a look at that.' (Brendan's family were later evicted from Chief Street in 1970, but at this stage he was staying with me.) The two Shorelands trundled across the pitch and turned sideways on, in line with the way the parallel streets were running along Glenard, with the two turrets with the 30/30 machine guns turned round. They had the whole district covered with their Brownings.

The people had taken all the buses out of the depot and they were placed along the top of every street in the district. I had been round in Old Ardoyne, but the CDC instructed everyone to go back to defend their own streets: 'We will make it that they have to take each street individually.' I thought this was madness. I remember thinking, 'This is nuts. Remember 300 Spartans here boys! Let's make our stand in Old Ardoyne. Give them as little room as possible and let them come on.'

So we had all gone back to our own streets when the word came in at about 6.30 p.m. that the Brits had come into Old Ardoyne and were on the Crumlin Road. Everybody relaxed. Brendan McKeown and I walked round to see what the story was, and the Brits were on the other side of the Crumlin Road with the Loyalists at their back, all facing into Ardoyne. I remember saying to Brendan McKeown, 'What's wrong with that? Why are they facing in towards us? We haven't attacked anybody. The Loyalists are the ones doing the attacking, but what do you expect from a pig but a grunt!'

Brendan wasn't a Republican at that stage, and he said, 'No, you are wrong. You are paranoid.'

I replied, 'I am not fucking paranoid. What would you expect but this typical English response?' This was what I would have expected from them.

The Army came around that Sunday and wanted to clear the barricades. They marched down our street, Strathroy Park, with their tin hats on and their bayonets fixed on to their SLR rifles. The 'good Catholics' were smashing the caches of petrol bombs that we had placed at the bottom of each path to allow for ease of access when we were running up and down the street. Bishop Philbin had also been around that day encouraging people to remove the barricades. I remember thinking, 'Go on you smug old bollocks!' He was for turning the other cheek. I even remember my ma, who was ex-Cumann na mBan, saying, 'Well the bishop says...'. They were all out kissing his ring, and I remember at that stage my anti-clericalism was starting to really bite with me. With Philbin it was, 'Turn the other cheek. Do the Christian thing,' but then he fucked off back to his house on the Somerton Road, and we were still in Strathroy Park.

It was the same with the women bringing them out cups of tea. McKeown had said to me, 'What do you think of that?'

I replied, 'It sticks in my craw, Brendan.' When Brendan and I came back to the street that night, you had these older men pouring the petrol down the grates, not great for the sewerage system either! Brendan and I were shouting at them, 'Hold on a minute. We might need these tomorrow.'

They replied, 'No! The Brits are in and we are safe now!'

That was the whole attitude. Maybe we were conspiracy theorists, but I wasn't convinced that was the end of it. To be honest though, if the Army hadn't come in it would have been a case of another glorious Irish stand. We would have been wiped out because at that stage the Loyalists were increasingly encroaching into the district.

Interestingly, when I was over in the National Archives in Kew a few years ago, I was reading *The 39th Brigade*. This contained the Brits' logs for those few days, and I was appalled when I read of the amount of CS gas and ammunition that they were giving to the peelers as they were coming in to stabilise the area. They were arming one of the protagonists, the RUC. Patrick Rooney, a nine-year-old boy, had been shot dead in Divis Flats with the 30/30, and here the Brits were giving the peelers 30/30 ammunition. It was what it was. No great surprise. It was commendable to the boys in the Republican movement who decided to hold their fire and to wait until they got a bit healthier, and meantime the Brits were doing their job for them in turning people against them by their actions. The escalating actions of the Brits led to greater recruitment into the IRA. There was a big influx of young men of my age into Na Fianna Éireann at that stage. That was the start of the radicalisation of Ardoyne.

Normalisation of Violence

Over the next few years, gun battles became a regular part of life in Ardoyne. When it came down to the gun battles, there was a great rise in solidarity. Basically everyone opened their back door, allowing the people involved to move through the houses rather than down the death traps that Berwick Road and Etna Drive became. In Old Ardoyne you could also move from house to house without the Brits being able to see you from the mill. So there was that solidarity that eventually died out as people got 'war weary'.

When you read about what happened in the rural areas, like parts of Tyrone, they took powerful poundings. In Crossmaglen, you had guys on active service for up to twenty years. If you went on active service in Belfast, you were lucky to get six months because by that stage you were either interned, on remand or shot dead.

Given the number of casualties the Army were suffering in Ardoyne, they put the Paras into the district for almost two years solid and that, to an extent, eventually broke the people. You only saw that spirit reviving again in 1974 with the burning of Long Kesh by the prisoners, then the hunger strikes, and then the death and funeral of Larry Marley. That's when you saw the people pulling together again.

Reflections on the Conflict

I look at all the guys who died as a result of the Troubles. The truth is though that I lost more classmates who were with me from P1 right through my school life to prescription drugs and alcoholism, to lung cancer and bad hearts, than I did through the Troubles. Yes, there was that physical confrontation with the British authorities in Occupied Ireland, but I was living in Ardoyne, a working-class area. It was the same in 'the Lower Whack' (the Lower Falls/Pound Loney area). They weren't only killing us with lead and plastic bullets; they were also killing us with housing conditions, health conditions, the whole failure of the health service to deliver. There was that social struggle that a lot of Republicans wouldn't look at because they were only interested in the armed struggle, but there is no chance of advancing towards a socialist republic without education. Unionists and Nationalists in the North of Ireland have to come together for the sake of education, and then go into a united Ireland.

Ardoyne Kickhams

Ardoyne Kickhams played a major role in my life in Ardoyne. What was great about Ardoyne Kickhams for me was that in the face of many clubs who were nearly fracturing due to differences in politics, we maintained a great ethos in the Kickhams, down to people like Frank McCallan, Jimmy Fennell and Harry Maguire. When you went into Ardoyne Kickhams you left your politics at the front door. You were there to play Gaelic football. Young boys and girls came in to play our Gaelic games, and they were proud to play their Gaelic games and they developed a great affinity for our club.

I always thought that if the Brits had the opportunity to make something vanish in a flash, and they had a choice between Sinn Féin and the GAA, they would have chosen the GAA, because the GAA, for me, has done much more to inculcate Nationalism and the sense that we are a separate nation from the English.

Ardoyne Kickhams paid a terrible price during the Troubles. We had seven playing members killed, but if you also include the brothers and sisters, the fathers and mothers of our members, we are talking up to 200 deaths. If they weren't killed in Ardoyne, it was over in the likes of the New Lodge or Ballymurphy. That is frightening. If you then consider the number of people wounded or imprisoned, it becomes really astronomical.

A big day for the Kickhams was 23 August 1969. The sun was splitting the trees. It was the Saturday after the Brits came in, and we played in the under-16 county championship final. There is a famous photo that was taken of the team in Casement Park. The club had got a minibus 'from somewhere' and were driving us over from Ardoyne to Casement Park. The Falls Road was still smouldering as we drove through it – mills, buses and burnt-out cars – but the most important thing for us that day was to play the match and to win. It was a while before we realised that what we had witnessed was not good fun, but that people had been killed and others had lost their homes. It was the first part of the double we were going for

– the league and the championship. We won 0–9 to 0–4 and we played really well, but we were beaten in a play-off for the league. It was the best underage squad the club had seen in a long time, and big things were expected of us. It was the first team photograph that I remember being in. It was all very professional, but great gas! Our Ciarán is in the photo, and he was shot dead. Ciarán is kneeling in front of Raymond Mooney. Raymond was shot dead coming out of the church. Gerard Rosatto is also there. His father was shot dead. Mickey and Frank McCallan are in it. Their brother Calum was shot dead. There are all those connections.

Then some of the lads started emigrating away from Ardoyne. Tommy Ferguson was the first to go, and then particular friends of mine, Davy and Danny Wasson. They were both in the team photograph that day, and Davy was captain of the team. Davy and I had played vocational schools football together and had been friends for a long time. I remember the night he left very well. Some of the lads went down to the boat with him, but I was chasing a girl from up the Falls at the time, so I didn't get down! It was a terrible feeling though that one of my best friends was leaving home at eighteen and I would probably never see him again.

Over the next four to five years we lost a lot of good players. Liam Corr, Big Mossy, Roy Kerrigan, Martin Mallon – all moved out of the district or emigrated. We also had the harassment by the security forces in Nationalist areas once the Brits discovered that there was a difference between soccer and Gaelic football and that we going to play Nationalist games. The club had acquired its own minibus by this stage, and when that became known to the security forces it was always a cert to be stopped, players taken off the bus, names taken, frisked and just general harassment. The sectarian assassination campaign was going ahead and a lot of members were bereaved. The assassinations hit Ardoyne particularly hard. We are a very close-knit community where people all know each other. Regarding the Gaelic club, most people had joined from around the age of nine or ten, so we would see each other grow up. The McCallans for example, Frank and Mickey, who had played on that 1969 team, were about the third or fourth generation of their family to play for Ardoyne. Their younger brother, Callum, who came up through the club, was assassinated in his early twenties. The pain of seeing someone like Callum growing up and then killed wastefully, to see my friends suffering because of events like that is very difficult.

As time went by you thought you became hardened to the Troubles. There was a familiarity about them that to an extent bred contempt. Initially when a gun battle started and shots were fired in the area, people and children would run into the house to get away from the gunfire. Then as time went on there was curiosity about it, and when people heard gunfire they would run out of their houses towards the gunfire to see what had happened. We became very complacent about it all. We would be playing over in the west of the city against a team from the country, like Ahoghill, and a gun battle would break out. The lads would have this great wind-up where they would shout over to each other, 'That's an armalite.' 'No, that's an SLR.' This used to take the country men to the cleaners.

Tommy McAuley was one of our top players on the senior team, and he was shot in the back by a Loyalist assassination squad as he got off the bus coming from work. We played a game about three weeks afterwards against a team from the country and they asked, 'Where's Tommy?' We responded, 'Ach, Tommy was shot, but he's ok. He's not dead.' You could see the difference in attitude.

Tragedy Hits Home

My brother Ciarán was on that under-16 squad with me in 1969. Our Ciarán always said that he would never see eighteen. That was always a claim of his. It used to scare the shit out of Cathal Goan when Ciarán started talking like that. On New Year's Eve 1973 Ciarán, then seventeen years old, came up to my house in Cranbrook Gardens after midnight, gave me a big fucking hug and said, 'That's it kid. This is our last one.'

I said, 'Are you at that crap again?'

He said, 'No. I am serious. This is my last New Year's.' He was killed the following October. He had called it from when he was about fourteen. He was convinced about this shit. He had been giving me the old James Dean bit: 'Die young and leave a good-looking corpse.'

Ciarán had a great move on the girls in Kelly's Bar. He would have been chatting away to a girl and then would say, 'Guess what age I am?' He told me that this was his ploy. I told him that it was madness. What woman is going to go for a guy much younger than her? But they did. They invariably did! He was deadly for the women, and when he was lying in the window for his wake, there were these broken-hearted women coming in. He was a serious case. He had the big Gilbert O'Sullivan hair. When he had the hair cut he looked like Gilbert O'Sullivan, but when it grew out he went more Hendrix or Phil Lynott. He also drove around in his white works van, and he wouldn't pass anyone from Ardoyne at the bus stop. I saw him pull up into Old Ardoyne, and maybe up to nine guys would get out of the back of that old van. He was a remarkable guy. About 6'1" at that stage with more growing to do.

Ciarán was killed by Loyalists after he was picked up on the Cliftonville Road and assassinated by the Protestant Action Force on 13 October 1974. He was seventeen years of age. Sadly, Ciarán was full drunk when he was picked up by two well-known Loyalists. He was a big lad and he could fight. He could certainly punch his weight. Had he been sober that night when they picked him up, he would have beaten the fucking crap out of the two of them when they tried to put him into the car. But he was drunk. He didn't know what was going on. He had knife wounds on his chest and arms, consistent with puncture wounds inflicted by a pen knife. He had been badly beaten in the community centre where they brought him before taking him to a quarry near a road called the Horseshoe Bend. He had slipped out of his coat and made a run for it. The first bullet that hit him got him in the back of the leg and he fell. He sat up, put his hands up and had bullet wounds in one of his hands and an exit wound in the elbow. He was hit six or seven times, although only one of the wounds was fatal. He was the third Catholic from Ardoyne murdered in four days.

I went to identify his body. The police took us from Musgrave Street station to the Laganbank morgue. It was a horrible place. When we entered the room to identify his body, there were five bodies along one wall which were toe-tagged, and they obviously knew who they were. There were two bodies along the right-hand wall with no toe tags but with sheets over them. Ciarán had very curly hair, and I could see the hair sticking up from under the sheet of the body nearest to me. Having slept in the same room as Ciarán for as long as I can remember, and knowing what his hair looked like sticking up from under a sheet, I knew even before the policeman had pulled down the sheet that it was Ciarán. It was a powerful size of a funeral. He really struck a chord with the people of Ardoyne.

When Ciarán was killed the RUC Special Branch sold me a pig in the poke about what had happened to him. The version of his death I narrated for *Ardoyne: The Untold Truth* was totally fabricated by the Special Branch. They had convinced the family of their version before I engaged with the Historical Enquiries Team and found that had been an absolute crock of shit that the RUC had handed out. They had put out black propaganda to put fear into the district.

Ciarán's death left me with a lot of pain. Things like that were inflicted upon families for no other reason than people imagining that they are a threat. Every time there is a death it brings it back to me. People and families on both sides have suffered.

I continued to play for the club after Ciarán was assassinated, but it got progressively harder to field a team. As a result of the Troubles we lost our home pitch in Ballysillan, so we were travelling away to all our games. There was one year we received an award from the GAA for never failing to field. It was tough, and by the late 1970s there were seven lads from that 1969 team who had emigrated to foreign parts, four or five were living in the South of Ireland and one, at that stage, had been shot dead.

A Proud Lunatic Asylum!

The thing that I find very sad is that we have a wealth of human resources in Ardoyne, but the ones that do well tend to move away. It's a bit like the demise of St Gabriel's School from 1969. The numbers had reduced dramatically by the time it closed down, and a number of those who were still on their books had been 'referrals' from other schools. St Gabriel's had enough problems of its own without taking people with problems from outside the district. That was the nail in the coffin for St Gabriel's. I loved that school. I pulled my old school record out. It is very funny: 'This boy is probably watching films that are too advanced for him.'

I would always borrow George Bernard Shaw when he described Dublin as 'an open-air lunatic asylum'. Ardoyne was a bit like that. It was stuffed with so many characters it was unbelievable. I just loved it. You went back into the Gaelic club after a match, and people like Malachy Donnelly, Old Bulliver, Hugh McCallan and all the boys who played for the Kickhams in the 1920s, the 1930s and the 1940s would be there. People used to ask why I was always standing up at the bar talking to the older guys. I would say, 'The devil always has the best yarns!' They had wonderful stories. I had a great love for them all.

I remember standing in the club one Saturday night at a sing-song at one of the Fleadhs, and my ma's old contemporaries were all in from the mill, the likes of Bell McRoberts and the old Cumann na mBan women. The noise level was fine until the women got a couple of drinks. Then they thought they were back in the spinning room or the shuttling room of the flax and linen mills, and the volume just got louder and louder. Then they started doing the tic tac, using hand signals like betting at the race course to communicate against the loud noise, 'Alright Bell? How's your Andy? Is his stomach ok?'

'Yea, yea, he is in bed with his stomach at the minute.' It was hilarious. I was standing at the Fleadh one night with Peter Brown, the piper. He said to me, 'Jaysus Paddy! There's a lot of noise coming off those auld boilers!' Ardoyne – just a fascinating place to live in!

13

Malachy Toner

The Boy from Armagh

I was born in 1948 about five miles outside Newry in Whitecross, County Armagh, not too far from Markethill. My father was a farmer and up until 1954 that was my life. I was two years at the primary school in a place called Tullyhearn. It was a typical old national school, with two classrooms where the mistress taught the junior class and the master taught the senior class. The junior and senior classes though were an amalgamation of different ages, so we had about four classes in the junior classroom, and four in the senior. The teaching staff was a husband-and-wife set-up and, to be honest, neither of them had an interest in teaching. The husband was a gambler and played poker with the parish priest, the butcher, the baker and anybody else who wanted to join in. As a consequence, our lunch break lasted two hours – it was a great life!

My father then fell into bad health, and his brother-in-law met him one day and said, 'I know the place for you. There is an off-licence for sale in Belfast. Sell the farm and move down to Belfast. There is no heavy work involved in it. All you are doing is work as a shopkeeper.' So in November 1954 we moved to Cambrai Street on the opposite ('Protestant') side of the Crumlin Road. Such a change. From getting up in the morning and walking three miles to school, I was now getting out of bed in Cambrai Street to be looking at a house across the street from me that I could almost touch. It was a complete change.

The off-licence that my father had bought had been owned by a family called McMullan from outside Loughinisland, County Down. They owned the off-licence, but a guy called Paul McCartan ran it for them, and he lived on the premises. The night that we arrived in he was packing his bags to go, but we had arrived to begin a new life in Ardoyne.

New Place, New Friends

One of my earliest memories of Ardoyne is of being brought to the boys' school in Butler Street. At that stage we had the old Nissen huts. The principal was a teacher called Miss O'Farrell. There were six of us in my family: myself, four girls and my brother, Charlie. When we joined Holy Cross Charlie was going into his first year at school. I remember my mother saying to Miss O'Farrell, 'Malachy is a bit nervous about where we are living. Is there anybody you could put him into contact with he could go to school with?' At that time I had no idea what kind of street Cambrai Street was, but it turned out that we were the only Catholic family living in it. Miss O'Farrell said to my mother, 'I know a family who live near you on the Crumlin Road. The father is called Larry McEvoy and he is a shoemaker. His son is Hugh McEvoy, and Hugh will take Malachy to school.'

My mother would leave me at the top of Cambrai Street, just on the Crumlin Road. Hugh would have walked down from his home to meet me, and away we went to school. The first day at lunchtime he said to me, 'Come on, we are going home for lunch.' Now that didn't happen when we lived in Armagh as it was three mile walk up to the house, and then the journey back! So Hugh brought me to the top of Cambrai Street and said, 'Right, away you go.'

I said, 'Go where?'

'Down there,' he said, 'you live down there.'

'I might,' I said, 'but I am not walking down there on my own!'

That was in 1956, and Hugh and I became great mates. I met other fellows at the school, like Joe McStravick and Mickey Hale. We were all good mates and Mrs Quinn was our teacher. I began to enjoy school then, and got close to the McEvoy family: Lawrence, Jackie, Kathleen and Jean. Kathleen and my sisters also became great friends.

We had a cousin called Stan Shields who lived in Galway, and sometime in the late 1960s he came up to stay with us for a holiday and he met Kathleen McEvoy. They started going out together and were eventually married on 20 September 1969. It was one of the last wedding receptions in the Mount Alverna Hotel at the top of the Whiterock Road, where the filling station is these days. We were visiting them just a couple of weeks ago on their 50th wedding anniversary and Kathleen was showing us photographs of the wedding, in which she was standing at the bottom of her driveway with soldiers standing beside her as she was getting her photograph taken: a reminder of the craziness that was descending upon us.

Getting Familiar with Difference

During the time we lived in Whitecross in Armagh I didn't know what a Protestant was, and yet families like the Frasiers (Willie Frasier) only lived a couple of miles from us. I hadn't a clue who they were. I knew they were farmers but had no idea about their background, and everybody just seemed to get on well with each other. So when we arrived in Cambrai Street, we were the only Catholic family in the street, and again there wasn't any antagonism. The earliest incident that I can remember, and it was reported in the newspaper, was about six months after we had arrived in Cambrai Street, when my brother, Charlie, had been sitting on the front doorstep of our accommodation at the off-licence. This fella came along and said to Charlie, 'I heard you are a Fenian.'

Charlie said, 'No, I am not a Fenian. I am a Toner from Maytown in Whitecross!' It was the first time we had ever heard of a Fenian.

The next thing, Charlie got friendly with this wee fella called Billy Tate. Billy was one these smart wee fellas who knew everything, and one day he said to Charlie, 'Charlie, my mother says that you support Davy Lowry.'

Charlie came home and said to my ma, 'Who is Davy Lowry?' We couldn't work out who Davy Lowry was, until we eventually worked out that he meant De Valera! So this was obviously the talk that was going on in the background about who and what we were.

I think in those days there were probably only about two people who had a telephone in Cambrai Street. We had a telephone in the off-licence, and in the late 1950s and early 1960s there were a lot of shipyard workers in the area. Shipyard work was getting less and less, and a lot of these men had to go over to places like Newcastle and Glasgow to find work. So there would be a queue of women at night coming in to ring, or to wait on a phone call from their husbands, who could have been away from home for up to six months. At this stage we were all the best of friends, but we began to notice as we got a bit older that when for example we would go to Mass on Sunday these same people didn't talk to us. They ignored us. If they saw us walking up Cambrai Street, or up Heather Street and along Chief Street, they would close the door. During the week everything was fine, and if they needed to make a phone call they were the best of friends. If they needed a bottle of whiskey at twelve o'clock at night they would rap the door, and on a Sunday when the off-licence was supposed to be closed they would be round looking for us to give them a bottle of whiskey through the side door. That was the kind of life we were leading.

When we first arrived in Cambrai Street, bonfires set around the beginning of July were being built about fifty yards from our house. As we moved into the 1960s, the bonfire was gradually moved up the street until it was right outside our front door at the corner of Heather Street and Cambrai Street. The outside of our house was painted with gloss paint, so for about a four-year period we had to put a claim into the Northern Ireland Office every year to get the house repainted after it was blistered from the heat of the bonfire. A contractor would come out and paint the house, only for it to be blistered again the following year. We had no doubt that it was being done to show that we were Fenians, or supporters of 'Davy Lowry'! That cooled down again after the 'Twelfth' period, and the same guys who had organised the bonfire would be playing football with us in the street.

One of the things that we had to be careful about was when Charlie and I were playing hurling. I left Holy Cross Boys' School when I was about ten and went to St Mary's Primary in Divis Street, and then on to Hardinge Street School. Charlie did the same, but ended up going to St Mary's Grammar School. We were both playing hurling, and we used to get the brown carry-out bags from the off-licence and put them over the base of the hurl and tape it up, so it looked like we were just carrying a hockey stick. So that's how we went to our matches with the hurling team. It wasn't that anyone had ever said something to us, but we just knew that there was the chance of something happening.

We were friends with the Mullan family from Ardoyne. They were big Republicans. Hughie Mullan's father died around 1968, and the funeral was going from Ardoyne over to Milltown Cemetery. When his remains came out of Mass at Holy Cross, Ardoyne, I saw these men with the old-style caps on. These were the 'old IRA' who were providing a guard of honour. They walked down the Crumlin Road, and Charlie and I were walking down the Crumlin Road behind the coffin. I said to Charlie, 'What are we going to do when it goes to Cambrai Street?' The men behind the coffin were going to walk behind the coffin down Cambrai Street (where we lived), but luckily they stopped at Flax Street and took the IRA gear off and got into cars. Charlie and I then left the funeral and went in the other direction, because although we wanted to be at the funeral, we didn't want to be seen as part of it by the people who lived around us!

Trouble in the Air

The first sign of any real trouble was before the Malvern Street shooting. Peter Ward was murdered and two other men were with him. One of the men, called Levington, escaped, but the other man was injured. He was from around the Beechmount area, but for some reason he had gone to Holy Cross Boys' School. He was a year older than me and was a good friend of Lawrence McEvoy, which was how I got to know him. Before the shooting happened we had windows broken in the off-licence and in our living accommodation. Paint would be thrown at the windows. We had a big sitting room with a large window, and my mother came down one Sunday morning and opened the curtains and pulled up the venetian blind. She thought the venetian hadn't gone up because it was still all white! The outside of the window had been completely covered with white paint. That was in about 1966, even before the Troubles started.

After the murder in Malvern Street, good families who lived directly opposite us were still very friendly towards us. One family was called Moreland and another called Berry. In between there was a guy called Gibson, but he was not friendly. He never said anything to us in those early days, but we could see that the connection was not there. Apart from the coolness I mentioned that we experienced when we were going up and down to chapel, the rest of the street were fine towards us. However, the number of incidents began to increase after the Malvern Street murder.

Outbreak of Violence

My father had been born in 1904, so was coming up to pension age by 1969, and we had been talking about selling the off-licence in Cambrai Street and moving up to the Woodvale Road. That was great for me, because I was at the age when I was playing football for Ardoyne. I had mates like Frankie McKeown, Paul Gowdy, Stevie Dobbin, Gerry Cullen, and I was going to be living nearer to them. The family had been talking about moving house from about late 1967, but on 2 August 1969 I remember being up in the old clubrooms of Ardoyne Kickhams at the top of Butler Street. It was a Saturday night. I was 21 years old. I was walking down the road with Frankie McKeown, who then lived in Chief Street, and I said to him, 'Do you fancy nipping down to the Wheatfield for a bottle of stout before I head home?' So the two of us headed down to the Wheatfield Bar, where the manager was a guy called Frank Roland. The bar was on the corner of Leopold Street. It was a fantastic bar. We went in and ordered two bottles of stout and were standing at the bar. Next thing, Frank Roland came down and said, 'You two boys better get home. I have got a call from a guy in a bar on the Shankill Road that there is big trouble coming up from the Shankill Road.' That was about ten o'clock, and Frankie went up to Chief Street and I headed for Cambrai Street.

Due to the premises being attacked so often, we had already put wire mesh on the inside of the windows so that anything coming through the windows wouldn't get any further. Along with my sisters and my da, I made sure that the wire mesh was secured because we thought we were in for another stoning that night. We went upstairs and put wardrobes against the windows. I don't know why we thought we were going to be attacked more that night than on others, but it turned out that a mob came up the street and instead of throwing stones as usual, they threw petrol bombs. Luckily enough, these were thrown as they were passing the house, and the mob was intent on heading further up the road towards other Catholic premises. A family called Matthews had an off-licence in Bray Street that was managed by Teddy McMahon, who in later years owned a clothes shop on the front of the Crumlin Road. Another family called Kelly had an off-licence in Disraeli Street and Enfield Parade. The mob was on their way to attack these premises as they passed us. We called the police and we were able to get the petrol bombs out when they arrived. The police said, 'Look, this crowd will be coming back and we will be about the place', but they stayed for about ten minutes and then they were away again.

The crowd did come back, and the same thing happened again. There were windows broken upstairs, but luckily none of the petrol bombs came into the premises. The police arrived again the next morning, 3 August, and said that things were so bad that they would advise us to leave. So we started to make plans to move. We knew a few guys who could help us. Peter O'Hare worked for a firm called the Happy Nappy Company. They did the laundry of the old towelling nappies. These were the days when you left the towelling nappies in a bucket in the house, but Peter would come and take the soiled nappies away and bring them back when clean. John Lappin was doing a service on a van that belonged to Moss's butcher's shop on the Antrim Road that had been given to him by Tom McMullan. So I went to Ardoyne and told a few friends that we had to get out of Cambrai Street. Peter O'Hare came with his Happy Nappy van and John came down with his Moss's mini-van, and we got our clothing and a few other necessities, as we thought we were going to be able to come back later with a proper vehicle to clear the place properly.

However, the police rang my da on the Sunday night/early Monday morning and said that the place was on fire. We went back later on the Monday morning and the whole place was gone. We left and went to an aunt's house on the Ormeau Road, where we stayed for a few weeks until we got rented accommodation in a place called Coolnasilla, off the Glen Road. Eventually we moved back into a house in Mountainview, and that's where my mother and father lived until they died.

Impact on Family Life

The impact of these incidents on our family's life was fierce. We were homeless. I was sleeping in my aunt's living room. I then got an offer from Peter O'Hare to live in his house on the Cavehill Road and I ended up staying with him until we got the new house in Coolnasilla. A great guy.

I remember going into the town with my father and he was looking for a place to rent in a safe area. I felt sorry for him. He was 65 years of age and he was walking around town, going into different estate agents, looking for a place for his family to live. One of the things I remember is going into an estate agent and my father saying, 'I am looking for a place to rent.'

The reply was, 'How many are in the family?'

'There are eight of us,' he said.

He was told, 'You have no chance. No one wants eight people going into a rented house.' Lucky enough though, the eight of us ended up moving into the house in Coolnasilla Park East.

We didn't know how things were going to end up for us. We had lost everything. We had trouble getting the statement that we needed from the police that there was 'a riotous assembly' in order to put a claim for compensation into the Northern Ireland Office. We also had to get evidence from the suppliers for the stock that was lost in the off-licence. It was a terrible time for my mother and father. Lucky enough, the uncle who had advised my father to buy the place in Cambrai Street knew a man called Paddy Hunt, one of the larger wholesalers in the drink trade. Paddy Hunt met my father and said, 'Look, there is this old law to do with the Blitz that happened in Belfast. If a licensed premises is affected by the Blitz you can move your licence within three miles of your old premises.'

So eventually my father was able to move his licence from Cambrai Street to a shop between Bray Street and Chief Street and was able to open an off-licence there. We thought that was brilliant and that we were back in business again. As it turned out, about six months later a bomb was thrown into the back of the off-licence and the back of the shop was wrecked. The incident was reported in the *Irish News*, and it told how my father was put out of Cambrai Street in August 1969, and then in February 1970 this happened to him again. When my parents bought their house in Mountainview in 1973, a bomb was once again thrown by Loyalists into it. That had a big effect upon them, but there was never any investigation carried out into it.

The old police station was in Leopold Street, and from 1964 until 1969 we would maybe have had about ten policemen who drank in our off-licence in Cambrai Street. I could even give you the names of some of them who used to come in. My da used to say to them, 'Where are you on duty tonight?' I remember one occasion in 1969 when one of them said, 'I am in the Highfield estate but it is a bit cold, so I think I will stay in here.' That was how they carried out their duties in the 1950s and the 1960s, and we knew some great characters in the police. My da was very friendly with one policeman, a guy called Sam Davidson from Ballymena. Sam was a detective, and he was a real character. Another guy called Wilfie Wilson was a constable and was often on duty in the Highfield estate.

There was another guy called Cummings and he was from Scarva. I always remember him coming over to my father when we were living in my aunt's house on the Ormeau Road. He had an envelope in his hand and said to my father, 'Charlie, I have a bit of savings. If you need it, there it is.'

My da said, 'No. I will be alright. I have enough money to do us.'

That was the type of young policeman who was there at the time. I also remember him telling my da that if he was making any report about what happened to him and knew anybody who was involved, then don't mention their names, just say that there was 'a mob'. He told my da, 'Don't mention any names, as this will get back to the Woodvale Defence Association.' These were the forerunners to the UDA. 'Anything you say', he told my da, 'will go straight out of Tennant Street police station to them.' I didn't believe him and thought he was just having us on, but now we know that it did happen.

Escalating Violence

I was going back and forward from the Ormeau Road to Ardoyne and I could see things getting very bad. I remember going across town around 12 August. There was nobody about. There was no one on the Crumlin Road. My recollection of the Troubles actually starting was the riots in Derry on 12 August, and then they were followed by the Hooker Street riots. I can remember the different people involved in them. Skinny Lizzie, who had a shop in Hooker Street, would put the Union Jack up outside her shop. I can remember the start of the stone-throwing and the rioting between Hooker Street, Disraeli Street and Columbia Street. That area then became an interface between the two sides of the community.

On Friday 15 August I was living on the Ormeau Road but I remember going back over to Ardoyne and a priest saying that it was the smallest number of people he had ever seen attending Mass on a holy day of obligation. The Catholic people were staying on their side of the Crumlin Road and were not venturing over to the chapel which was on the Protestant side. I was standing at the corner of Butler Street with Frankie McKeown. This was when the McKeowns were still living in Chief Street before eventually being put out of their home a few days later. We saw these men coming up the road. They were 'B' Specials but all of them were wearing masks. During those nights of August they were making their way up the Crumlin Road as far as Ballysillan and they were attacking homes of Catholics.

Teammates Making Different Choices

I knew a lot of guys who got involved in the Troubles, although for some of them I only heard about their involvement in later years. I had played football with them for many years, and some of them I am still very friendly with. I remember 27 June 1970 when a riot had started on the Crumlin Road, and my sister Deirdre and I were due to work in the off-licence near Bray Street that Saturday afternoon. We were walking up towards the top of Brompton Park and this car came round from Twaddell Avenue at speed. It had come from West Belfast, and when it stopped a couple of guys got out and came round the side and opened the boot. You should have seen the guns that were in it. Some of the guys I had played Gaelic with were involved in that incident. That was my first experience of gunfire in Ardoyne.

I played football with some of the guys who got involved in the IRA, but that was their choice. I didn't want to be involved in what I saw developing. I didn't think it was right that no matter what was happening to you that you would shoot someone. I made a conscious decision that was different to theirs, but I still remember being asked to do things for the IRA though. I worked for the GPO, which then became BT (British Telecom). My wife, then my girlfriend, Nancy, lived in Owenvarragh Park in West Belfast. I remember she had a friend who worked with her in the hairdressers in Belfast. Her friend said to her, 'Your boyfriend works in different hotels in Belfast because of his work. Would he be doing work in these hotels?' She mentioned the names of a few hotels in Belfast.

Nancy said, 'Well you better ask him yourself. I am not sure what he does.' This was about 1971.

So I was in Owenvarragh one night and the friend comes to the door and says to Nancy, 'There is a man here who wants to know if Malachy will go out and talk to him.'

I went out and the man was sitting in the driver's seat with his head turned away from me. He said to me, 'Get in the back.' I got in the back and he introduced himself as an intelligence officer from the IRA. He said, 'We will not introduce each other. We all have our own breaking point, and if we are taken in and questioned I don't know you and you don't know me.'

He told me that the place they wanted to get information about was the Royal Avenue Hotel. The IRA knew that there was a room in the hotel were people were coming up on the train from the South and meeting the Special Branch in this room for whatever reward they got. That was the first time I had ever heard about 'touts'. I wasn't able to help him, so he didn't want to know me again!

We have so much information now that we didn't have then, so it's hard to compare choices that people made. Different programmes are telling us more and more about what was going on. I went to the Civil Rights marches, but for me that was about housing and about confronting the discrimination in Derry. I thought that if we protested people would listen to us and the discrimination would stop. I witnessed the different stages of O'Neill trying to change things, and of Paisley going to stop all the changes.

When Brian McCargo joined the police reserve I didn't think that was such a terrible thing, because there was talk that things would change if Catholics would join the RUC. Even when the UDR was formed there were Catholics joining it, believing that this would stop the rioting and the shooting between different sides of the community. People genuinely believed that these decisions would help to change things.

I didn't think that the men I knew who got involved would end up shooting people, bombing places. I never thought at that time that these things could happen. I could hear people like Gerry Fitt, Paddy Devlin, Frank McAteer telling us that we were on the right road now and that all these injustices are going to change. So my thinking was that violence was not going to help get us anywhere. I have to say though, that although I may not agree with what some of those people did, I can understand their choices, especially when I think of incidents like Bloody Sunday, various other incidents around Ardoyne, or particular people being singled out simply because they were Catholics. People were being picked up by the Shankill Butchers, like Ted McQuaid, chairman of the Ardoyne Kickhams Gaelic club, and brutally murdered simply because they were Catholics. It's hard to remember my particular reactions to specific events, but I know that I didn't want to be involved in violence. I was just hoping that it was going to stop and that men would not see the need to get involved in violence. I hoped that what I saw happening around me would be over soon, but unfortunately that was not to happen.

A Terrible Price to Pay

While every incident had its own impact, I could see the effect it had on other people more than on myself. I can remember Fr Ailbe in the early 1970s when people were living in Silverstream. He would be in our house in Mountainview and he would say, 'I have just heard that someone has been put out of Silverstream.' As a priest he would go to Silverstream. To be honest, the majority of the people in Silverstream would have been antagonistic towards him, but he was brave enough to go in there and help those people, to arrange for a van to go in there and help to get them out.

There were tragedies in which someone I knew had been shot, like Ted McQuaid. Ted and I were great mates. Tommy McAuley was also shot coming from work. He was badly injured, but luckily enough he survived. People like Terry Toolan, with whom I also played football. He was shot and killed. I remember that very well. I remember going to his funeral and his whole family were affected by Terry's death. This community played a heavy price.

A Community Apart

I am very proud of being from Ardoyne. While I did not want to be involved in shootings or bombings, I knew guys who were, and they are still my friends. I play golf every Wednesday with Hughie Mullan. If you hit a ball out of bounds in golf, or you think you are out of bounds, you play a provisional ball. If that happens when I am with Hughie I say, 'Hughie, I am playing one of yours!'

Gerry Cullen was a great friend who died in June 2018. He had been living in Nenagh, Tipperary and I would go down to visit him and would meet his friends. His wife, Máire, rang me about six months after he died and said, 'There is a guy going up to Belfast. He was a great friend of Gerry's but I don't think you have met him. You met his brother, Brian White. Will you meet him in Belfast?'

So I met him in the Hilton, down near the Waterfront. He asked me to show him around Belfast. I said, 'Right, I am going to take you to Ardoyne.'

He asked, 'Why are you bringing me there?'

I told him, 'Well, Gerry loved Ardoyne, so that's where we are going first. There is no better place to start.'

14

Cathal Goan

Early Years

I was born in 1954, the fifth child of eight born to Seamus Goan and Ita Rice. Family life for me started in Andersonstown. My earliest memories of Ardoyne are going to visit my grandparents, who lived there when we lived in Andersonstown. I have a memory of occasions like Christmas, but my biggest single memory is my older brother taking me over to see Granny and Grandad after I had made my First Communion. With the proceeds of whatever I was given, I was able to go to down to Woolworths and buy a wooden sword, which was broken the next day. I remember not being impressed by the quality of goods from Woolworths as a result. I was at school in Holy Child Primary School, which I think at the time was one of the biggest in the area. It was already too small for the burgeoning population of Andersonstown, so our class was relocated to under the stand in Casement Park.

When I was eight years of age we moved to Ardoyne to live with my grandparents. It was the winter of 1963, and there had been an enormous snowfall. The snow was kind of exceptional at that stage. It was a big adventure. In the middle of it all though, my grandfather had gone missing. He was found about three or four days later in Templepatrick, about twelve miles from his home on the Crumlin Road. It was clear that he had been suffering from some kind of memory lapse, so my father took it into his head that the best thing that could happen was that he and his wife and eight children should leave their relatively modern Housing Trust house with a bathroom, toilet and three nice bedrooms in Andersonstown to move to a Victorian house in Ardoyne which didn't have a bathroom. It had a bath, but the toilet was outside in the yard.

So, that's what happened. We moved lock, stock and barrel in February of that year. My mother, father and eight of us children moved in on top of my granny and granda. They were both getting on in years and died within five years of us moving in, so they were lucky enough to be spared the experience of the Troubles.

The snow was still on the ground in Ardoyne when we started our new school. The local primary school headmaster was a man called Charlie Morris. I think my father must have been with us the day we started our new school, as he said, 'I taught your father as well.' I remember thinking that was something special, going to the same school that my father had been to. It was a good school and I was very lucky.

Are You a Catholic?

I don't even know that I was necessarily aware of the terms 'Catholic' and 'Protestant' at that time. I remember though that when we came to live in Ardoyne we used to go down to the Ormeau Baths on a Saturday morning. We would get the bus down and go for a swim at about 8.30 or 9 a.m., and we had to queue up to go into the baths. I remember a man asking us what religion we were, and we said we were Catholics. He continued, 'But are you Roman Catholics? Because I'm a Catholic, but I'm not a Roman Catholic.' I hadn't a clue what he was talking about.

So my memory of Ardoyne at that stage was of beginning to become much clearer that there was 'them and us', or some sense of 'them and us' than there ever had been in Andersonstown, which was just one big homogenous Catholic block. I began to discover there were places which were defined as Protestant, other places that were defined as Catholic, and some that were mixed.

Uninvited Guests at the Party

I think that in the mid-1960s, for the most part, the atmosphere around the Twelfth was generally festive, but it wasn't our party and we weren't invited to it. It was a bit of fun, these lunatics beating the hell out of drums, jumping up and down, and making eejits of themselves in my view. And then also, there was a kind of sense of they were 'Orangeys' and we weren't. I don't know that it was particularly deeply felt, but even during that period I was beginning to become aware of a sense that there was something else going on.

In Ardoyne we lived on the front of the road, right opposite Holy Cross Church. On 12 July the bands would have stopped outside the church on their way down the road to the parade or to the Field, and beat even more hell out of the drums than they would normally. Marching bands were literally within six feet of our house. As we were sitting in the front room, they were beating the hell out of their drums just the other side of the window, so we couldn't but be aware of it. I suppose the expression that we would have come to know at that stage was 'Croppies lie down': just a general reminder that this was their sacred turf and we were there on tolerance.

Living in Ardoyne you became aware of 'cautionary tales', and you absorbed them almost by osmosis. We became aware of the need to be careful of who you met, and of what you said in front of them. Then we got all these stories of fellas being stopped and asked what school they went to, or asked to say the alphabet. Strange how even the way you pronounced the letter 'h' indicated your religion! If you gave the wrong answer you got clattered. So all of that became part of growing up in Ardoyne.

Childhood Memories

Our playground would have been the Ballysillan Playing Fields, which was just a walk up Ardoyne Road. It was a great spot. We would also go up to a place we called Harmony Heights, where there was a waterfall behind a factory that made some kind of fabric, and occasionally you could see whatever effluent they were putting out into the stream as it would change colour. The river would become the most violent red or unimaginable blue just at a switch. That's the area that subsequently became redeveloped and known as Glencairn, a big Loyalist estate for people from the Lower Shankill.

Ardoyne Kickhams, the local GAA club, had its base just around the corner from our house. This was before they got their own rooms down at the bottom of Butler Street. It was not much more than a glorified little room at the back of Frank the barber's shop, so I got to know people through that as well. My father had played for Ardoyne, my older brother would have played a bit, and my sisters were involved in the camogie teams as well. So there was a sense of being involved in the community, even if we were relative blow-ins.

The GAA club was for the most part a Catholic environment. There was only one lad I can think of immediately who was a member of our GAA club who was a Protestant, and at that stage nobody passed any remark. Fifty years later I say to myself, isn't it an awful pity that we didn't have more of that, then maybe we would have had less of the bitterness. The fact that he was a Protestant wouldn't have been anything that anybody got wired up about until the Troubles started. Then these 'badges of honour' became very much more important. It wasn't that everybody was saying, 'Oh, he's a Prod!', but somehow or other these things began to be said in a way that wouldn't have any great importance attached to them before the Troubles.

Looking back at it, my sense is that life went on pretty much as normal, except for about five or six weeks during the summer, when a substantial portion of the population went daft but at some level, conscious or unconscious, we negotiated our way through all this nonsense.

Political Awareness

My father had been a member of the IRA, and he had been interned during the Second World War. However, he very rarely spoke about his experiences. Anything that I know about this was gleaned from occasional remarks over the years. We knew that he had been interned and I, for whatever reason, remember feeling this was something that I should be proud of. Maybe my sense of Irishness at that stage was framed in that context of my father being put away for his country. I don't ever recall him advocating a particular line in politics other than him saying that the person he respected most was our local Northern Ireland Labour Party MP, Vivian Simpson. He seemed to have a lot of respect for Vivian Simpson.

My first memory of conflict beginning to take shape would have been an awareness of Ian Paisley and the riot in Divis Street over the tricolour flying in the shop window in 1964. Then we had Seán Lemass coming to Stormont to forge understanding with Terence O'Neill and all that 'brouhaha' from Loyalists about nothing in the aftermath.

It seemed that, as Catholics, we were somehow or another implicated in all this gloom and doom that Paisley seemed to be constantly predicting. That was something I became more aware of and it seemed to me then, rightly or wrongly, that places where kerbstones hadn't been painted before were now being painted, and that flags were being flown from places where they hadn't been flown before. For some people, there seemed to be some higher sense that this place was under siege, and it was important for people to wave their flag, but again I would have had a sense that this was all nonsense, that this was all hysteria and, at some stage, they were going to stop this codology.

I remember my brother Seán and I used to go to a health clinic off Agnes Street, further down the Crumlin Road. Seán had something wrong with his breathing, and I had something wrong with my feet, and we would get one day a week off school to go to this physio session together. I was always aware that when I went down to a place like Agnes Street, because we were coming from Ardoyne there was a chance that we might get stopped and get thumped for being a 'Taig'. Soon that became more than just an irritant. There was a real sense of anxiety, but in the normal course of events, because I didn't have to go to such places, I just did my best to avoid them.

These are just the things come in to my head. The next thing was the shooting of Peter Ward in 1966. I remember clearly my father being very upset by that because when we lived in Andersonstown before I was born, we lived in the same street as the Ward family. I think my father stood for Peter Ward when he was confirmed or christened, I can't remember which. Peter Ward was only eighteen years of age. He was shot in the Malvern Arms by Gusty Spence and the other UVF guys. So these things were beginning to intrude into my consciousness.

Then the following year Austin Currie organised the 'sit-in' in Caledon over the unfair allocation of houses. I remember being fascinated by him doing that, and just beginning to have an awareness of politics. I was thirteen at that stage, and the whole business of civil rights was coming more and more to the fore. Then in April 1969, there was a riot down the Crumlin Road. The riot squad was called in, and there was a row and a baton charge. I subsequently heard that the reason for it was that there had been a row in the pub at the corner of Hooker Street. A run-of-the-mill kind of Saturday night squabble, and instead of responding as normal by sending a sergeant and two constables, the police decided to send in a riot squad and enflamed the whole situation.

As 1969 progressed, tension was beginning to become more heightened, and that summer the situation became much more dangerous. There was rioting in Derry first of all, and then it started on the Falls, then into Ardoyne; 14–15 August saw two consecutive nights of rioting, and my memory is of my father and older brother Ciarán, who could drive at that stage, getting my mother and my younger siblings over to Andersonstown to stay with some relatives. I was fifteen at this stage and, for whatever reason, I was judged old enough to stay behind. My father, my older brother, some neighbours and myself were in our house, and we were looking at the RUC, along with thugs, lighting petrol bombs and throwing them into houses of neighbours. So my reaction to that was that this was out of order and that the RUC were contemptible.

Those Victorian houses we lived in had shutters on the inside. The shutters were closed in case anything came through the window. We all gathered in what would have been my granny and granda's bedroom, a room looking out on to the Crumlin Road. We watched it all unfold in front of us on the street right outside our window. As the Ardoyne song says, we watched 'the so-called long-haired ones' pushing the RUC and their camp followers back, because it wasn't just the RUC they were fighting against. Guys in civvies were throwing sticks, stones and petrol bombs with impunity at the lads from Ardoyne, and they were running up and down the road. All we had in the house was a couple of hammers and buckets of sand in case the petrol bombs came through the window. Every so often Daddy would tell us to stand back from the window in case they saw us looking at them and they would throw something at our house.

I can't remember which night it was – because it all becomes a blur now almost 50 years later, and then you hear things afterwards from people and you don't know whether you actually remember it happening, or if you have absorbed it into your own narrative of the event – but at some stage the police started using live ammunition. It became very scary when you heard the Sterling submachine guns and these little whippet cars. Around two or three in the morning the rioting stopped, and the whippet cars, it seemed to me, were raking the place with gunfire. That may not be what actually happened, but certainly you could hear gunfire and it was only one kind of gunfire. There was nobody shooting back at them. A man was killed in Herbert Street, Sammy McLarnon. He was standing in his living room. He was just an innocent man caught in his own house.

Throughout all this period there was talk of getting the United Nations to intervene. Bizarre when you think about it. It was 16 August when British troops came down the front of the road. I can remember the most telling thing for me was they all were lined up in the middle of the Crumlin Road and they were all standing with their backs to the chapel, looking at our side. My father came out from our front door and said, 'Why are you facing us? We are not the ones rioting. You should be facing those bastards!'

He was right, and there was a real sense at that stage that this place is finished. Even as a fifteen-year-old I was hearing people like Bill Craig talking complete nonsense about the State being under threat from these imagined IRA men. The only thing that happened as a result was that what was then imaginary became reality, because of the way the entire situation was mishandled.

Starting with Paisley's racist incitements way back as far as 1964 and 1965, and then when all of this happened, you had this rubbish stuff being published in the *Protestant Telegraph* about IRA snipers using the spires of Holy Cross Church to target Protestants. Now, because of the position of the shutters the only thing they could have hit from the spires was the ground, but don't let the truth get in the way of creating panic and hatred. The *Protestant Telegraph* published all this complete nonsense and wrote about brothels being run by nuns. Just complete, utterly poisonous garbage that was being promulgated at the time.

The IRA

There was no IRA in Ardoyne at that time. In fact I wrote a piece for a book published a few years called *Remembering the Troubles* by a guy from the Falls Road called Jim Smyth, Professor of Irish History in Notre Dame. He is a former prisoner who did brilliantly in Trinity, and then Cambridge, and he edited this book of different perspectives on the Troubles. I did a piece just remembering some of this, but it was more to do with the fact that my father was proxy-bombed by the IRA in 1974.

I remember being a fully paid-up subscriber to the notion that we had these IRA (I Ran Away) signs written on the gable walls, only to subsequently read in Brian Hanley's book *Secret Army* that there were no such signs anywhere. It was all imagined, although even now if you ask me I can still see them. Brian is probably right, all this memory was reconstructed afterwards, but there was definitely no IRA in Ardoyne at that stage. That's not to say that almost immediately people starting talking about it. Very, very immediately, and because my father was one of the '40s men', we obviously became aware that both at an organised level and at an informal level between the IRA and local defence committees there were people saying, 'This is not going to happen again.' The simple fact is that people were adamant that they were not going to allow people to burn their houses and homes again. The following year, for precisely the same reason, I joined the Fianna. I was turning sixteen, and my head was turned with the notion of being a patriot. Of course, I had to do it very covertly, because I knew my father would have been very opposed to it.

It was then not very difficult to find somebody who knew somebody who could get you involved in this kind of thing, and so I joined the local branch of the Fianna. This involved going to various houses in the district in a clandestine way and being given lectures about handguns. I never actually handled them but was given lectures about them and also about what one may do if you were arrested or other kinds of stuff. I would get involved in selling the Republican newspaper, *An Phoblacht*, but all the time I was doing this without my parents' knowledge. Then my father found out. I think a local priest had seen me in the company of people he knew were members of the Republican movement, so he must have said something to my father. I was confronted by my father, who was very direct about me not doing to my mother what he had done to his by getting involved in something where you don't know what the outcome would be. My father had broken his own mother's heart when he was interned in the 1940s, and he was adamant that he wasn't going to let me do the same. My father worked at an emotional level, and what he said worked. So I left. I suppose this would have been in the middle of 1970, and my career as a freedom fighter was very, very short!

Riots Escalating

The riots that began on 14 August escalated very quickly. I remember Mickey Rosatto from Havana Street. I didn't know him well at this stage, but I got to know him later. Mickey was one of the so-called 'long-haired ones'. He was two or three years older than me. The 'long-haired ones' saw themselves as defending the district against the RUC and the Loyalists hoards. Mickey was shot as they were pushed back into the district. They realised there was gunfire, and Mickey was running down into Brompton Park. He was running and felt nothing when he was shot until someone said to him, 'Jesus Mickey, you've been shot.' He then lost consciousness and when he woke up in the Mater Hospital the fellow beside him was one of the Loyalists. So he very quickly learned to keep his mouth shut.

My brother Ciarán, my father, and two or three other people were in the house that night. I can't remember who they were, but we were frightened stiff. Afterwards it became even crazier. You had very respectable people with no associations of any kind with the Republican movement like my dad had, all insisting that guns had to be found somewhere in case this ever happened again. They were adamant that the Loyalists and the police were just not going to get into Ardoyne. They just were not going to get in, and I suppose the perceived need for the IRA became obvious.

We lived two doors away from the corner of Butler Street, so we could see right down the front of the Crumlin Road. The chapel had large grounds down to Chief Street, and the girl's primary school was on Chief Street. There were a number of Catholic families living in Chief Street, but after that the road was largely Loyalist, or Protestant. I am sure these were people who didn't consider themselves anything more than decent Protestants, but there were thugs in there as well, who were allowed to behave with absolute impunity during that period.

I think there was barricade in front of Butler Street, so the Loyalists were not getting into Butler Street. I couldn't swear as to where the barricade actually was, but it was near our house. The buses were also across Herbert Street and Hooker Street, and maybe down as far as Brookfield Street, but that didn't stop the burning. Most of one side of Hooker Street was burned to the ground. A large part of Brookfield Street was also gone. There was a Loyalist woman who lived in Herbert Street, Skinny Lizzy. She was put out of her home. I am not trying to say that we were any less sectarian than the people across the road, but my memory of her is that she really enjoyed sticking it up the Taigs by waving her Union Jack and flying her flag down at the corner of Chatham Street and Herbert Street. It was all gruesome stuff.

Tessy Donegan was a lovely wee woman who had a sweet shop in her front room, just down below the Co-Op on the front of the Crumlin Road, near enough to Chief Street. Tessy was a wee saint. Her home was gone, also burnt to the ground. So there was a real tit-for-tat that went on during that period. I remember two days later seeing Martin Bell, the BBC guy, standing up at the corner of Kerrera Street doing a piece to camera. I remember thinking, 'Jesus! This is great. All the news people are here. We are celebrities!'

I met a man from the *Sunday Times* Insight Team, which was a revolutionary thing in print journalism at that time. Harold Evans was the editor. He had the Insight Team swamp Ardoyne in those first couple of weekends. I remember showing a couple of the reporters round. At the time I was just an over-opinionated, talkative fifteen-year-old – so manna from heaven for journalists to describe as 'one source said'! I was that 'source', a fifteen-year-old gobshite, as I showed them around Hooker Street and Brookfield Street.

Fr Marcellus, Fr Ailbe and some of the younger priests from Holy Cross monastery played a crucial role in the community remaining firm. At some level there was a tacit acceptance, even if not with whole-hearted enthusiasm, that guns had to be used. My memory of the priests was that at least they were standing in support for the community against the threat. The community was united in that we were going to have to stand our ground. Things were so clearly wrong. That, for me, was the reason why I couldn't do anything else but join the Fianna.

Due to the rising fear and tension most of our neighbours would have left their homes by 14 August. Families like the Shannons, whom we knew, I think had all gone, so we were probably the first house above Butler Street who actually stayed. The Trainors and the Mallons may have still have been there, but a lot of people had got out of Dodge, staying with relatives over in Andersonstown, which was seen as a safe place at that time.

I vividly remember the smell that filled the air in the wake of the riots and the burning of the streets. The strong smell of smoke and charred ruins. This was all so unimaginable. From that weekend in August, the whole thing became just a huge conflagration. People were shot. People were killed. I remember the gunfire. I remember being afraid. We closed the shutters that covered the inside of the windows of our big Victorian house in case the windows were broken. Those shutters were never opened again. There was no daylight in that room ever again until the house was knocked down some twelve years later.

These kinds of riots, or different manifestations of them, happened for years at the front of the road. The kids from Everton and Summerdale, the two Protestant schools, walked down the front of Crumlin Road, so there was always a row with local schoolchildren, and the row would have developed into a riot. Then at teatime, the Protestant kids would have better sense and go home and get their tea, but the Taigs kept rioting, the eejits kept rioting. That was our telling of it to ourselves. Yes, the access to the front of the road could be problematic at times. It seemed to us that there was a riot outside the house for two or three years, non-stop.

Over the Brink

All of a sudden we had gone from a scenario where Nationalists were unhappy with how things were, and where Unionists were saying, 'Fuck you. This is good enough for you...' to a situation of complete destruction and death being visited on the community, and it had all happened in a very compressed period of time. I thought, 'My God, what is happening here?' And that's how it stayed for another 30 years.

You can be as philosophical as you like about it, and I am conscious that I had the luxury of moving away and had the space and the time to become less reactionary and more analytical about things, but the people who stayed at home were putting up with all of this. At some stage you indulge their sense of loyalty to the armed struggle, which seemed to me from early on to be pointless, but then moved on from being pointless to being just wrong. Whereas a lot of my older friends didn't see it that way at all. They thought, 'What else can we do? This is the only way we are going to get anything.' I believe that attitude had emerged from the complete and utter mismanagement of what should have been relatively straightforward social problems at the time, like 'one man, one vote'. How could anyone have a problem like that? Or give people the houses they deserve, but the place was so absolutely sectarian.

I suppose I began to question the order of things from around the time of the outbreak of the Troubles. I remember thinking, 'Well, democracy is all very well but this is not getting us anywhere.' So as I say, within the frame of reference that I had, the logical thing for me to do at that stage was to say, 'Well, I will play my part to seeing an end to this.' Hence my choice to get involved with the Fianna, but it didn't last very long, and I don't know that I was ever made for that anyway. But I knew that so many guys who were of my age, even a year or two older, who got involved with the Republican movement. Did they go in with a sense of altruism or did they go in with a sense of, 'I've had enough of this'? Whatever their motivation, fellows of the same age as me ended up behind bars, sometimes for doing nothing, and sometimes for doing perfectly awful things, and it could have been me.

I don't know that it's possible to reconstruct my thoughts at the time completely, but to the extent that I do remember some of them, I would have been angry about what were perceived to be the injustices that were done to the Catholic community. And in truth, most of them weren't just perceptions, they were real. It was the way things were, and it was bad, and I fully understood and shared the communal sense of anger about that.

Lack of Understanding in the Wider Community

I have this really strong memory of going back to school in September 1969, full of anger and surprise at what had been happening on the streets outside our front door, feeling sure that people at school would have felt exactly the same way. What I hadn't taken into account was that the sectarian trouble was confined to Belfast, and to particular areas, like the Lower Falls, the Market, and Ardoyne, but otherwise life continued the way it had. To my shock, all the guys wanted to talk about was the fact that man had landed on the moon while this was all going on. It's a terrible thing to say, but I have no memory of the landing on the moon. Just whatever happened that summer had passed me by. All I was thinking about was what was going on outside my front door.

I also have a memory of when the Troubles started, although my mother subsequently denied this, that the BBC news was at one o'clock, while on Radio Éireann, or RTÉ, radio news came on at half one. My mother would stay on BBC until about twenty-eight minutes past one, and then put on Athlone(RTÉ), so that we heard 'the truth'. So, that was a good reflection on her view that the BBC didn't always tell you what was going on outside your front door in the way that it should have done!

Ardoyne Friends – Same Memories, Different Paths

The events of August 1969 impacted massively upon the community of Ardoyne. While the people may have shared that experience, they didn't all react in the same way. I was friends with Brendan (Bik) McFarlane. Bik was a couple of years older than me and we were altar boys together. I have a very clear memory of going to the Savoy Cinema further down the Crumlin Road from our local flea pit, the Forum. The Forum was a completely safe environment for us, but the Savoy was at the corner of Cambrai Street and was a bit dodgy in that there would be people from both communities there.

Anyhow, Gerard Matthews and myself decided to go to the Savoy to see *Ben Hur*. I think I was about twelve at the time, so this was 1966/67. As we were coming out of the cinema a couple of fellows confronted us with, 'You wee Fenian bastards!' Our knight in shining armour was Bik! He arrived on the scene and the boys melted. I have no memory of what he said or what he did, but they were just suddenly gone.

I was never a good footballer, but I was always around the GAA club and Bik and his brother Gerard were handy footballers. Something that fascinated me at that stage was that Bik could pick up any instrument and just play it. He just had a musical ability. He was interested in music and myself, Pat Murphy and a friend called Jim McCullough were very interested in music at that stage and we would meet Bik through that. Then he went off to become a priest. He went off to Wales and again we would have been quite close. He was in and out of our house all the time. I think himself and my sister Máire might even have had a brief encounter! But he went off and he came back within the year. Shortly after that he got married. Bik's home was in Balholm Drive. I remember being there very often and I would have seen him right through the Troubles until 1974, when Ciarán Murphy was killed.

Bik had been involved in a small kind of group who had been involved in an unconnected way with the IRA, but who were active in Republican activities, and I think he went over to the Provos at that stage. I was actually doing my Finals the following year, 1975, and my brother Ciarán came in to meet me to tell me that Bik had been arrested coming back into Ardoyne following the blowing up of the Bayardo Bar. He came to tell me as he didn't want me to hear it on the radio. We were devastated about the deaths that had happened – and whatever about it being a Loyalist or a UVF place, most of the people who died in it had nothing to do with anything. The boys were caught coming back into Ardoyne. Silver Hamilton, who had been in the same class as me in Holy Cross, and Bik, and I can't remember who else was involved in that. Silver Hamilton was a real character! He lived at the bottom of Butler Street. On one occasion the water cannon arrived and Silver came out of the house with a bar of soap, stopping in front of the water cannon pretending to have a shower. I had thought he was a total wag! Now this.

Brian McCargo took a very different path from Bik. I remember the McCargos. When my family first moved into Ardoyne, the GAA clubrooms were just round the corner from our home. Beside us was Frank McAreavey's barber's shop, known affectionately to all as Frank the Butcher for reasons that were very apparent! Frank had what was for all the world a stable yard. There was a big green stable door on it, and a door within that door. That was the entrance to the GAA clubrooms. So that's where they would all gather for matches, and I would say that the older members had a couple of dozen bottles of stout under the benches. There was a toilet and a dartboard, and so when I was playing under-13s that's where we would meet before games. Seamie White would take us all off for training and matches and so on. We got to know the older men like Gerry Cullen and guys like Pat McCargo and his brother Brian, whose nickname was Budgie at that stage.

After the Troubles started there was a commission examining the behaviour of the RUC. Arising out of that there was an initiative to get Catholics to join the RUC as they were so vastly under-represented. Brian was one of those who decided that 'This was for me!' There would have been a mixture of 'Fair play to him' to 'Stupid bollocks!' reactions. There was that division of opinion. He was a nice man. I never actually met him afterwards, but I put people in the way of meeting him when I began working with RTE and they were looking for people with a different perspective. So Brian did pieces with Nick Coffey for a programme I was working on at the time called *Today Tonight,* exploring the difficulties for Catholics who had joined the RUC. Brian could never come home, because when the shutters came down they came down with such ferocity.

When Ciarán Murphy was murdered, his sister Eithne was married to a Catholic RUC man who had joined around the same time as Brian. He couldn't come to the funeral. Even though attempts were made to talk to people who were in a position to do something about it, 'Stay away' was the response. So that was the difference; when the shutters came down – the fierceness of it – F*** them! That was it – there was no middle ground. I would say that probably when Brian and other Catholics joined, they did so with the best of intentions, but there was no coming back. They couldn't have known what was about to happen and the ferocity with which they would be viewed.

Personal Impact

During all that period, I think everybody at some part of their being had, for want of a better term, a permanent presence of butterflies in their stomach. You were always slightly on tenterhooks, but there are a few particular experiences that stand out for me.

I remember times coming home from friends' houses when there was a blackout in Ardoyne. All the street lights had been put out by order of the British Army to prevent sniper attacks, and coming home at night in pitch black was fairly terrifying. In response to that the people had put up lights outside their front door at the instigation of Fr Myles, but there was a lot of intimidation from soldiers.

On one occasion, when I was still at college, my father had got me a job as a bread server. I was a helper on lorries that went down the country with bread during the night. We would have pulled out of Belfast at maybe 8 or 9 in the evening and delivered bread down to country depots for Hughes' in Newry, Cookstown, Dungannon, or as far as Ballinamallard in Fermanagh. We were always wary that you could get stopped by a patrol of the UDR and that you might end up in a ditch. 1974 was the year of the Miami Showband massacre. You certainly didn't go out at night during that time without thinking, 'Something awful could happen to me during this.'

I remember we were coming back into Belfast at about six o'clock in the morning, and we came up the Grosvenor Road to go across onto the Springfield, to go up to the Hughes' Depot. We were hijacked: 'On behalf of the Irish Republican Army, we're commandeering this.'

The man who was driving the lorry, Frank McDonald, a former internee, said, 'Oh, for God's sake lads, we're after spending hours delivering bread in the country.'

The response came: 'F off you F'er! Give us this van!' So we were unceremoniously dumped from it and it was dragged across the road and used as a barricade.

Father Proxy Bombed

It was Saturday 31 August 1974. I was down around Desertmartin delivering bread for Hughes' bakery at that time. As we swung back into the bakery at about two o'clock in the afternoon a colleague of my father's, a man called Jack McGee, called me and said, 'Your father's been involved in an incident. He's been involved in a proxy bomb and was forced to drive a bomb to the BBC.'

My first reaction was, 'Is he alright?' He was all right, and I then wondered, 'Who would do this to him?'

He was delivering bread up the Glen Road to one of the Kennedy's bakery shops when some these fellows approached him and said, 'We're commandeering your van in the name of the Irish Republican Army.' He told them to f*** off and they said, 'No, you're going to do exactly what you're told or we'll blow you away.' So they took the keys and his license from him and loaded his van up with explosives. He was then put in the van and ordered to drive it. One of them accompanied him in the van down as far as the bottom of the Grosvenor Road. He then got out and said, 'Drive that to the BBC. We know where you live, and your wife and your kids better look out if you don't do exactly what you are told.' So he drove up Bedford Street and there was an Army personnel carrier coming the other way. And as soon as he saw it, he stopped and jumped out and said, 'There's a bomb in this van.'

The Army sent for the robot they used to defuse car bombs. There were two explosions and the van was blown to smithereens. Then my father was arrested. He pointed out to the cops that he hated the Provos, but that held no sway and he was very closely questioned about the attack. My father would have felt that the guys who carried this out were no better than RUC and the British Army, but, while he hated the Provos, given his own Republican background he felt no obligation to cooperate with the RUC.

He was arrested a number of times after that in the middle of the night and taken down to Tennent Street to be questioned, and then let go in the middle of the night as well. I think that eventually got the better of him. I think he had what you might call some kind of post-traumatic disorder, and he suffered from very bad depression after it. I think he felt that what he and comrades of his age had done thirty years before meant nothing.

Reflections on the Conflict

The biggest thing for me is that the loss of life was completely needless. I am not saying that the struggle to have civil rights would have been easy, and I think there is such an entrenched sectarianism in the North that it is difficult to say how progress could have been made, but I think that it would have been possible without killing each other. There was such savagery.

During the period of the Troubles I would have thought that violence was not getting us anywhere, and all that it was doing was deepening the sectarian divide. North Belfast was a killing field and a lot of Catholics were being murdered, and, as we know now, there was a lot of collusion at that time between security forces and members of the UVF and the UDA. So the community had a real sense of being under siege. People needed to feel that there was somebody who was going be there to defend them and if they were doing that then they were doing something good. However, I think the violence ultimately contributed to a deepening of sectarianism rather than solving anything.

The overriding thing about that weekend in August 1969 is the speed with which it went from being the kind of social disorder what could have happened in any urban society in the world where you have people who are underprivileged, under-employed, poor and living in rotten conditions rising up and having a riot, into a deep-seated sectarian war where there was awful savagery. When you think back on Lenny Murphy (leader of the Shankill Butchers' murder gang), he was indulged. The security forces knew what he was doing, and they left him alone to do it for years. How many years of collusion was there between the RUC and gangs who were murdering people simply because they were Catholics? At the same time you had the Provos, who were allegedly fighting for freedom, taking people out simply because they were Protestants. Can any of us honestly say that either of those actions advanced anything? So you wonder at the end of it, what was that all about? What was it about?

Is life in Ardoyne now any better than it was when we were kids? Is there the same level of dysfunction, or maybe even worse than it was then? I know that Catholics can point out that we were educated. Our parents put a particular emphasis on getting the 11+ and you can look now and see the disparity between the approach taken by working-class Catholics and working-class Protestants at that stage. There was such a concentration on education at that stage and you can see the patterns emerge from that to the extent that I am sitting here now in a house in Donegal that I was able to buy eventually as a second home because I had an education. That emphasis on education made me different to a fellow who might have been born on the Shankill whose height of ambition was to get a job in the shipyard.

The thing about all this is that there is nobody of my age who lived in Belfast, Catholic or Protestant, who doesn't have some version of the same thing that has happened to them. We are all scarred in one way or another by that. The stupidity of it, the crassness and the viciousness of it, but we have survived in some shape or form while others didn't, so we should be thankful for that much. Our stories in Ardoyne are probably a bit more extreme than other people's, but versions of the same stories and experiences are all over Belfast and probably other parts of the North as well. Certainly North Belfast was a very dangerous place during that period.

Ardoyne Today

While many people left Ardoyne, many of my friends like Pat Murphy chose to stay. When I have gone to see them we usually end up in the GAA club for a few drinks. There are people who stayed at home and who lived their lives in their own way, and who are still the same decent, quiet people. They still have the same interests in the things I have, like Gaelic games. The banter of the place is still alive and strong. So none of that has changed, and yet the place is not doing as well as it should be.

There are lunatic elements still there masquerading as Republicans, that's all you can say about them. They are involved in drugs and every kind of skullduggery, undermining any hope people have of a decent social fabric. When you reflect on that for a while though, you realise the same can be said about Ballymun or parts of Coolock. This is what happens in urban living in a society where opportunity is not evenly distributed. Is Ardoyne any worse than those places? I would say on balance probably not, but it has come through an awful lot.

The experience of the Troubles must have had an impact upon me, because at some level or another we store all these things. What sense we make them I don't know, but having seen the things I saw, and seeing the people I knew who were killed or ended up in prison, there's obviously still a lot of unresolved issues. I don't know that it's possible to resolve them ever, other than to think that I would not want it to ever happen again. I now have a lot of sympathy with my father's view when he was talking to me about the folly of getting involved and hoping that nobody does it, regardless of the circumstances, because it's a huge price to pay.

From my experience of living in Ardoyne I would like to think that I automatically know that there is another side to everything, because the place I came from was misrepresented right down to its very name. On every news bulletin I heard, people constantly referred to 'the Ardoyne', and I would think 'There is no such f***ing place! It's "Ardoyne"! ' It was a complex place with lots of different stories and lots of different people doing decent things, and decent people getting involved in all sorts of madness, and I was involved in that myself. I have a degree of thankfulness that I was one of the lucky ones, thanks to my father, who didn't get caught up in getting interned or getting put away. But I would be very loathe to condemn anybody who went through all that, and, if the truth is told, I would also be slow to condemn anyone from the other side who was being wired to the moon by the bile they were getting fed, not just by Paisley, but Bill Craig and all those other merchants of paranoid sectarian poison.

I suppose the overriding thing I feel all the time is gratitude. I know some brilliant people in Ardoyne. I escaped. I don't mean getting out of gaol, but I escaped, and I probably would have gone anyway, Troubles or not. I wanted to see different places, do different things, but I do have that sense that 'I escaped' if that is not too negative, but I also have great affection for so many people still there.

I can remember people like Brian McCargo and all the bigger lads in the Gaelic club: Paddy Dobbin, Stevie Dobbin, all those fantastic characters. Ted McQuaid, who was our neighbour, later murdered by the Shankill Butchers. I am grateful for the sense of community cohesion that the GAA offered us all as we were growing up. The Gaelic club may have been a shebeen, but that's where all the social events happened. We went down on a Saturday night to hear the old guys sing the same songs, week in and week out, drinking awful pints of Harp. There was great fun in it all and a real sense of solidarity. In that way I am always very proud to say that I am from Ardoyne. There was, and is, a strong sense of solidarity despite it all.

Final Thoughts

Feast of the Assumption – 15 August 2019, 9.02 p.m.

I am not long home from Mass in Holy Cross Church, Ardoyne. This evening's Mass was celebrated in memory of all who had lost their lives as a result of the conflict in Ardoyne. At this time fifty years ago tonight, Ardoyne was being attacked by the full force of the RUC, 'B' Specials and Loyalist crowds. Buses had been hijacked earlier, and were now being used as barricades in every street in the district, and the soon to be familiar sound of gunfire was in the air. Houses were burning, and a real fear that the parish was on the brink of being overrun and destroyed could be felt in streets now covered in rubble and broken glass.

As I sat in the body of the church just two hours ago Fr Eugene McCarthy, the rector and parish priest of Holy Cross, summed up for many the tragedy endured by this community over fifty years:

> *'The people of Holy Cross suffered deeply over the course of the Troubles. Their suffering went deeper and deeper yet, and when you thought it could get no worse, their suffering went deeper still.'*

There is a deep attachment between the people of Holy Cross, Ardoyne and the Passionists. Maybe it was their strange habits that made them, and consequently us, different from the rest of the diocese. I think though it was more about their sheer down-to-earth humanity and the compassion that people received from those whom they considered as 'their own'. As the white sign stood out against the black habit, so these men were a sign of hope when times were tough.

The Passionists came to Ardoyne in 1869. Even as children growing up in the parish, we knew they were different. While others called their priest by their surname, we were on first-name terms with ours, and such wonderful names they were: Alphonsous, Ailbe, Honorious, Conrad, Fernando, Marcellus.... As altar boys, we got to know the characteristics and quirkiness of each one.

What was it though about these priests in black habits and white signs, that somehow got under the skin, and seemed to draw a deep loyalty from the people of Ardoyne? Whether it was in the rebuilding of burnt-out houses, the construction of factories and jobs, the walking down riot-torn streets or accompanying children through waves of hatred on the way to school, the hours spent counselling and listening to stories of hurt and loss, we knew we were not just a parish – we were a Passionist parish. We were proud of that. It seemed the Passionists were also proud of us. Men who literally put their lives on the line to minister to a people in times of conflict and trauma.

August 1969 marked a turning point in the experience of the community ministered to by the Passionists living in Holy Cross, Ardoyne. Since that summer of 1969, Ardoyne has witnessed the deaths of 99 parishioners, and over 400 men and women from the parish were imprisoned for Troubles-related offences. As violence hit the streets and homes of this small community we became a people who identified with the prophet Isaiah when he used the phrase 'familiar with grief' (Is 53:3), and in the people of this Passionist parish the crucified was no stranger. This is a community, though, that not only endured suffering, but that has also inflicted much hurt upon others. It is both a wounded and a wounding community. Such suffering has left an indelible scar on the face of this community.

The first vow a Passionist takes on the day of his profession is 'to keep alive the memory of the Passion'. On the streets of Ardoyne this vow was not expressed through pious prayer or devotion, but in the lived reality on a daily basis of people seeking hope in the midst of pain, affliction, conflict and death itself. If there is any community that keeps alive the memory of the Passion, it is the community of Holy Cross, Ardoyne.

The remembrance of this painful time in the history of this community has the potential to reopen old scars, and retraumatise people who have already endured more than their fair share of pain and suffering. However, there are two ways in which to look at a scar – as a reminder of the pain endured, or as a reminder of the healing received. My hope is that this book will be an act of remembrance that will contribute to the healing of this wounded community.

Most of my daily work over the past number of years has been working with the Passionists and other community partners to build peace within this community, and ensuring that what we experienced as children growing up in the parish is not repeated for those who come after us. My work is particularly focused on bringing hope to the young people of the community. Unfortunately that aim is not shared by all, and within the Ardoyne district there are still those caught in the addiction of violence, the sickness of sectarianism, and the scourge of gangsterism. On more than one occasion, I have been challenged with the fact that I don't live in Ardoyne, and therein lies their blindness. They don't recognise that it is not about living in Ardoyne, but it is everything about being from, nurtured by, belonging to and having the DNA of the community of Ardoyne flowing through your veins. People who left Ardoyne fifty years ago and have never been back will still very proudly proclaim that they are Ardoyne people first and foremost. Others moved into the district fifty years ago, but they will never be 'from' Ardoyne, because for them it is just a place where they live, and not about the life blood that flows through their veins.

Journeying towards a New Future

Healing and reconciliation cannot be built upon playing on the mistrust and suspicion between communities. We need courageous religious, political and civic leaders who are prepared to take the risks of reaching out and building new relationships where faith, identity and culture are fully embraced and cherished by all. We ignore the past at the risk of recreating it in the future, but facing up to the past must not only include looking at violent acts, but also the violent, unjust political structures and systems that facilitated discrimination and embedded inequality.

In J.R.R. Tolkien's *The Fellowship of the Ring*, Frodo reflects with Gandalf upon the situation in which he finds himself and says, 'I wish none of this had ever happened.' This is a sentiment that many people from within this fractured community will identify with in relation to the recent conflict: 'I wish none of this had ever happened!' But in response to Frodo's lament, Gandalf reminds him, 'So do all who live to see such times, but that is not for them to decide. All we have to decide is what to do with the time that is given to us.' In dealing with the legacy of the past conflict we are also faced with that same choice: how can we, together, use the time that has been given to us to promote the healing of this wounded and wounding community?

There are people who tell us that we need to move on from the past and to forget about the awfulness of the conflict visited upon this community. Perhaps though one of our problems is that we have forgotten too soon the horror of the conflict we endured, and in doing so have robbed ourselves of the energy we need to create a new shared community together. It is no accident that among those most committed to peace today are those most affected by and involved in the experience of the conflict, now working towards a new vision.

I want to borrow a story I heard a number of years ago from Fr John Friel CP. He inherited it from a friend in Derry.

In Belfast there are two gods, a masculine god and a feminine god. The masculine god is orange and he marches to the beat of vibrant drums. He loves to tell stories of forefathers and of battles fought and won. His songs are angry, and tell of faithfulness and fidelity and a heritage hard won. His favourite colours are red, white and blue, and he dreams of a future when his loyalty will be rewarded by a restoration of power and privilege.

The feminine god is green. She is somewhat melancholic, and constantly laments a fourth green field and calls her sons and daughters to mourn over what has been lost. Her songs are sad and speak of betrayal and victimhood, and of innocence stolen away by the oppressor. She dreams of a future when the fourth green field will be restored and the foreigner in her midst will be banished forever.

Both gods share allegiances from their followers that amount almost to worship, and in the middle of this struggle between these two gods are the crucified ones. The one who is shot, lying by the side of the road. The one who is tortured. The disappeared. The one who receives brutal beatings and is kneecapped. The one who is expelled from his home and his family. The one who was a victim of collusion and false imprisonment.

The story cautions us as to how allegiances to worthy causes can become distorted and violent, and often result in the reopening of old wounds on the streets of this wonderful city. Speaking in Sri Lanka in January 2015, Pope Francis said:

'It is a continuing tragedy in our world that so many communities are at war between themselves. The inability to reconcile differences and disagreements, whether old or new, has given rise to ethnic and religious tensions, frequently accompanied by outbreaks of violence... It is no easy task to overcome the bitter legacy of injustice, hostility and mistrust left by the conflict. It can only be done by overcoming evil with good and by cultivating those virtues that foster reconciliation, solidarity and peace. The process of healing also needs to include the pursuit of truth, not for the sake of opening old wounds, but rather as a necessary means of promoting justice, healing and unity.'

Along with the recorded deaths attributed to the Troubles, so many more people were to become 'the forgotten victims', people who died 'too soon' as a direct result of living through and with the trauma of conflict and division. Women endured the trauma of partners and children killed or imprisoned, and were left with responsibilities that ought to have been shared. Children had precious shared childhood memories of their fathers stolen and replaced by visits to Long Kesh or Crumlin Road Gaol. As I listened to the memories of people from this community of their experience of conflict, I heard of unborn children who never experienced the freedom to breathe outside the womb of their mother due to the cruel cost of trauma endured. Their deaths were never recorded in any books, but are etched in the still aching hearts of mothers and fathers.

Despite, or maybe because of, the shared experience and trauma, there is something special about this small square mile of earth in the north of Belfast called Ardoyne that has nourished a fierce pride among its inhabitants. We did not just endure conflict, we overcame it. While this little island of Ardoyne undoubtedly became a prison without walls for some, it empowered many others to launch out into the deep and to cross oceans and continents to make this world a better place due to their presence. The stories told by the people within this book are mere examples of the fierce pride and talent of 'Ardonians'. Many of those now in exile will give a response similar to mine when asked where I am from:

'I live in Ballymena. I come from Belfast – but I was born in Ardoyne!'